Male Bisexuality
in Current Cinema

Male Bisexuality in Current Cinema
Images of Growth, Rebellion and Survival

Justin Vicari

McFarland & Company, Inc., Publishers
Jefferson, North Carolina, and London

LIBRARY OF CONGRESS CATALOGUING-IN-PUBLICATION DATA

Vicari, Justin, 1968–
　　Male bisexuality in current cinema : images of growth, rebellion and survival / Justin Vicari.
　　　　p.　　cm.
　　Includes bibliographical references and index.

　　ISBN 978-0-7864-6160-8
　　softcover : 50# alkaline paper ∞

　　1. Bisexuality in motion pictures.　2. Homosexuality in motion pictures.　3. Men in motion pictures.　I. Title.
　　PN1995.9.B57V53　　2011
　　791.43'6352663 — dc22　　　　　　　　　　　　2010044516

BRITISH LIBRARY CATALOGUING DATA ARE AVAILABLE

© 2011 Justin Vicari. All rights reserved

No part of this book may be reproduced or transmitted in any form or by any means, electronic or mechanical, including photocopying or recording, or by any information storage and retrieval system, without permission in writing from the publisher.

On the cover: A scene from the 2004 film *A Home at the End of the World* with Colin Farrell, Dallas Roberts and Robin Wright Penn (Warner Bros./Photofest)

Manufactured in the United States of America

McFarland & Company, Inc., Publishers
　Box 611, Jefferson, North Carolina 28640
　　www.mcfarlandpub.com

To the memory of
PARKER TYLER
(1904–1974)
and
JACK SMITH
(1932–1989)

Table of Contents

Preface   1
Introduction: Searching for Bob Elkin   7

Part 1. Personal Visions

1. Fifteen Minutes of the Future: François Ozon's *A Summer Dress*   31
2. To Bend Without Breaking: Bisexuality and Adaptation in the Films of André Téchiné   39
3. Tentative, Tender ... and Trendy? Gregg Araki's Teen Trilogy   51
4. Rock Star Bisexuality in Todd Haynes' *Velvet Goldmine*   64
5. For Whom the Bi Tolls: Craig Lucas' *The Dying Gaul* and Ozon's *Water Drops on Burning Rocks*   72

Part 2. Alone and with Others

6. Making the Man: The Bisexual Hero   91
7. Illegible Patriarchies: Bisexualizing the Family   108
8. Fazes and Mazes: Inside the Triangle   142

Part 3. Matters of Love and Death

9. The Schoolboy Crush and Its Ambiguous Object   161
10. Turning It On and Off: "Bi for Pay"   174
11. Allegories of AIDS   186
12. In His Wake: The Strange Power of the Dead Bisexual   204
13. At the Limits of Heterosexuality: The Woman's Viewpoint in *Anatomy of Hell*   219

Conclusion: "It's All Good"	232
Chapter Notes	235
Works Cited	239
Index	243

Preface

This book analyzes a variety of films about bisexual males. In all of these films, bisexuality is treated both as an actual practice and as a complex metaphor for a number of things: the human need to adapt to changing environments, the questioning of rigidly traditional male roles and identities, the breakdown and regeneration of family structures, the limitations of monogamy, and the stubborn affirmation of romantic love.

I wrote this book because I wanted to explore the subject of male bisexuality in cinema and found very little serious scholarly research on it. In film theory, as in so many other areas of life, bisexuality (particularly for males) seemed unseen and unrepresented. Wherever a film gave evidence of male bisexuality, critics often re-categorized it and explained it away as a more familiar and "comfortable" scenario. Either a heterosexual male was dabbling, or a gay male was having trouble coming out. The idea that something serious, real, complicated, and enthralling might be taking place in the space *between* the two primary identities of gay and straight was overlooked (or the films themselves were).

In an ongoing David and Goliath battle, homosexuality and heterosexuality have been squaring off for socio-sexual territory since the late 19th century. They are the two main categories we have for sexual behavior, even as we sometimes acknowledge that sexuality itself is hard to define, nebulous, a "gray area" subject to nuance, mood, fantasy and opportunity. Nonetheless, we cling to the gay and straight labels even, or perhaps especially, where the labels seem to be in question.

Bisexuality has been most controversial where it seems to be a rejection of the two primary labels and of the ongoing power struggle between them. Culturally, we seem to have a vested interest in reducing human behavior to obvious dualisms (male/female; gay/straight; and so on)—and also, needless to say, in perpetuating the idea of struggle at the heart of identity, e.g., that

1

the various forces are in tension with each other, mutually exclusive and antagonistic. But what if "gay" and "straight" were not antipodes but rather complements, mirror images, merging points along a continuum which is, finally, more circular and cyclical than linear? What if the problem wasn't so much that some of us are gay and some of us are straight, but rather, that all of us, as a species, are far too dualistic and linear in our thinking? What if our affinity for dualism and linearity was preventing us from seeing an essential truth which bisexuality proposes — that it is possible for one person to be open to giving and receiving love with both genders?

As a film critic, I was immediately attracted to the idea that bisexuality, as a subject, could be used to challenge precisely those dualistic and linear narrative clichés which the best films have always striven to subvert. Bisexuality opened up the possibility of reading films beyond the narrow strictures of "boy meets girl" (or "boy meets boy," for that matter). It seemed as though the more I looked, the more I began to see.

In writing this book, I have almost exclusively avoided making reference to Freudian and psychoanalytic theory. Though a visionary in many respects, Freud was also very much a product of his time: just as he could not encounter a strong woman without diagnosing "penis envy," so he could only understand same-sex activity as being, in some way, neurotic and regressive. Bisexuality is post–Freudian, or anti–Freudian, if for no other reason than because it represents a radical de-sublimation of what Freud would have considered "pre–Oedipal drives." Therefore, I have found psychoanalytic theory in general less than useful in understanding bisexuality as an affirmative life choice or a natural human tendency.

Writing about bisexuals can be as tricky and fraught with sensitivity issues as writing about any social, cultural or sexual minority. Even though my intent has been to examine *films about* bisexual males, it is inevitable that I have ended up writing, to some extent, about the actual experience and nature of bisexual males, and one never wants to write about such things inaccurately or unfairly. On the other hand, even the most cursory investigation into the subject led me to conclude that there is no such thing as a single monolithic bisexuality, and nowhere is there a pre-written code of bisexual mores and behaviors. This is partly what continues to make the subject of bisexuality fascinating and stimulating — it is neither traditional, like straight culture, nor rigidly politicized, the way gay culture often can be.

Bisexuality may be more of a bellwether for sexual liberation than even homosexuality itself. We are still in the beginning stages of seeing true acceptance for gay people in American society. Gay activists' struggle to destigmatize the gay label has often disowned the struggle of bisexuals to more or less do away with labels altogether. Heterosexuals often misread bisexuals as nothing more than a subgroup within the homosexual population. According to this misreading, the liberation of bisexuals is often seen as dependent upon the liberation of gays. But the fact remains: sexual minorities will never be liberated piecemeal. Either heterosexuality will consent to become one in a crowded constellation of adult-consensual identity-choices, or it will remain oppressively dominant, rendering everything else visible or invisible as it sees fit. Bisexuality actually leads the way in challenging heterosexual hegemony because the bisexual male, within his own psyche and life, has *already* relegated heterosexuality to only one among other choices. Every bisexual is a living microcosm of a future society in which the choice between gay and straight will not only cease to be controversial — it might cease to be at all.

I acknowledge that many now think it is reductive to speak of there being only two genders, male and female, thereby discounting transsexuals and androgynous persons. Gender studies have become remarkably sophisticated in their efforts to create the most diverse of all possible spectrums, on which anyone who identifies as a mix of genders, and anyone who is attracted to such a mix, can be included. However, movies have been less radical, less all-encompassing in their depiction of bisexualities. Partly, there is a conflict in representation, to the extent that films about bisexual males also contain homosexual male characters: for a generation now, it has been considered important to depict gay men in films as masculine and "normalized," like straight men (in other words, not effeminate), even if the reality of gay personality remains diverse. Moreover, to make it clear that the subject *is* bisexuality, a film will often emphasize the more traditional aspects of gender: the woman is a "typical estrogen female," the men are "typical testosterone males." Movies have emphasized gender virtually since their inception, and it could certainly be argued that they have always glamorized gender difference too much, at the expense of androgyny. And yet, there remains an ingrained assumption in cinema (and I must confess I share it to a certain degree) that male bisexuality implies "twice the testosterone." The clear-cut choice between "the Woman" and "the Man" dramatizes the bisexual male's central dilemma — "Whom do I love?"— as well as his potential liberation, if he comes to see the categories as essentially arbitrary, interchangeable from the standpoint of emotional response and sexual pleasure. It could be argued that the genders themselves are never completely interchangeable, since they correspond to specific pleasures (and specific people). At any rate — and again, more for the purposes of this book than anything else — it has made more sense to employ the following as a working definition a male bisexual: an identified man who loves and has sex with one or more identified women and one or more identified men.

Likewise, my decision to limit this book to bisexual *males* was in no sense an attempt to slight the real struggles of bisexual women. In terms of cinema, the presentation of female bisexuality is often so different from the presentation of male bisexuality that the two subjects can be only vaguely considered in light of each other. Many films about bisexual women have been lightweight and exploitative, with *Basic Instinct* (1992) as perhaps the lowest point of the genre. Whether used to excite male heterosexual fantasy or to incite male heterosexual fears, films about bisexual women are still largely relegated to a cinematic ghetto where males control the nature of the discourse. The proliferation of gay male cinema, on the other hand, has caused the subject of male bisexuality to be treated more seriously in a number of films, even if these films are at times somewhat dishonest and exploitative, too. But in general, whenever a man explores bisexuality, it is rarely treated lightly within culture; even the most offhanded films about bisexual males tend to dramatize the subject in a way which is, at the very least, thought-provoking about what male bisexuality could mean to monogamy, patriarchy, love, sex, and masculinity itself.

In my research I am indebted, in particular, to two pioneering books which helped shape my own thinking about bisexuality. The first is *Dual Attraction: Understanding Bisexuality*, by Martin S. Weinberg, Colin J. Williams, and Douglas W. Pryor. This remarkable study is the product of extensive surveys and interviews conducted over a period of decades with self-identified bisexuals (male and female) associated with the Bisexual Center of San Francisco. The authors' research began in 1983 and ended in 1988, after the AIDS crisis had begun to force bisexuals to reevaluate some of the freedoms they had formerly enjoyed. AIDS and its dangers had stigmatized Bay Area bisexual men and women, and driven their tentative attempts at forging a community into a kind of diaspora, marked by the closing of the Bisexual Center itself. The appeal of *Dual Attraction* lies in the thoughtful and unreconstructed testimony of the bisexual subjects who lent their life stories to the project. It was invaluable for me to hear bisexuals speaking in their own words (albeit anonymously), some of whom I have quoted here in order to clarify, amplify or contest certain points presented by the films.

The second book is Dr. Marjorie Garber's mammoth cultural study, *Vice Versa: Bisexuality and the Eroticism of Everyday Life*. Her thesis is that bisexuality is everywhere, but denied and ignored by our society. Her belief that all labels are inherently misleading and false did much to open my eyes to the fact that bisexuality is often a struggle against labeling complex human beings with reductive, one-dimensional "tags." Her writing on the nature of erotic and romantic triangles is also distinctive and illuminating; she believes the triad, rather than the couple, is the true geometry of love in our culture (in art and in life), for reasons which speak to a certain innate universal bisexuality. A third figure is often needed to bring two other figures together, in a kind of symphony of projected desires; all three points of a triangle, regardless of gender, are involved with all of the others — the flow of desire running like an animating electrical current in all directions.

I have also consulted two other works of scholarship: *Bi Any Other Name: Bisexual People Speak Out*, edited by Loraine Hutchins and Lani Kaahumanu, and *Getting Bi: Voices of Bisexuals Around the World*, edited by Robyn Ochs and Sarah Rowley. Both are anthologies of life stories and testimonies of bisexuals: they are heartfelt and meticulously inclusive, and reward repeated readings with nearly endless insights.

Finally, this book has been inspired and informed by personal experiences: my conversations, friendships and relationships with bisexual males. None of these experiences appear directly in the book, but nonetheless permeate it, in the same way that the masculine man who confounds expectations, who opens himself to the possibilities of love in all its forms, has been a source of fascination to me throughout my life, and an abiding muse to my creative existence. I wrote this book for him.

Introduction:
Searching for Bob Elkin

There are as many definitions of bisexuality as there are bisexuals.[1]

Bill Condon has spoken of the reaction which his film *Kinsey* (2004) received for its prominent male kiss: "People groaned, kids groaned, during this kiss, and I thought that was really interesting. You know, I had been a teenager when I saw my first male kiss onscreen, which was in *Sunday Bloody Sunday*. Shocking, then; a lot of people talked about it, because it was a full-on kiss... It was just interesting to think that thirty-five years later something like this would still be disturbing to people."[2]

While it might be a bit sad that certain audiences remain as put off by same-sex kissing as ever, it is nice to have a certain artistic synergy between John Schlesinger's *Sunday Bloody Sunday* (1971) — a pioneering treatment of male bisexuality, still in many ways ahead of its time — and *Kinsey*, a post-millennial treatment of, among other things, the same subject. But even with this synergy, one important distinction should not surprise us: the male cinematic kiss of today is more like a stranded gesture (neither wholly new nor wholly acceptable) rather than a piece from an unfolding revolutionary tapestry, as it was in 1971. During that vaunted Age of Explorations (the late 1960's and early 1970's), men were walking on the moon; and here on this planet other men were also journeying light years. In the same year that *Sunday Bloody Sunday* was released, members of the influential art-rock band Roxy Music were raiding disparate wardrobes for leopard skin and leather, velvet and sequins, forging a playful, campy, and at times sexually ambiguous style of dress that was both retro and futuristic, romantic and avant-garde. Other films of that period — including Schlesinger's *Midnight Cowboy* (1969), which won a Best Picture Oscar in spite of its X rating, Pier Paolo Pasolini's *Teorema* (*Theorem*, 1968), Nicolas Roeg and Donald Cammell's *Performance* (1968), Luchino Visconti's *The Damned* (1969), Harold Prince's *Something for Everyone* (1970), Michael Sarne's *Myra Breckenridge* (1970), Ken Russell's *Women in Love* (1970) and *The Music Lovers* (1971), Bob Fosse's *Cabaret* (1972), as well as Paul Morrissey's films with Joe Dallesandro, John Waters' early films, and much of Rainer Werner Fassbinder's work — featured major characters in sexual flux, often in rebellion against narrow categories and identities.

No home, in those days, seemed to be without its inevitable exploding closet. We are still fascinated by, and still trying to fully understand, that era, a seemingly magical time when the interests of homosexual and bisexual men happened to sync up, in an unprecedented way, with the financial interests of pop culture. "To be young and bisexual in the seventies meant in part to find the media and the music industry describing a life that uncannily matched one's own desires, and, as all popular media do, also created them."[3] Indeed, in popular culture, from Mick Jagger's "Memo to Turner" in *Performance* to Ziggy Stardust to *The Rocky Horror Picture Show* (1972), the figure of the bisexual male represented a bastion of vast sexual freedom, bordering on a thriving state of anarchy.

Those familiar representations had both metaphorical and non-metaphorical implications. When used as a metaphor, male bisexuality has always been particularly potent and versatile. The bisexual as space alien: passing judgment on our planet for its miserable lack of variety, getting mired here, falling prey to our harsh atmosphere. The bisexual as superman: able to see through straight people's squeamish objections, able to accomplish impossible seductions in a single bound. The bisexual as secular Christ: preaching love and tolerance, standing out from the lonely herd, finally being made to suffer for the sins of a corrupt and hypocritical world. In a word, the bisexual as outlaw: breaking all laws of identification and commitment, robbing from the sexually rich, perhaps, to give to the sexually poor.

But this last point is less clear than it might seem, regarding the question of who the "sexually rich" and "sexually poor" actually are. In fact, this question occupies the center of that transvaluation of dualisms which bisexuality promotes. The biggest danger in trying to understand bisexual experience is the tendency to interpret it unilaterally rather than, appropriately enough, bilaterally. I am thinking about the tendency of privileging one side of bisexual experience — either the hetero- or the homosexual — over the other, to view the bisexual as either a heterosexual dabbling in the gay life, or a gay man playing at heterosexuality. What is most decisive about the bisexual as a film character, for example, and what makes him so radical, so accruing of metaphorical significance, is the fact that he undoes and deconstructs classifications and labels. Wherever he goes, his "dissatisfaction," his search for something more, something else, never fails to remind each part of the world, normally enclosed in its superior isolation, that other parts of the world continue to exist. The bisexual male is a walking dialectic in action.

This is why we need to consider the bisexual male as someone who is not fickle or indecisive by definition, but instead as someone who experiences an attraction to both sexes as his normal, possibly innate condition, the way a straight male feels it is normal to be attracted to women and a gay male to be attracted to men. The partner of a bisexual male might be wary of his propensity to "cheat" with either gender, since couples are often taken up with policing each other's interaction with the world, although such jealousy and possessiveness are never healthy and in fact lead to valid questions about whether monogamy is a natural or even desirable state. But at any rate, the assumption that a bisexual will cheat simply *because* he is bisexual is surely as insulting as the assumption that a heterosexual or homosexual man will inevitably cheat because of *his* orientation.

And even if we are presented with a nonmonogamous bisexual male, this might only mean that we must revise our views of monogamy accordingly. (This is the "Apples and Oranges" theory: for one apple to get set aside for another apple might indeed be a reflection on the quality of the first apple, whereas an apple getting set aside for an orange only speaks to a legitimate taste for variety.) Admittedly, in the world of abstract theory, nonmonogamy can be more stimulating and easier to follow than it is in the day-to-day world, where real feelings are involved. Certainly in films, bisexual characters and their appetite for variety have made for fascinating reexaminations of monogamy as institution and daily practice. In *Sunday Bloody Sunday*, for example, we learn a great deal about Bob Elkin (Murray Head), a young man who is romantically and sexually involved with a young woman, Alex (Glenda Jackson), and an older man, Dr. Hirsch (Albert Finney), but the one thing we never learn is which lover predates the other in his emotional life. Indeed, this very issue, which might be crucial to understanding a conventional story of exclusively heterosexual "cheating" (or exclusively homosexual cheating, for that matter) is never raised, precisely because it is not an issue for Bob. Bob is not cheating on Alex with Dr. Hirsch, or vice versa. He does not seem to have one single primary relationship, which he then becomes deflected from, according to the traditional "Boy meets girl" continuum. Neither of his lovers can be defined as a response or reaction to the other. Rather, they both constitute separate, distinct, complete worlds, which Bob visits in turn the way a spaceman-traveler might visit different planets, planets which are connected through Bob but which have only the vaguest knowledge of each other. (Ultimately it might be the strangeness of *life on earth* — as witnessed by a kind of "stranger passing among us" — that becomes apparent in many dramatic stories about bisexual relationships.)

What we are touching on, here, is an important larger point: just as individual and collective lives exemplify narrative arcs, so the art of narrative has always been a way of giving recognizable shape to inchoate social identities. (And the bisexual character, therefore, constitutes a moment of revolutionary action in both society and narrative.) This is why film is a powerful arena where issues of acceptance and toleration are put to daily tests. In the taxonomy of visual representations, we recognize elements of the living world better once they have been catalogued by movies: nothing exists as fully as it does until it exists within a film, and can therefore be pointed to as unique evidence of a phenomenological experience often too fleeting or complicated to be pinpointed when it occurs in life.

Movies and life are perhaps best thought of as parallel realities, the former a complex intersubjective illusion which has little direct consequence, the latter a complex intersubjective illusion that has enormous direct consequence; the two can be made to bleed over into each other, and they can even be made, now and then, to intersect, like train tracks that sometimes switch into each other. They can be testing grounds for each other. But one thing obtains: to be shut out of the movies, or always depicted unflatteringly in them, is to experience a special kind of pain which only the members of a heavily saturated media culture can know. It stands to reason that if the intricate mimesis of films can reflect lives which people already live, then they can also help inspire lives which people might possibly live. We have always learned how to present ourselves to the world, how to exist among others, how to select our identities, from the movies. As writer-director André Téchiné has said: "People say the same things, think the same things, and, what's more serious, desire the same things that they've seen in the movies. They have the same obsessions."[4]

Like an enormous visual encyclopedia, film defines elements of reality by giving them an archetypal representation. Good Guy, Bad Guy, Damsel in Distress: in this primal triumvirate, the generic descriptors alone are enough to conjure images of men and women from specific films. But where, in this hall of mirrors, can the bisexual male be found — or is his identity too inherently complicated and contradictory, too threatening, perhaps, ever to be reduced to an archetype? The very question exposes the bad faith of archetypes themselves, because, even though they have the power to fixate an identity in the public consciousness as indelibly as figures on a chess board or face cards in a deck of fifty-two, they presuppose that identities are best precisely *when they are fixed*: static, unchanging. And it is part of the nature of bisexuality to rebel against just this impactedness, this state of being narrowly defined.

It is ironic, to say the least, that films have not depicted bisexual males nearly as often or as accurately as they should have, since film in general has always been permeated with bisexual awareness, bisexual attraction, bisexual innuendo, and what I would call innately bisexual ways of looking at the world. The camera, a great democratizer of desire, applies its flattering, devoted, longing stare to male and female actors alike. The great voyeurism of film is that it enables one to peek into the "hidden world" of what men and women do; a mimesis of multifarious desires unerringly divines and elicits the multifarious desires of its potential audience, which is to say, the entire world. One of the first films, Edison's *The Kiss* (1896), presupposes an interest in seeing both a woman and a man as romantic objects: this film, like the hundreds of thousands of others with onscreen kisses that followed in its wake, does not segregate desire into "the woman's point of view" and "the man's point of view" (anyway, this would not have the same charge, since it would mean the actor or the actress was kissing the camera lens itself!), but instead depicts, in medium two-shot, what we can only call a bisexual point of view. The magic of film is that it works on the Superego to relax the dictum that we cast our eyes only where it is "appropriate" to do so. With *The Kiss*, a scopophilic truth is born: one does not mentally edit out half the shot, half the action, to focus on either the female or the male — indeed it never even enters the mind to try to do so, since it is precisely the *interaction*, the shared space in which the two sides merge, which becomes of primary interest.

That pair of good sports who locked lips for Edison's camera were not even movie stars. A further quantum leap in bisexual looking/desiring was accomplished by the glamorous stars, as many attractive men as attractive women. In theater posters and playbills, as well as Variety Photoplay campaigns, the male stars may have been billed as bait for the women in the audience and the female stars as bait for the men; but this smokescreen dissipated, probably almost immediately, to a more anarchic if still often undisclosed reality, in which everyone was looking admiringly at everyone else. The camera has always noticed and recorded with equal intensity the sexual glamour of female and male actors, that "cross-gender magnetism, an object of [the] performing self that is in fact characteristic of all the greatest stars of [the 20th] century."[5]

It has long been my contention that the roots of the gay liberation movement of the 1960s and the 1970s began some thirty years earlier, when very young gays across the U.S. stared up out of the dark at Dick Powell, Buster Crabbe, Johnny Weissmuller, Errol Flynn, Lew Ayres, Paul Muni, Clark

Gable, John Garfield, Zeppo Marx. Gay poets such as Frank O'Hara and John Wieners, and gay film theorists such as Parker Tyler, give persistent and convincing testimony to the ways in which Hollywood mediated, sharpened, defined, and helped liberate homoerotic desire. In poems such as "Ave Maria," O'Hara links the iconography of Hollywood as secular church with that of Hollywood as capital of polymorphous perversity.

Long before Warhol made film a way of recording omnivorous bisexual desire ("the most beautiful boys," "the most beautiful girls," the unisex term "superstars"), Hollywood had founded an empire upon the same principle. Shrouded inside the protective darkness of the movie theater, private as dreaming but public enough to feel like validation, with that tingle of carrying a brimming glass through a jostling crowd, desire could multiply, flow in simultaneous directions. It could be genderless, borderless, all around and inside oneself at the same time.

But even while the movies were covertly engaged in teaching the world how to look bisexually, they were also overtly engaged in selling narratives whose primary arc still began "Boy meets girl" and ended "Boy gets girl." Whatever misunderstandings and conflicts ensued along the way to provide suspense between the "meeting" and the "getting" (and to mimic the timespan of respectable courtship), the focus of desire remained single-minded, a one-way street: *one boy wants one girl.* Today, when queer cinema has become a booming cottage industry, the basic plotlines of gay-themed films remain little more than a translation of the classic heterosexual narrative — only this time, "Boy meets boy" and "Boy gets boy." It is, partly, the predictability itself that reassures, the sense that complicated human life is reduced, condensed and encapsulated into a ninety-minute metonymy, whereby the ups and downs of one ultimately successful love story can stand in for a host of yearnings for meaning and certainty. Just as it is the fear of death we unconsciously seek to stave off in that ubiquitous "They lived happily ever after," so it is sexual ambiguity that is considered the enemy of a film audience's cozy complacency, its peace of mind and its willingness to buy tickets.

A work which addresses the anti-linear possibilities of bisexual narrative is *Amores Possíveis* (*Possible Loves*, 2001). In fact, this sexy, experimental Brazilian film, directed by Sandra Werneck, might well define the Bisexual Narrative in all its complications, its repetitions of the same man's romantic moments with different (and different-gendered) partners. Carlos (Murilo Benicio) waits at a movie theater on a rainy night for his date, Julia (Carolina Ferraz). As time passes and he appears to have been stood up, the film cuts to a series of "possible loves" and future lives for Carlos. First, he wakes up in bed next to his wife, Maria (Beth Goulart); they have their desultory breakfast ritual before Carlos goes off to his successful law practice with his partner Pedro (Emilio de Melo). Later, Carlos wakes up next to Pedro; in this possibility, Carlos married Julia and had a son, Lucas (Alberto Szafran), with her, but then left her for a gay man, creating great animosity on Julia's part. In a third scenario, Carlos is a bachelor Lothario and mama's boy who wakes up next to a ditzy one-night stand whom his overbearing, protective mother (Irene Ravache) promptly chases away.

These three scenarios could not be more different, and the fact that Werneck cuts back and forth among them rather than letting each one play out individually lends a dream-like quality to the film, which functions as a kind of allegory about the natural curiosity young people feel about who they will become in life, and whether or not they would have been happier with their first loves. With the stubborn reoccurrence of an *idée fixe*, Julia features in all three scenarios. Married Carlos runs into Julia by accident, and, as they catch up with each other, he initiates an affair with her, and later leaves his wife for her. Bisexual Carlos finds himself increasingly drawn back to Julia, in spite of her rage against him (at one point, she tells him she longs for him to die of AIDS). Overcoming her anger, he tells her he wants to leave Pedro and reunite with her. Bachelor Carlos joins a dating service to help him find his soul mate: he is given an electronic "localizer," which works like a divining rod to lead him to the right woman; it leads him straight to his first love, Julia. But although the idealistic Carlos is obsessed with Julia in all of the scenarios, his attempts at having a relationship with her fail in realistic terms. It is the kind of fantasy that remains a fantasy, even when it "comes true."

In *Possible Loves*, bisexuality exists as one more option in a life given over to wondering: "Who am I? What kind of love would make me the happiest, the most fulfilled?" Werneck is to be commended for including bisexuality in a romantic film aimed mainly at a heterosexual audience; as one of her characters says, regarding sexual preferences, "We must consider every possibility, no prejudices." *Possible Loves* is fearlessly told as if sexual orientation itself were mutable, as if the narrative of a single life could contain numerous possibilities, among them bisexuality. We are happy to follow the likeable Carlos through all the various identities he grows into, and through. Werneck's cross-cutting can be dizzying; we also grow attached to the secondary characters in Carlos' lives, and regret seeing them lose out to the force-of-nature Julia. But these things, too, are true to the experience of many bisexuals — their lives inevitably grow complicated as they become attracted to more than one gender, and they often end up having to make decisions which unintentionally hurt one or another of their partners, and which make them feel as though they are being untrue to their bisexual selves. If Julia is the love of Carlos' life, then this worn cliché of romantic cinema is mitigated by the film's belief in inevitable detours and twists along the way — indeed, the detours and twists end up being what constitutes real life and happiness more than the idea of clinging to an illusion, belief in the single Great Love. By its very title, *Possible Loves* plays upon the openness of bisexuality to possibilities; and in its intricate narrative it questions the workings of fate in human lives, which bisexuality also does to a certain extent: are we predestined only to feel and experience what goes along with one narrow gender or orientation, or can we change that biological or social destiny?

Needless to say, the bisexual narrative, with its permutations, oscillations and trade-offs, cannot be reduced to simple terms. Michael Mayer, the director of the bisexual narrative *A Home at the End of the World* (2004), has described his film in this way: "This is one of those stories that's, I think, impossible to sort of reduce to a little nugget or a sound byte. You just can't, it's too complicated."[6] As welcome and refreshing as it is to hear a director commit to telling a story that has any degree of human complexity, the actual truth of the bisexual narrative is that it can never quite be complicated enough to reflect the realities behind it. Rather than obeying a strictly linear logic, the bisexual narrative automatically doubles, bifurcates — boy meets girl, same boy meets boy, boy falls in loves and has relations with girl and boy, boy is asked to choose, boy does not choose, or boy chooses but feels cheated. And behind all of these actions, there are often unanswerable, barely even asked questions of how and why, who and when. You get the picture. Twice the romance, in theory, should be twice as romantic; in practice, it isn't very romantic at all, at least not in a classical sense. The sentimental cliché of the Great Love — the love that demands all sacrifice, all fixation on the single flawless image of the beloved — meets its ultimate Waterloo in the bisexual. The idea that one can have two Great Loves is anathema to the very concept of the Great Love itself.

Also, because films tend to trade primarily in known quantities, visible and definable phenomena, literal meanings, they are unlikely vehicles to explore and express the often unquantifiable and unseen inner landscape of bisexuality. Films externalize, they are the triumph of appearances, of the physical world. Wherever bisexuality exists as an evanescent question, a fleeting mood, a feeling, it has often escaped the framing of the camera's eye. "Put in terms of a conundrum, we might say: How can something fluid be something solid?"[7] Given that we each forge an entirely personal sexuality — freely ranging, open to new possibilities, while nonetheless tethered to certain core sensory stimuli, memories, fetishes and scenarios — how, again, can film capture the infinite cloudscape of any sexual awareness, much less bisexual awareness? It is no wonder that many films have opted to deal only with the surface, with the most overtly sexual (and sexy) aspects of bisexuality, rather than the agonizing or joyous teasing out of feelings, that psychosexual equivalent of the Proustian madeleine which jogs the incomplete repression to spontaneous life.

* * *

Dr. Alfred Kinsey was the first scientific researcher to attempt to quantify the presence of bisexuality in human sexual behavior. First published in 1948, the famous Kinsey Scale measures gradations of sexual preferences:

(0) Exclusively heterosexual
(1) Predominantly heterosexual, only incidentally homosexual
(2) Predominantly heterosexual, but more than incidentally homosexual
(3) Equally heterosexual and homosexual
(4) Predominantly homosexual, but more than incidentally heterosexual
(5) Predominantly homosexual, only incidentally heterosexual
(6) Exclusively homosexual

The majority of the numbers — from 1 to 5 — measure different emphases of bisexuality. The number 3 represents the golden mean, as it were, of bisexual experience, what we might call true bisexuality. However, the word "equally" has been misunderstood. It does not assume an exact one-to-one ratio of male lovers to female lovers or an equal length of time in which a person acknowledges or acts upon heterosexual and homosexual impulses. It can best be understood as meaning: to whatever extent they each manifest themselves, the hetero- and homosexual attractions are *equally genuine*. Each holds up as real in and of themselves, whenever and however they occur. To be entirely "with" a female partner when he is with her (focused on her, thinking about her, not in denial) and to be entirely "with" a male partner when he is with him (focused on him, thinking about him, not in denial): this, to me, is the meaning of the sometimes contested word "equally," and the meaning of true bisexuality in males.

True bisexuality, like true north on a compass, can be hard to locate exactly. Is it an open-ended refusal to choose? Is it a merry-go-round where one hops from the tigress to the lion and back again before the calliope fades, a musical chairs of relationships ("serial monogamy")? Or is it something even harder to imagine, the wish or attempt to settle down simultaneously with a man *and* a woman? (And is bisexuality about "settling" for anything?)

There is an exchange between a woman and a bisexual male in *A Home at the End of the World* which summarizes both the allure of the bisexual male as well as his perceived "weakness":

Claire: You are a strange and mysterious creature... Is there anything you couldn't do?
Bobby: I couldn't be alone.
Claire: No. No, you couldn't, could you?

One of the first stereotypes that is shattered when one reads the testimony of bisexual males is the notion that they do not ever look for real love. In fact, this is far from being the case. "I am a romantic. If I fell in love with a man, and our relationship was developing that way, I might become strictly homosexual. The same possibility exists with a woman."[8] The key word here is *possibility*, since one of the most liberating aspects of bisexuality remains the fact that the bisexual has more avenues available to him for finding love and pleasure. "Many combinations of behavior, feelings, and self-identification are possible."[9] Ideally, this translates into a kind of self-awareness that is always expanding, always learning, always evolving. "The erotic discovery of bisexuality is the fact that it reveals sexuality to be a process of growth, transformation and surprise, not a stable and knowable state of being."[10] Like Darwinian adaptations, endowed with ever-renewing skills to live longer, richer, more productive lives, the bisexual would seem to be nature's perfect design: no loneliness, no waiting—he can see beauty in all, and rather than waste stray impulses, he rolls them together into a nest-egg of erotic creativity guaranteed to warm a body on a cold winter's night.

So what's not to love? Seemingly nothing. And yet, controversy often attends the implicit challenge the bisexual issues to erotic signifiers (labels). The very openness to possibility that makes bisexual males thrilling and attractive to some seems to make them inimical to others. "Bisexuality consists of a mingling of sexual feelings, behaviors, and romantic inclinations that does not easily gel with society's categories of typical sexuality."[11] Partly it is bisexuality's Protean nature that seems to encourage people to read into it rather than accept it at face value, and to judge it as "more one thing than another"—with the placement of emphasis on either the straight or the gay side depending largely on the viewpoint of the beholder. A certain amount of open-endedness in one's own identity might be required to acknowledge and embrace it in others. Is bisexuality, for this reason, an often invisible identity, as Dr. Marjorie Garber has wondered? To what extent does such a refusal to see the validity of the bisexual stem from the unconscious belief that the bisexual himself may be too suggestive, too fluid and labile, for his own good—or for our own? Bisexuality is often hijacked to suit other people's cross-purposeful interpretive agendas, and to be fair, it sometimes lends itself to such hijackings in its very amorphousness; yet, as a metaphor or as an image, male bisexuality derives much of its special expressive resonance precisely from this Protean nature.

Indeed, the more one looks at the subject of bisexuality, the more one is forced to conclude that, although it is the fluid, nonlinear, hybridized aspect of bisexuality which can make it exciting and provocative, it is also this same aspect which can make it seem not merely undefined but actively threatening toward anyone with a vested interest in a fixed sexual identification as a way of life (still the majority of people). Both the heterosexual and the homosexual ends of the spectrum have raised red flags at the presence of bisexuals. "Bisexuals always risk being stigmatized from two directions: by heterosexuals for their homosexual inclinations and by homosexuals for their heterosexual inclinations."[12]

We might expect the staunch heterosexual to frown on the bisexual male's quotient of gayness, for the same reasons that he frowns on gay people — but what about gays themselves? Wouldn't they welcome bisexual men as at least *half*-brothers-in-arms? Eve Kosofsky Sedgwick writes: "Since Foucault, it has been common to distinguish a modern concept of 'homosexuality'—delineating a continuous *identity*— from a supposedly premodern (though persistent) concept of 'sodomy,' which delineated discrete *acts*."[13] The identity itself becomes invested in protecting the acts, giving them serious, continuous meaning within a societal context. Self-labeling as homosexual, and the risk incurred when someone comes all the way out as a gay person, have been seen as essential to the process of gay self-acceptance. The willingness to declare oneself openly gay is also tied, as a bid for greater mainstream acceptance, to the assertion that gay orientation is always innate and immutable: if a person truly is "born that way," then he should not be shunned or persecuted for an identity which is beyond his choosing. Of course, the idea that sexual orientation is wholly unchosen (like race, for instance) has never been entirely valid, since there is always a point when a person chooses to accept, announce and act on his sexual orientation, no matter how fixed or innate it might be. Societal acceptance of homosexuality must come; but it will never come in a conditional or "manipulated" way; instead, same-sex activity must be accepted even when it might appear most arbitrary from a heterosexual viewpoint. This is the only true acceptance.

"Whether an explanation for sexual preference is biological, psychological, or sociological, the basic presumption usually is that sexual preference is set early and changes little through life."[14] It has been difficult enough getting the world to entertain the probability of a biogenetic factor for homosexuality —

could there be a bisexual gene as well? Bisexuality suggests that unconventional sexual lifestyles may be as much a matter of experience and willingness (therefore at least partly constructed) rather than wholly essentialist and inborn; but why must it be any less valid or authentic for that? In general, the late 20th century campaign to reduce complex issues of human behavior to biological imperatives — not only in sexuality but in other areas, such as the treatment of addiction as a "disease" or the use of neuro-chemical medicines to treat disparate psychological disorders that would have once been treated mainly with psychoanalysis — has often proven to be regressive and infantilizing, disregarding the role of self-will and curtailing the primacy of the creative imagination. We must learn to trust once again the testimony people give about who they believe themselves to be, not merely the lines they chart on graphs or the CAT scans they produce.

The problem with comprehending any of these issues in a clear, fair and open light is that societal shame and prohibition still surround non-heterosexual lifestyles. We simply do not know what people would do — or admit to doing — if they felt completely free to express homosexual or bisexual impulses. Bisexuality can require the same coming-out process as homosexuality, and is just as traumatic: "It took me a long time," one bisexual male has stated, "to acknowledge my bisexuality, and even longer to accept this part of myself."[15] But if heterosexuality remains "the norm," our mania for simplified dualisms (is there, perhaps, a dualist gene which overrides everything, even sexual preference, in the human DNA?) has determined that homosexuality, not bisexuality, must represent "the loyal opposition." Because heterosexuality is so all-pervasive, reaching into families, schools and other social institutions to turn every embryonic gay identity against itself, it has become common to defer all same-sex activity to the default option of closeted homosexuality: "He is secretly gay, he is in denial, he only sleeps with women as a cover," and so forth. "Some homosexuals saw bisexuals as people who were really homosexual but afraid to admit it, or as unloyal lovers who might switch to the other sex on a whim."[16]

Of course, these anti-bisexual attitudes presume, inaccurately, that bisexuality is not a true identity, and that bisexuals incur no risks of their own. "Many bisexuals referred to the persistent pressures they experienced to relabel themselves as 'gay' ... and to engage in sexual activity exclusively with the same sex. It was asserted that no one was *really* bisexual, and that calling oneself 'bisexual' was a politically incorrect and inauthentic identity...."[17] In the sexual arena it turns out there are repressive laws even where we thought these might have been done away with as a matter of sheer principle.

"I learned to accept the fact that there are a lot of people out there who aren't accepting. They can be intolerant, selfish, shortsighted, and so on. Finally, in growing up, I learned to say, 'So what, I don't care what others think.'"[18] With this testimony we are placed squarely back at the bisexual as outlaw, his most attractive, redemptive and far-ranging quality being that he stands apart from the conformist masses, he does not fit into any given mold. According to this, we might hope to find bisexuals as leaders spearheading social and political revolutions; however, we might also expect to find that they are so individualistic that they do not fit easily into even the most radical of groups and networks.

In fact, it is far from easy to live such a life — always on the fringes, often alone, never finding a permanent place where one belongs. Again, what makes bisexuality provocative as a metaphor can make it frustrating as an actual social option. Bisexual image and bisexual reality must never be confused with or wholly subsumed into each other, but must be understood in constant relation to each other. Far from being overpowering and charismatic personalities who silence all quibbles by conscripting everyone in sight into one enormous, non-stop orgy (the *Rocky Horror Picture Show–Interview with the Vampire* branding of predatory, superhuman bisexual men), actual bisexual men have admitted to very human-sized doubts and second guesses. "A few [bisexuals] wondered whether they were lying to themselves."[19] "When I'm with a man or a woman for a period of time, then I begin to wonder how attracted I really am to the other side."[20] "I know I have strong sexual feelings towards men, but then I don't know how to get close to or be sexual with a man. I guess that what happens is I start wondering how genuine my feelings are...."[21] "There were times when my attractions to women were so strong that I didn't feel attraction for men and vice versa."[22]

If bisexuals themselves are sometimes confused by their own contradictory urges and attractions, it is no wonder that outsiders have had a difficult time trying to visualize them, without simplifying them in one way or another, nudging them into whatever established category seems to need their "swing votes." It is hard to see the spaces between: between bodies, between identities, between certainties. Bisexual nature sometimes exists in the deepest part of the self, even, perhaps, unacknowledged by the self. And the bisexual male — stranded in social history, judged half saint, half devil — continues to defend his lonely tower. How could his lifestyle be just "fickle," "wishy-washy," "fence-sitting," when it has become as persecuted as any unconventional sexual orientation in the AIDS era? It is in this persecution, and in his isolated, confused, often unfulfilled yearnings, that the bisexual appears to us today. Where once stood a sign of surplus desire, of erotic energy overflowing the boundaries of a single body, a single gender, there now stands a sign of sincere and helpless *intention*: to love and be loved. In place of the bisexual as space alien, as outsider, we need to make room for the bisexual as creator spirit: sowing seeds of lust for both sexes is perhaps the ideal gesture of humanist appreciation for this populous, multifarious world. Ultimately, the bisexual male occupies a kind of fulcrum position from which we might contemplate the nature of all human identity, exclusive or inclusive, sexual and otherwise.

* * *

In practice (rather than in theory), is there ever true equality in bisexual attraction, or is there always one gender who holds pride of place, so to speak, in any given person's psyche? In 2005, research teams in Chicago and Toronto studied the arousal patterns of self-identified bisexual males watching sexually provocative images of women and then of men. The expectation was that the bisexual males would be aroused equally by both types of images. In an article entitled "Straight, Gay or Lying?: Bisexuality Revisited," which appeared in *The New York Times* on July 5, 2005, Benedict Carey writes: "The psychologists found that men who identified themselves as bisexual were in fact exclusively aroused by either one sex or the other, usually by other men."

The inflammatory title of the article itself, in its dismissive reduction of bisexuality to "lying," speaks to a familiar aspect of the contemporary discourse on sexual identity. Indeed, it often feels today as if the most politically correct option in terms of the gay rights movement is to view those men who profess to be bisexual as "lying" in order to deceive the world about the fact that they are really gay. The queer movement often seems to lay claim to any man who commits a homosexual act, wanting to promote the idea of homosexual orientation not only as essentialist but as an all-or-nothing proposition (if you have any tendencies toward being gay, then you are gay, de facto). In this, however, they display little difference from a classically homophobic mother, for instance, who clings to the idea that her gay son is really straight because he once dated a woman. In this sense, the Chicago-Toronto study cannot see the bisexual forest, as it were, for the trees: we need to look beyond cultural bias to see that a person's decision to label himself as bi may tell us much more about who he is, in the long run, than how he responds sexually at any given moment.

The article goes on to say: "But the men in the study who described themselves as bisexual did not have patterns of arousal that were consistent with their stated attraction to men and to women. Instead, about three-quarters of the group had arousal patterns identical to those of gay men; the rest were indistinguishable from heterosexuals." Note how neatly these numbers conform to the kind of politically correct assumptions I have been talking about: *three-quarters are actually gay*. "'I'm not denying that bisexual behavior exists,' said Dr. Bailey, 'but I am saying that in men there's no hint that true bisexual arousal exists, and that for men arousal is orientation.'" This last statement presupposes a false syllogism: if an orientation is a complicated nexus of cultural identification, experience, and the willingness to self-label, then how can it be reduced to a simple physiological response? Arousal might be equal to orientation in the animal kingdom, but human males are more complex in their socialization processes, including the subtle use of language and shades of meaning to define, express and codify fleeting emotions.

Strangely enough, the article also informs us that "a third of the men ... showed no significant arousal watching the movies [at all]." Unlike the men who were "exclusively" aroused by the men or the women in the films, these men are not called liars, however; simply un-aroused. The fact of arousal itself becomes a reason to be suspicious of the self-labeling of the aroused males. Regardless of the reasons why a man might or might not become erect in a semi-public setting, "[the un-aroused males'] lack of response did not change the overall findings...." Seemingly eager to jump at certain conclusions (that males who become aroused might also tend to lie, or that bisexuality does not truly exist in males), Dr. Bailey implies that nothing short of a tireless, unceasing supply of erections toward anything and everything shown to them could convince him that the bisexual males *were not* lying.

The Chicago-Toronto study ties in, depressingly, with all of the societal prejudices elicited by bisexuality. It is telling in the way that it attempts to invade, colonize and quantify the most private of inner landscapes, the masturbation fantasy; and yet, do masturbation fantasies hold the entire key to anyone's sexual make-up? "Seated alone in a laboratory room," we read in the *Times*' article, "the men ... watched a series of erotic movies, some involving only women, some involving only men." The methodology of this particular study may have been flawed in that the videos showed only women or only men, since the researchers would not have been able to separate out the amount of response to a man versus to a woman in a video that showed both genders interacting together. But in spite of, or related to, this particular methodological problem (and indeed, measuring amounts of attraction to one gender as opposed to the other is a constant area of uncertainty, according to the testimony of actual bisexuals), what we must begin to view as suspect is precisely the habitual attempt on the part of non-bisexuals to separate the genders, and to pit them against each other. Psychologically, the separation of genders in the erotic films shown in the Chicago-Toronto study may have already influenced the difference in the subjects' arousal rates. When bisexual males offer a compelling argument to bring the genders closer together, to see them truly as complementary to each other rather than antagonistic, it seems telling that society often responds by hysterically pushing them to opposite corners again, reifying the essentially heterosexual-based *difference*, with which the majority of people (gay men included) seem to be more comfortable.

Certainly, this is one major reason why some people tend to view bisexuality as a complex (if incomplete) mimesis of heterosexual desire by partially closeted gay men: this preserves the notion of straight identity as inherently privileged (everyone *wants* to participate in it on some level) while placing the bisexual "safely" in the gay camp (he was the Other all along). The idea that someone could be straight and still want something else, that being straight might not be enough for some people, is deeply disturbing to the heterosexual status quo.

What are we afraid of admitting to ourselves? What are we afraid of losing? Heterosexuality is the only sexual identity that is not called upon to explain itself, to uncover its own meaning; rather, it is perceived as being implicitly meaningful, and more than this, as a fountain of meanings defining the world around it. (Adam was the original Namer, etc.) Homosexuality, on the other hand, is burdened with the innately homophobic perception that, wherever it occurs, it must explain and justify itself, must define itself. The most primal cultural wound of coming to gay awareness is still the moment of recognition, not when a man says, "I am gay" (for this is already progress, implying self-acceptance), but even before this, when he senses his own difference and the negativity it is likely to produce in others (negativity which he already feels toward himself, and which he registers on his own internal, culturally calibrated scale) and says, "I am not straight." Before any value can be added to his gay identity, the gay male must first undergo the pain, imposed by heterosexual culture, of feeling himself excluded from, and depleted of, the implicit heterosexual meaning which everyone is presumed to have and to want. Doubtlessly this pain might be more transient and momentary today than it once was; but it is likely to remain the starting place of every gay identity—the awareness that one must always somehow journey from the straight world to the gay one. The bisexual, intriguingly enough, enacts this moment of the initial crisis of meaning again and again, as if it was precisely the act of throwing the implicit meaning(s) into crisis which attracted him in the first place.

One of the larger heterosexual blind spots defined by the Chicago-Toronto study is that we must also be wary of reducing male sexual preferences only to matters of blunt physical arousal. In the patriarchal world, the male erection is the be-all and end-all, creator and consumer, a machine of endless self-reification, needing nothing but its own presence to complete itself as a sign of desire: the male erection may be the only human physical response that is universally a complete substitute for language. But bisexuality opens up the possibility of a post-patriarchal world, in which male sexuality has the chance of becoming as diffuse and sensitized as what we often conceive of as "female desire"—in other words, extra-genital in nature. Bisexual male erogenous zones multiply, as do the cultural loci where desire can be expressed and given meaning. (The meanings of word-signifers also multiply in bisexual self-reference, as in *"Two loves have I..."*) There is a lack of reference in popular imagination to any kind of coherent bisexual culture; in fact, the very words sound odd when placed together, though there is no reason why they should. It is my hope that some of the films discussed in this book—by directors such as François Ozon, André Téchiné, Pedro Almodóvar, Gregg Araki, Michael Mayer, Pascal Arnold and Jean-Marc Barr, Alexis Dos Santos and others— might begin to form a canon which dramatizes the elasticity of human sexual identity and the gray areas of erotic life. It seems to me that men who identify themselves as bisexual need encouragement to explore and understand their often confusing and contradictory feelings, rather than dismissed with the allegation that they are lying about one or another aspect of themselves.

Instead of always being the "cool guys at the party," who can snap their fingers at a moment's notice and have anyone they want, bisexual males might, more often than not, feel as though they are trying to follow a fleeting zephyr which no one else around them even notices. Internalizing the discouraging attitudes of both the heterosexual and homosexual communities, many bisexual men may experience their deepest yearnings alone, bewildered and without an outlet. To an extent this is because there is, of course, a component of all sexuality which remains elusive. "Eroticism is what escapes, what transgresses rules, breaks down categories, questions boundaries. It cannot be captured in a manual, a chart, a lab test, or a manifesto."[23] To another extent, however, this is because bisexuality is as much driven by romance and love as any sexual identity, while frustrating the standard progress of these emotions with the refusal or inability to choose. After all, a hero can only ride off into the sunset with one person...

Or can he? *That* particular ending might be yet to be seen. To return to Bob Elkin in *Sunday Bloody Sunday*, we see that the exact opposite occurs: he leaves both his female partner Alex and his male partner Dr. Hirsch to move to America and make his fortune as an engineer. Bob's ultimate escape from making a choice, from settling down with either man or woman, has been read by critics such as Vito Russo and Dr. Marjorie Garber as a brave, bold choice in itself, rather than as a deliberate evasion. This is certainly true as far as it goes. At the same time, a certain amount of deliberate evasion is part of the nontraditional pattern of choices which Bob implements. *Sunday Bloody Sunday* offers an all-important key to the bisexual male's allure, at least as a cinematic image: he does not have to live out any particular lifestyle in its grubby day-to-day sense. He is above the same weary routine that drags the rest of us down. As a bisexual, Bob can avoid all the mundane pitfalls of both hetero- *and* homosexuality. In one scene, Dr. Hirsch (without Bob) meets up with an ex-trick on the street who is drunk and angry, even violent; Dr. Hirsch gamely offers to score dope for him. This is redolent of a certain type of urban gay male experience, stereotypical as it might seem — but Bob is spared having to deal with any such unpleasantness. When we see Bob and Dr. Hirsch together, they speak exaltedly about art and making their "famous trip to Italy." Bob gets the best of gay life in the same way that he gets the best of straight life. He stays apart from people long enough that they are always happy to see him when he does turn up again, always ready to start with a fresh, clean slate. Bob is exempted from precisely the constant state of proximity-to-each-other which characterizes the drab or downright obnoxious married lives of the film's numerous heterosexual couples. ("I can't stand people carrying on," he says at one point, trying to escape from a party where a husband and wife are drunkenly feuding.)

Both Alex and Dr. Hirsch accuse Bob of selfishness — not merely because he tends to think of himself first or because he ultimately makes himself "unattainable," though these things play their roles, but because he never has to embody any of the compromises which befall love when it extends itself beyond the bon mot, the seduction, the orgasm. It is Bob's particular genius to know what he wants, not working at love over a difficult period of time, but instead effortlessly reaping the benefits of a kind of free-floating charisma, an electric spark that never has to last longer than it takes to register its frisson.

It can be difficult to maintain romantic feelings in a relationship that is set up to be nonmonogamous, as Alex discovers when she cheats on Bob with another man. Hoping to prod Bob into jealously declaring his love for her, she finds him typically blasé, even grateful perhaps that she has evened the score. "You really don't mind about that, do you?" she asks, a bit astonished, her sense of propriety tested yet again. "We're free to do what we want," Bob affirms, grinning boyishly. Bob is not a hypocrite: he makes a highly principled commitment to the refusal to commit. "Darling," Alex says (Glenda Jackson's weary, gruff, from-the-hip delivery is put to excellent use in *Sunday Bloody Sunday*), "other people often do what they don't want to do at all." Bob groans and turns away, his utopian spirit disappointed by her insistence on turning the conversation back to questions of adult responsibility.

This revises much of what we think of as the paternalistic purview of the traditional hero: that he must be responsible for others, must take care of them the way a father might, must guide them toward doing the "right things" with their lives. In fact, Alex and Dr. Hirsch are both distinguished as people of superior intelligence, independent, laissez-faire perhaps to an uncommon degree in matters of the heart. They are also sophisticated enough to know about each other's existence; they even use the same telephone switchboard exchange, suggesting that it is their destiny, as it were, to always share the same connections. After Bob leaves for America, Alex seeks out Dr. Hirsch. The supportive points of the triangle briefly reach out to each other, but it is a stiff and awkward encounter; without Bob the two have little in common. They are distantly, almost indifferently kind to each other, as if not wishing to look too closely into the mirror each holds up to the other. There is no reconciliation between the gay and the straight world, even if we would like to think it is the bisexual male's project to build one.

But is that his project? With his wide, soulful eyes, Bob remains, throughout the film, an attractive riddle: is he truly an innocent, set apart from the mundane world like one of his own efficient mechanical designs, or is he only selling the mask of innocence to ensnare soft-hearted "victims" like Alex and Dr. Hirsch? Bob expresses the eternal dilemma of the bisexual male, one whose implications are felt in succeeding generations of films. To one extent — the fact that he unites the gay and straight worlds in his own flesh, his own life, mind and spirit — he is, or could be, a valuable liaison in matters of our common humanity, and a powerful testament to human adaptation and resilience. However, to the other, more likely extent that he ends up dividing gay from straight, sowing mainly mistrust and resentment, can the bisexual male truly be accepted as a liaison? Or is he instead perennially doomed to remain on the outside of human interaction, using busy movement back and forth to create the impression that he stands at the center of all things?

Penelope Gilliat's script gives Dr. Hirsch the last word. He is doggedly learning Italian, as if still in preparation for the "famous trip to Italy." Speaking directly to the camera, he simply says, "I miss him, that's all." He affirms that Bob was neither courageous or resourceful, but that the two men had something real, and that "apart from missing him," Dr. Hirsch remains happy with his erstwhile companion. Dr. Hirsch accepts and loves Bob for how he is, not for how he might like him to be; and because the film ends with Dr. Hirsch's words, it is as if he is claiming the relationship, and Bob himself, with the filmmakers' tacit approval. The seed of how we tend to read bisexuality, today, is sown here: Bob is more gay than straight, he belongs with the man, it is the woman, Alex, who does not fit into the schema, and so forth.

Perhaps there is no truer indication of how far gay politics have moved away from male bisexuality than the fact that queer director Jon Shear has a gay character in his film *Urbania* (2000) recite Alex's break-up speech with campy relish: "I've had this business: 'Anything is better than nothing.' There are times when nothing *has* to be better than anything." What does it mean when contemporary gay men stake their self-awareness, their identity, and their bid for mainstream acceptance, on being more like the woman in *Sunday Bloody Sunday*'s classic bisexual triangle, rather than Bob or Dr. Hirsch? Presumably the character who is most abused and betrayed, Alex seems to speak for all those whose love has gone unrequited, and who have tried to love deeply and passionately but had the wool pulled over their eyes, so to speak. But why is Dr. Hirsch's love less visible — or Bob's, for that matter?

These questions, as raised by *Sunday Bloody Sunday*, were some of the ones on my mind as I watched the films described in this book, films from the 1990s and the first decade of the 21st century. In these examples of bisexual cinema, I have looked for meanings in the bisexual male's relations to men and women, to the gay world and the straight world, to himself and others. I do not know if the films, or I, managed to answer any of these questions. Since the mid–1990s there has been an increasing number of films about bisexual male characters; many of these have arisen from, or ended up becoming part of, the ever-expanding category of "gay cinema." Unlike the spate of sexually adventurous, "gender-bending" films in the Age of Explorations, these recent films do not possess that power of novelty which would make them into bona fide cultural events: they are not a galvanized or galvanizing movement, or even necessarily interconnected in a way that speaks directly to our times. And yet, in this lack of momentousness, contemporary bisexual cinema does speak to our times, in that it is no longer seen as noteworthy, in and of itself, for pushing sexual envelopes or eroding taboos. There is, of course, a form of progress there, in that what was once shocking has now become more unassuming, matter-of-fact. Like life, bisexuality just happens, and like bisexual males themselves, bisexual characters and bisexual cinema simply exist.

Actually, not *so* simply. Along with the sense that these recent films are no longer opening volleys in a cultural battle to win visibility and recognition, there is the sense that we have peeled back enough large outer layers of bisexuality and sexual ambiguity, as it were, that the details now matter more than the big, blunt gestures. *How* a character enacts his bisexuality matters more than the simple fact that he is bisexual. If anything, sexual identity issues have become far more variegated over the last decade as a result of a well-intentioned quest for greater and greater inclusiveness. Wishing to avoid stereotypical generalizations, and to be truthful to the multifaceted experiences of "two, three, many bisexualities," we have reached a point where bisexuality in film can appear, and play out, and signify in a vast number of different ways, even if some basic structures and issues obtain from one film to another.

What has been confirmed to me, and what I find most exciting about bisexual cinema — about bisexuality in general — is precisely that it does raise questions, questions that shake up our assumptions about sexual pleasure, identity and labeling, patriarchy and its discontents, the human capacity for and rebellion against monogamy, and the very ways in which social orders are structured. My intuition tells me that it remains more important to keep asking these questions, to keep drawing and re-drawing the circle, in a spirit of permanent sexual revolution, perhaps, than to find concrete answers. The avoidance of the rigid, the petrified, the overdetermined is something which bisexuality can teach us, and something which can make us more alive to human possibility in all its forms.

PART 1
Personal Visions

Long live doubt; through doubt comes insight. — Derek Jarman

1

Fifteen Minutes of the Future: François Ozon's *A Summer Dress*

> The first time I had actual intercourse, an orgasm with a woman, it led me to realize I was bisexual, because I enjoyed it as much as I did with a man, although the former occurred much later on in my sexual experiences.[1]

The anonymous bisexual male quoted above had achieved orgasms with men, but felt that a missing piece of his own particular identity puzzle was put into place when he finally achieved orgasm with a female too. Clearly, he had found concomitant, complementary reasons to seek out orgasms with women as well as men. Is this so unusual? If males and females are part of the same humanity, are in fact aspects of each other, couldn't it be considered more healthy to embrace both of those aspects? And even if it is not necessarily *unhealthy* to be sexually exclusive (whether purely heterosexual or purely homosexual), might it not represent a breakthrough to a richer psychical balance to acknowledge the attraction of both sides?

As a film director, François Ozon consistently creates characters who represent a wide spectrum of sexualities. In fact, Ozon has suggested in his films that bisexuality can be a completely natural tendency, even a necessary stage of sexual development, promoting the growth of one's capacity to love others. This is the theme of *Une Robe d'été* (*A Summer Dress*, 1996), a fifteen-minute short film in which a young man's sexual encounter with a young woman helps him become more comfortable with his ongoing sexual relationship with another young man.

Not only is *A Summer Dress* about bisexuality, it has even been filmed "bisexually," in the sense that Ozon switches his visual language from the opening "homosexual scene" to the ensuing "heterosexual scene" and then everything "in between"—as if cinematic styles themselves could be said to have flexible and shifting sexual preferences. *A Summer Dress* begins with a shot of eighteen-year-old Luc (Frédéric Mangenot), sitting in a deck chair. More exactly, the shot is a close-up of his lap, centered around the outline of his penis in his swim trunks, indicating the film will be organized around Luc's sexual life. The camera pans up to his face: his eyes are closed and his arms are raised above his head. The offhanded voyeurism of the shot, mingled with a certain rough-hewn quality in the somewhat abrupt pan, recalls gay American underground films. Indeed, stylistically, the entire opening of *A Summer Dress* evokes that intersection of camp taste and avant-garde sensibility in the work of Jack Smith, Kenneth Anger, Andy Warhol, George and Mike Kuchar, and Paul Morrissey.

Now, a second young man, also in swim trunks, walks in front of the seated hero. This is Sébastien (Sébastien Charles). We see him only as a disembodied pair of legs, a shadow cast upon Luc. He asks in husky English, "Do you love me?" to which Luc grumbles wearily, "Oh shut up!" Then, Sébastien—still just a pair of legs—begins to play a tape of Sheila's French version of the 1960s soft-rock ballad "Bang, Bang, My Baby Shot Me Down." Facing the camera in medium close-up, Sébastien lip-syncs and dances to this song. Throughout this scene, Sébastien dances in a very provocative way, with the moves of a drag queen: he shimmies, wiggles his ass, runs his hands over his thighs, and mimes theatrical gestures such as covering his face with his hands or placing his fingertips against his temples to play-act "having a nervous breakdown." Sébastien is doing this dance *for* Luc, as we clearly see when he forms a gun with his fingers and aims it at Luc during the "*bang bang*" chorus. Sébastien plays directly to the camera, a self-aware performance which again places us in the world of gay underground film. One is reminded of the bikers presenting their bodies for the camera (and subliminally, of course, for each other) in the "Blue Velvet" sequence of Anger's *Scorpio Rising* (1964). Mike Kuchar has defined camp as occurring precisely "when you see the mechanics of movies. It becomes evident, while you're watching the story, also that you're watching people act."[2] These shots of Sébastien have the disarming openness of any performer communing with his audience, drawing us into an intimate web of empathy and complicity in which Sébastien communicates not only his attraction to Luc but also a certain gay pride.

However, the exchange between these guys is ambiguous. Sébastien, in the throes of his sexy, campy dance, makes an all-out attempt to capture the attention of bored butch stud Luc, who is a fixed point of lethargy, stillness and disinterest, trying to tune Sébastien out while doing as little as possible. This is strongly reminiscent of the Warhol-produced films which Morrissey made with Joe Dallesandro. In a similar exchange of sexual energy/passivity and interest/disinterest, the listless, hyper-masculine Dallesandro was paired against a host of hysterical male, female and transgendered suitors.

According to this pattern, energy is female (woman, drag queen, effeminate homosexual), inertia is male; the female element does the desiring, the male is desired; the female acts, the male is acted upon. Literally, this is a kind of sublimation, into non-sexual activity, of the sexual position of giving a blowjob to a man while the man "lies back and enjoys it." But although Ozon references this axiomatic formula in his opening homosexual scene, he will come to reject its main implication — that male desire is always narcissistic, withholding, self-enclosed — later in the film. This is, in fact, the point of Luc's growth through bisexual experience in *A Summer Dress*. When it comes to male bisexuality, Ozon has a better understanding of its heterosexual component than Warhol and Morrissey did. The young male bisexuality which the Warhol-Morrissey films present largely as hip attitude, as scene-making posturing, is delivered by Ozon as a genuine feeling, a genuine way of relating to the world.

The lyrics of Sheila's song relate a story of seduction in which the female singer wallows masochistically in being "used and cast aside" by a man. In a long shot we see that the two men are on a patio in front of a bungalow. Luc gets up and shuts off the tape, saying, "I need peace! I'm sick of your fag songs." In spite of the intimacy suggested by Sébastien's proximity to Luc, and his vamping dance, the epithet "fag" makes us wonder who these young men are to each other.

Sébastien's rapt, yearning fixation on Luc trains us, the audience, to focus a similar sexual attention on Luc. Indeed, every performance presupposes an audience, and so, since he does not wish to be the audience, the object, of this one, Luc positions yet another audience, which could even be us, in our theater seats. "The neighbors are watching!" Luc says, peering vaguely toward the camera, indicating a scopophilic presence "out there" but characterizing it as hostile or malevolent, the suspicious opposite of Sébastien's total openness. Luc's sense of discretion, or panic, enters this scene-length monument to gay underground film as an incongruous note of discomfort, even protest. "Relax, we're on vacation," Sébastien says. "Fuck the neighbors!"

This opening scene is so aggressively "gay" in its visual instincts, its filmic and musical references, that the undecided Luc has no choice but to leave it. "Ok, you win, see you later," he says as Sébastien switches on the tape again. Sébastien makes a last effort to hold onto Luc, clinging to his neck and leaning against him, grinding his buttocks provocatively — or perhaps, given the extremes of Sébastien's camp and Luc's reticence, Sébastien is finally driving Luc away, forcing him to choose a side.

Luc gets on his bike and pedals out of frame, taking his seemingly heterosexual objections with him and surrendering the space of the frame completely to its homosexual iconography. Even after Luc's exit, Sébastien continues singing the next verse of the song, holding out his arms to the departed Luc as if he himself could not follow, tethered as it were to this manmade space of kitsch and queer performativity. (The open arms held in Luc's direction also signal an implied promise that Sébastien will wait for Luc.) In this verse the singer reveals that she has lost her childhood love to another woman, who has come into their cozy little world; in fact, this turns out partly to be foreshadowing of what will happen later in the film. Yet, the kind of sexual triangle which the song presents as melodrama will be presented as light-hearted and life-enhancing in the film.

Luc rides his bike to a deserted beach, where he kicks off his trunks and goes for a swim; then he falls asleep fully nude on a beach towel. In a reprise of Sébastien's entrance in the previous scene, Ozon pans on a pair of female legs walking toward Luc. This is Lucia (Lucia Sanchez). Like Sébastien, she pauses and casts a shadow over Luc's body. In the conversation that ensues, Luc smiles and giggles in awkward embarrassment, while Lucia radiates calmness and self-confidence. Throughout this heterosexual scene, in contrast to the previous homosexual one, Ozon's camera maintains a decorous, "respectable" distance from its subjects. No one plays directly to the camera, there is no self-conscious theatricality; in fact, the shots are all slightly angled to the characters' eye-lines, which creates a more natural impression. Unlike Sébastien, whose playfulness was arch, theatrical, noisy, dependent on the hidden meaning of words (song lyrics), Lucia's style is both more direct and more sly, and needs no mediation within the realm of culture: she plays, but does not seem to "play a part." Needless to say, her presence will disturb neither Luc nor any possible onlookers.

She asks him if he would like to go into the woods. "I want to make love," she says. He giggles again and shrugs. Lucia is liberated (or determined) enough to take charge of the moment: she pulls him by the hand and he trots along behind her. Though his body is solidly muscular, Luc's nakedness makes him seem vulnerable, especially when the couple climbs inside an enclosure formed by driftwood and low-hanging branches. To emphasize that Luc is "the man" in this encounter, he climbs on top of Lucia; this is not a male passively submitting to a female. Still, Luc's gay side is symbolized by a moment of triangulation: he notices a man, some distance away, staring from behind some bushes. For the bisexual Luc, the shadow of the choice not made (a man) becomes superimposed upon what is at hand (a woman). But unlike the threat of spying neighbors in the homosexual scene, the potentially disturbing presence of an interloper is easily quelled by Lucia, who says, "Forget it, close your eyes," and pulls Luc's face into a deep kiss. In contrast to homosexuality, heterosexuality has the social authority to claim the public sphere as its own. This authority is seen neither as false nor oppressive in itself: it simply is. We see that it was not so much the fear of being seen that frightened Luc up till now, but the fear of being seen *as gay*: shame and internalized homophobia, perhaps, have held back the full expression of his gay side. His fears are lessened in a situation where he will be seen as heterosexual.

The fact that the heterosexual contact makes Luc more comfortable with himself is further witnessed by his post-coital confession that this was his first time with a girl, and that he is actually on vacation with his boyfriend. This could be a moment of sexual crisis for Lucia, but in *A Summer Dress*, nothing between two lovers is ever a crisis: everything is understood and embraced as the almost Zen-like reason why they have come together in the first place; everything carries them that much further along in their shared intimacy, on their journey toward emotional self-awareness. "For a gay boy, you're a pretty good lay!" she laughs with sincere joy and appreciation, as if seeing Luc for the first time and liking what she sees. And we, too, as the audience, finally fully see Luc. In fact we only now fully understand that Sébastien *is* Luc's male lover — but, significantly, we understand this only from hearing him give the news to his female lover.

Back on the beach, Luc's clothes have been stolen. Lucia comes to his rescue by offering to lend him a blue dress with red flowers. He is incredulous, but soon accepts the dress as his only alternative to going home naked. "If you pedal fast," she jokes, "no one will know the difference." Luc promises to bring back the dress the next day.

On the highway, Luc makes an unusual vision: a butch young man, all bare legs and sneakers from the waist down, wearing the flower-print dress from the waist up. A passing car honks at him, he turns to give it a wary look; but as he bikes along, he seems, if anything, to grow amused by his own strange appearance, even slightly proud. He begins to sit tall on the seat of his bike and pedal in a seemingly carefree way, grinning to himself. This gender-bending masquerade links Luc to Sébastien's campy lip-syncing, and sure enough, when Luc gets back to the bungalow, he begins to seduce Sébastien without even taking off the dress. "Did the neighbors see you?" Sébastien asks, but now it is Luc's turn to be open and defiant. "Fuck the neighbors!" he says, starting to sing "Bang Bang" as he and Sébastien kiss. The song finally becomes *their* song, a duet, as Luc and Sébastien sing to each other between passionate kisses. In a further reversal of expectation, it is Sébastien who is the dominant one, placing Luc on the washing machine and penetrating him. We see that Luc displays a range of sexual behaviors and enjoyments: he can have sex with a woman as a man, actively, and with a man, passively, thereby dispelling stereotypes about how men are expected to play one role or another, not both. After sex, while Luc is showering, Sébastien holds the dress up to himself. The dress becomes a visual metaphor for both men being comfortable in their gayness — and, in true bisexual fashion, having their gayness enhanced by Luc's "borrowing" from his encounter with Lucia.

The next morning, Luc wakes up and dresses quickly. We see him riding his bike again, this time with the dress around his neck like a puffy collar. He arrives at the pier where Lucia is waiting and offers to give her back the dress. She tells him: "Oh keep it. You might need it again." Lucia's parting act of understanding toward Luc is to acknowledge that the dress belongs to him now. What he "might need again" is precisely the reminder that he can own and inhabit the feminine side of himself. Again, in true bisexual fashion he can access his feminine side only through the memento of his *heterosexuality*. Luc and Lucia kiss each other goodbye, and he watches her sail away with the dress still around his neck.

Like the bisexual man whose testimony began this chapter, Luc has struck a balance between his gay and straight sides. This life-enhancing balance is borne out by further research into the lives of bisexuals. I was struck by this comment from another anonymous bisexual male:

> One effect has been that it has been a turn-on for her [my female partner], hearing about it or imagining. On a couple of occasions when I've been away from home, I think I've returned to her happier and more relaxed because I had sex with someone I was visiting.[3]

While it may be a projection that this man's encounters with men are actually "a turn-on" for his female partner, his honest admission that he needs the gay encounters to feel "happier and more relaxed" in his heterosexual relationship is telling. The triangle in *A Summer Dress* is not founded on heartache and recrimination; instead, the three main characters are eternally curious, eternally optimistic, and eternally helpful to each other as they journey toward fulfillment and self-acceptance. There is no jealousy on anyone's part in *A Summer Dress*, neither is there any sense of wanting to artificially prolong or enforce commitment where it does not exist. In this, they seem to follow the logic of cinema itself: if something can be shown, it must be shown; and once it has been shown, it is never a bad thing.

Perhaps the relaxed optimism of *A Summer Dress* is connected to a certain kind of cinema, the dream-like short film in which the exigencies of narrative are compressed and generally subordinated to elements of ambiance, style and conceptualization. Because it eschews dramatic conflict in favor of a multiplicity of freely and successfully made choices, the bisexual narrative, in this case, attains a kind of blissed-out stasis which might not be able to sustain itself in a longer film. The moment of bisexual recognition, as well as its immediate outcome of bringing greater harmony to the bisexual's life, are what matter most in *A Summer Dress*; whereas in longer films, some dramatic conflict is invariably needed, requiring critical or negative aspects of the characters to be revealed. Indeed, when Ozon returns to the theme of male bisexuality in the feature-length *Les Amants criminels* (*Criminal Lovers*, 1999), no triumphant balance is achieved; instead, the bisexual hero is delayed in his self-discovery through an agonizing series of conflicts and traumas, and the ending is tragic.

In this sense, *A Summer Dress* seems to be a landmark short film as important as Luis Buñuel's *Un Chien andalou* (1929). This comparison is not a random one. Both of these films are psychosexual documents, organized around a series of dream-like images and focusing mainly on a polysexual trio. And both films are unapologetic, even insolent in the pursuit of their own cinematic truth, which they do not seem to care if the audience will accept or not.

Significantly, both films also share a central image of a young man wearing women's clothing and riding a bicycle, an image which is nonetheless handled very differently by Buñuel and Ozon. In *Un Chien andalou*, a man rides a bicycle down the street wearing women's accessories over his suit: a frilly white tutu, and a white bonnet and collar. (This collar is similar to the placement of the dress around Luc's neck in the final scenes of *A Summer Dress*.) The feminized cyclist wears a grimly serious expression on his face, and as he rides down the street, we see a young woman sitting in her apartment, looking up from her reading with a troubled expression, as if she sensed the approach of something dismaying. The cyclist crashes his bike into the curb and lies in the gutter, bewildered; the young woman rushes to his rescue and covers his face with concerned, tender kisses. She seems to love him, in spite or perhaps because of the fact that he is dressed androgynously. Here, as in *A Summer Dress*, a woman loves a sexually ambiguous man, but, as with the rest of the imagery in *Un Chien andalou*, this attempt at love only leads to confusion and, ultimately, disgust; for all sex roles, as well as all possibilities for romantic and sexual happiness, are largely scourged by Buñuel as either too sentimental or overly laden with the baggage of Western culture. (Even the tango, used so insistently and often ironically in *Un Chien andalou*—is it not ultimately as schlocky and flamboyant, and yet as catchy as Sheila's "Bang, Bang?" The violin that shrieks with the voice of repetitive denial in the tango has learned to quietly mourn its misbegotten love in the pop ballad, and both are examples of a heterosexual culture which, by exceeding its own kitsch quotient, provides inroads for the sexually unconventional.)

It is precisely this Buñuelian pessimism which is completely absent from the vision of *A Summer Dress*, where Ozon overturns and reinvents traditional sex roles in order to embrace the potentialities of new and ever-shifting ones. In Ozon's film, Luc discovers the confidence to overcome his insecurities and even take delight and pride in his feminine side; whereas in Buñuel's film, the strange stigma of the man's androgynous clothing returns again and again to disturb the couple's chance of happiness together, until the woman is finally forced to abandon him. The dress serves to make Luc *more attractive*, just as it serves to stabilize his conflicted ego so he can love both genders more openly and deeply.

The most fundamental difference between *Un Chien andalou* and *A Summer Dress* is that the former is a highly Freudian film: as a series of dream images it is open to Freudian interpretation and may have even originated within the Freudian schema. According to this schema, sexuality is fraught, a kind of obstacle course whose goal is "mature" genitality (procreative heterosexuality) but which is filled with the pitfalls of neurotic regressions, traumatic fixations, "perversions," etc. The treatment of bisexuality as authentic and serious human behavior is, for this reason, necessarily post–Freudian; there is no place for it in Freud's conception of "normal" psychosexual development. To reach the heterosexual genital stage and still seek pleasure in homosexual activity was, for Freud, the definition of neurosis, specifically a failed mastery of the Oedipal complex. This is why Freud could only imagine bisexuality "in his more whimsical moments"[4] — either as part of a primordial creation myth (Plato's tale of the hermaphroditic origins of the human species) or part of the dawn of an individual lifetime (the barely remembered, pre–Oedipal infancy).

Freud found it easier to explain acts of sadism and masochism between adults (as a manifestation of the Death Instinct) than acts of consensual same-sex love, and Buñuel as an artist largely follows Freud's lead in these matters. *Un Chien andalou* seeks and finds freedom from traditional sex roles only in acts of brutality, while *A Summer Dress* finds the same freedom in more sex, and more variegated roles. *Un Chien andalou* remains a staggeringly powerful attack on the ravages of sexual repression, and the inevitable way in which internalized puritanism gets channeled into unhealthy sexual violence. By contrast, *A Summer Dress* is post-repressive, post-puritanical, and no less powerful in the sense that its images also seem to be drawn from the unconscious — an unconscious in tune with instinctual, pleasurable and (in this case) bisexual impulses.

2

To Bend Without Breaking: Bisexuality and Adaptation in the Films of André Téchiné

> We like to think we are in control, if not of our entire lives, then at least of our emotions and affections. To have an unconscious that wants and desires things quite different, and often at variance from, those things we think and say we want is disquieting, to say the least.[1]

The kind of psychical disturbance of having a desiring unconscious at variance with one's public self can only be surmounted through an act of radical adaptation. One can, and often must, adapt oneself to living with the disturbance, to living in a constant state of uncertainty, but this does not necessarily mean that the disturbance resolves itself by coming into line with the public self, "those things we think and say we want," as stated above. In André Téchiné's films, people are constantly forced to adapt: to personal traumas and life-changing events, to collective crises like war and disease. His most powerful and affecting characters are misfits, transplants, foreigners, refugees, and also young people disabused of their idealism.

Within the universe of adaptations, sexuality is an often labile characteristic. Just as people travel a lot in Téchiné's films, so they constantly cross internal sexual borders. In *J'embrasse pas* (*I Don't Kiss*, 1991), Pierrot (Manuel Blanc) is a straight kid from the rural Pyrenées who goes to Paris and ends up as a gay hustler. Early in the film, he states that his only experience with gay life was going to see *La Cage aux folles*; later, after he has been working as a hustler, there is a scene in which Pierrot watches a TV program in which gay identity is being discussed. Pierrot is intrigued because he knows the TV host, Romain (Philippe Noiret); but the subject of the interview has more than a little to do with Pierrot's own life. Romain says to his guest, presumably an expert on sexual identity issues, "You go to war against those who think, 'I'm this' or 'I'm that.' You even go so far as to claim that no queer can say with certainty, 'I'm queer.'" The expert responds: "In effect, we have to think in uncertain, improbable terms, 'I don't know what I am.' So much research is required, so many tests."

What this seems to suggest is that no identity can be properly said to be fixed, everything is contingent and subject to the drift of change; we merely latch on to certain labels which "work" for us, which define and console us for periods of time. As befits the idea of adaptation, Téchiné's films bear witness to almost evolutionary processes in individuals, whether heterosexual, homosexual, or bisexual. Pierrot in *I Don't Kiss* is engaged in a de-evolutionary process, or a process of self-extinction, for reasons that may have something to do with his hatred of his father (his origins) but which are never made completely clear. There are subtle implications that Pierrot — with his emotional disconnection, and his early homophobia — may have survived childhood sexual abuse. Adaptation itself is a painful process, and in the end the character is not necessarily "happy": when someone's survival is at stake, his expectations tend to lower to the point where continued existence becomes a reason for contentment. Yet, almost always, in cases of adaptation, there are benefits to changing: again, ways of dealing with deeper, even more painful traumas. Therefore, at bottom, the nature of sexual identity, even basic identity itself, can be more undefined, more fluid and unstable, and at times, this very instability can yield, along with its inevitable pain and discomfort, key insights into how to survive, how to find love.

Always gorgeous to look at, Téchiné's films unfold slowly, probing in detail how an individual identity is formed. *Rendez-vous* (1985) is a mesmerizing account of how Anne (Juliette Binoche) comes to Paris to become an actress and, through her often traumatic contacts with various men, forges the necessary will to endure. The film ends right before she makes her decision to go onstage on opening night or give up on her dream and run from the theater, indicating that, for Téchiné, what she ultimately becomes is less important than how she becomes it. The adolescents in *Les Roseaux Sauvages* (*Wild Reeds*, 1994) have conflicted sexual identities resulting from the fact that, as young people, they are still developing: François (Gaël Morel) is reluctant to embrace his homosexuality, and so reaches out to Maïté (Élodie Bouchez), telling her, "You reassure me." For her part, Maïté is afraid of sex; she says she does not want to get too involved with a boy and end up getting hurt, like her mother was in her marriage. The film is partly about how

2. To Bend Without Breaking   41

François and Maïté help each other: she helps him accept being gay, and he helps her accept physical love from a boy, Henri (Frédéric Gorny).

We see that traumas leave deep, lingering scars in many of Téchiné works, such *Alice et Martin* (*Alice and Martin*, 1998), in which Martin (Alexis Loret) forges a dream-like existence as a model, only to be pulled up short by the memory of the patricide he has committed — itself a long-delayed reaction to his ruined childhood. But if irreversible human destruction is memorialized by Téchiné's films, he again takes note of the equally human capacity for survival, no matter what the odds. In *Les Égarés (Strayed*, 2003), the hero's name, "Yvan," turns out to be a fictitious identity for "Jean Delmas"; as an escapee from a boys' prison, the character's freedom and very life are shown to be dependent on his ability to pass himself off as someone else. At the end of *Les Témoins* (*The Witnesses*, 2007), which takes place during the early days of the AIDS crisis, four of the main characters celebrate the fact that they have survived by sailing a speedboat: the rush of forward movement itself is a ravishing relief after some of the film's most tense and sorrowful moments, and the point is that they are not necessarily "going anywhere"; all that matters is that Téchiné leaves them in a state of motion.

The drama of human adaptation can end in only one of two alternatives: death or growth. In their most dramatic light, the two can seem, even be, interchangeable. Before Pierrot comes to accept the idea of sleeping with men for money, he has a brief moment when he contemplates throwing himself from a bridge; later, he wishes he had never been born in the first place. In *Les Temps qui changent* (*Changing Times*, 2004), Antoine (Gérard Depardieu) symbolically dies, and is reborn, from his love for Cécile (Catherine Deneuve), who, to bring things full circle, had been his first love some thirty years previously.[2]

Téchiné rarely presents heterosexuality itself as obeying fixed norms, so insistent is his artistic project of making sexual gray areas a fertile ground for plots and characters. His heterosexual characters often make unusual choices of whom to love. One of the central love stories of *Les Voleurs* (*Thieves*, 1996) is between a gangster (Daniel Auteil) and a lesbian college professor (Catherine Deneuve) who becomes willing to "convert" to heterosexuality for him. Love is whatever someone says it is, and can be found wherever someone happens to find it. Moody and claustrophobic, *Ma Saison Préferée* (*My Favorite Season*, 1993) explores the repressed and unrepressed desires within a family whose members are presented as exceedingly neurotic and drearily typical at the same time. Interracial relationships are constant in Téchiné's films, as well as relationships between gay men; while in *Strayed*, Yvan (Gaspar Ulliel), a teenage boy with a criminal past, is the unlikely soul mate for Odile (Emmanuelle

Béart), an older war widow. He announces to her: "Girls my age don't interest me. Only you interest me. I'd like you to be my wife."[3] When she expresses disbelief and disapproval at the idea, he offers, "I'll do what you want," suggesting expediency as a reason for Odile to adapt to the new idea.

It is not surprising that male bisexuality is one of Téchiné's abiding themes, and what seems to interest the director most could be considered a kind of situational bisexuality (although not without some awkward degree of tenderness) in which a man who identifies himself as straight uses a certain rationale, or takes advantage of a certain opportunity, to engage in sex with other men. So, again in *Strayed*, we are only slightly surprised when the resourceful young Yvan finally has sex with Odile and tells her that he has never seen a naked woman before; he begins to penetrate her from behind, and she asks him why. "It's what I know," he says. "I don't know that," she says, but then tells him, "Go on." A clearer picture of Yvan emerges only after he is arrested by the police, and the rest of the family is taken to a refugee camp; they learn that he grew up in a boys' prison, where presumably he had had sexual relationships with other boys. This is in keeping with the hardscrabble ways in which Yvan has learned to make do, to satisfy his needs. (It is also part of Téchiné's vision of the inherent fragility of youth that this revelation does not make him seem any less pure in his love for Odile, or their tryst any less poignant; in fact, quite the contrary.) A similar scenario occurs in *Wild Reeds*, when Serge (Stéphane Rideau) seduces fellow student François at the boys' boarding school they both attend; Serge's use of situational bisexuality parallels his need, as someone from the lower classes, to be constantly looking out for opportunities for survival: "I try to get by as best I can. When you are poor, if you're not on the ball, you get screwed."

Serge (Stéphane Rideau, right) gives François (Gaël Morel) a ride on his motorcycle in *Wild Reeds* (1994). François falls in love with Serge, and although Serge is heterosexual, he sleeps with François, partly because Serge's survival, as someone from the lower classes, depends on his taking whatever he can to get by. Nonetheless, a close friendship also develops between the two young men.

Time and again, gay

sex becomes a resource, an extra reserve as it were, for the heterosexual male who needs it. In *I Don't Kiss*, Pierrot drifts into the life of a gay hustler after finding himself unsuccessful at every other kind of work or relationship. Pierrot has had one heterosexual affair, with an older woman, Mme. Lebord (Hélène Vincent), who drove him away by offering him money. What insulted him, coming from a woman whom he liked, is precisely what he looks for with men, the impersonal "give and take" of commerce. One option exists to balance out the other. "With women, it's complicated," he reasons, "at least it's clear with men."

There is a kind of wisdom to be gained through bisexual experience. In Téchiné's films, when a man sleeps with another man, it sometimes implies, on the surface, a reduction of feelings. In *The Witnesses* Mehdi (Sami Bouajila), a young husband and father married to Sarah (Emmanuelle Béart), embarks on a sexual relationship with the adolescent Manu (Johan Libéreau), which seems to be only about sex, or — as he puts it when he describes it to his wife — getting rid of his hard-on. But this idea, that intimacy with other men is strictly physical, without an emotional connection, is often revealed to be a kind of self-deception. In reality, below the surface, both Mehdi and Pierrot are changed by their encounters with men, whether or not they choose to acknowledge this. Mehdi is devastated when Manu contracts AIDS; even after sex between them becomes impossible, he still wants to see his lover, even watch him sleep one last time before he dies — a request denied by Manu's friend and caretaker Dr. Adrien (Michel Blanc), who is jealous of the fact that Mehdi was able to seduce Manu where he was not.

Bisexual experience helps to complete an identity that may have formerly been sketchy, uncertain, missing something. As a gay hustler, Pierrot becomes happier, more relaxed and confident than ever before; he dresses better, begins to style his hair, and even acquires a motorcycle. He describes hustling as "the only way I could feel free." He seems to have found his calling, so to speak. An old friend notes that Pierrot has changed: "You are much more handsome. You don't have the same look." Similarly, after his gay affair comes to light, Mehdi eventually seems able to relax more, to be more open with his wife Sarah. A certain emotional expansiveness — of personality, of heart — seems to come with sexual expansiveness.

* * *

The 19th century philosopher Benedict Friedlander "ridiculed those with an exclusively hetero- or homosexual orientation as *Kümmerlinge* [atrophied or puny beings]."[4] Téchiné does not champion male bisexuality *at the expense* of other orientations; he believes consistently that people love, and should be allowed to love, whomever they choose, no matter whom that might be. But even though the bisexual male characters in Téchiné's films may not necessarily experience themselves as stronger — Mehdi is often filled with shame and helplessness; Pierrot seems to consider himself a failure by the end of *I Don't Kiss*—they are arguably among Téchiné's characters who attempt to grow and change, and to adapt to the world, the most.[5]

Needless to say, what also changes these men is the fact that they have allowed themselves to emerge from the lie they tell themselves — that they are only one thing (straight) and not another. Here again, we find significance in the words of the TV interview which Pierrot watches: "The problem for man is not whether he's this or that, not at all." Indeed, at its deepest, the problem is never realizing the full potentiality of everything one can be. At the same time, the tendency of young people to rush into their lives head-first — grabbing at moments, falling in love hastily, getting hurt — has been explored with great sensitivity by Téchiné. Part of what makes Manu's wasting death from AIDS so horrifying in *The Witnesses* is that he contracts the illness as an adolescent, while he is just beginning to explore his sexuality, and dies within a year. Manu becomes emblematic of an entire generation mowed down in its first flowering.

The interrelationship of bisexuality with mixed cultural identity — as two metaphors which reflect and amplify each other — becomes important to the character of Sami (Malik Zidi) in *Changing Times*. The son of a French mother and a Moroccan father, Sami lives in Paris with Nadia (Lubna Azabal), a Moroccan woman, and her son Saïd (Idir Elomri); he has brought them on a trip to Tangier so that he can see his male lover, Bilal (Nadem Rachati). Although Sami does not have sex with Nadia, he is extremely close to her: he agrees to return to Paris with her when she becomes unhappy and strung out on pills. They exchange the following dialogue while taking Saïd to the park to play:

Nadia: I don't want to stop you from seeing Bilal.
Sami: Bilal is just a fling, you know. He's not essential. You're the most important thing.

Here we learn that Nadia not only knows about Sami's homosexual relationship, she is supportive and protective of it. They go on to say:

Nadia: Sometimes I feel like I'm ruining your life.
Sami: Are you kidding? If I didn't have you, I don't know what I'd do.
Nadia: You would live with a boy.
Sami: Don't say that. I'm happy with you. Seriously.

We cannot say that Sami is ashamed of his gay desires, or even particularly closeted. And yet, he does not wish to give up his close relationship with

Nadia — he does not wish to choose between what a man represents and what a woman represents. Sami is also physically affectionate with Nadia.

When Bilal confronts him about the bifurcated nature of his emotional life (partly out of jealousy, partly out of wariness at the ways of sophisticated European men), Sami can only say, "I need her." Bilal is less than sympathetic, leveling a shrewd, post-colonial diagnosis of Sami as a misbegotten cultural product, poorly assimilated, halfway between identities: "You don't know what you want. You don't make decisions. It's understandable, though. Half-Moroccan, half–French. Half-man, half-woman. It must be hard for you to figure it out."[6] It is an accusation often made about bisexual males, that they "don't know what they want," they "won't decide." (Whether it is better to decide once and for all, or to remain open, is, of course, a matter of viewpoint.) Nonetheless, Téchiné shows Sami as a well-intentioned, even a healing and salvational angel, inspiring a number of the other characters; though his own love life is complicated, his belief in the importance of love itself becomes a direct and indirect catalyst for one heterosexual relationship to form, and another to repair itself, toward the end of the film.

We note that Sami bears some resemblance to an earlier Téchiné character, Benjamin Sauvagnac (Mathieu Amalric) in *Alice and Martin*. Benjamin is a homosexual with a distinct taste for rough trade; yet he lives in a kind of cozy, intimate codependency with Alice (Juliette Binoche). Sexually, this living arrangement is platonic; nonetheless, it is more familiar and nurturing than friendship. They sleep together in the same bed. Like Sami in *Changing Times*, Benjamin does not conceal his gay experiences from Alice. When he is beaten up by a psychopathic trick he has picked up on the street, he immediately tells the understanding Alice all the details; his eyes light up, reliving the details of the sex and violence in conversation with her, as if his telling the story to her, and her listening to it, helps complete the act for him, brings it full circle into a kind of bisexual fulfillment. When Alice leaves Benjamin for his brother Martin, Benjamin acts like a jealous, jilted lover. Rather than reduce Sami or Benjamin to easy labels — "they are gay men afraid of completely coming out," "they are gay men who do not wish to be gay" — Téchiné allows for complex readings of them, in which their psychosexual natures are allowed to keep an indeterminate factor. This is part of the dignity which Téchiné sees in all of his unconventional characters.

Indeed, for Téchiné there is nothing tawdry about love (or sex) in any of its guises; though his films can be and often are romantic, this is not to say that he spares his characters very many illusions — but even this is part of how he upholds their essential dignity as human beings. Téchiné's special genius is to elevate the melodramatic story until it takes on the cold, diamantine luster of universal tragedy. Téchiné often refers to Shakespeare (whose fondness for sexual and romantic ambiguities is, needless to say, quite strong). Pierrot is likened to Hamlet in his indecisiveness, his divided self, his reluctance to take action. As a somewhat bullying way of prodding him to work harder in class, his acting teacher assigns him the "To be, or not to be" soliloquy. Over a period of days he tries to memorize the lines but struggles with simply grasping the words themselves — even as his life begins to spiral downward, fulfilling the text's fatalistic meaning. He is embarrassed because his classmates not only know the speech by heart, they have theories as to Hamlet's motivation; one young woman calls Hamlet "a big phony. Melancholy made him that way." Pierrot experiences her negative words as being about *him*, which of course they partly are. Pierrot, although a Hamlet-type himself, is painfully unable to articulate the character, just as he is unable to articulate himself, to express his own needs and feelings. He runs from the class, and the glimpse of self-recognition it gives him, just as he runs from all other situations in which some early revelation of what he will become is pointed out to him. In a self-fulfilling prophecy made true by the very force of his own denial, everything he proudly and solemnly vows never to do — chief among them, to sleep with homosexuals for money — becomes exactly what he does.

* * *

The reality that Pierrot can and does have sex with men is, in another nod to classical tragedy, like Oedipus' realization that he has slept with his mother, that the "uncleanness" he has despised has been part of him all along: the unexplored inner landscape turns out to be vaster, and more universal, than its owner suspected, precisely *because* he has refused for so long to look within. This is something more, however, than the unscratched itch growing more virulent and bothersome. With Pierrot it has to do with the complex mimesis he engages in with others: in spite of himself, when his back is pushed to the wall, he turns into the very examples of adult survival which he has witnessed but rejected as untenable and dishonorable. He assumes the traits of those very people he has insulted and spurned: the homosexual men and their hustlers, the romantic Mme. Lebord and her need to be loved at all costs. (When he begins hustling, he uses the alias "Romain," the name of the first gay man he met in Paris, and whose car he jumped from in a homophobic moment.) Cutting off more and more of his ability to relate to the world around him, and to people who are supposedly different from himself, Pierrot nonetheless grows, unconsciously, in all of those repressed directions. The final irony of the title — the hustler's code to forbid the intimacy of lips-upon-lips — is that this is finally the only exchange he does not surrender to: in every other conceivable way, sexually and non-sexually, consciously and unconsciously, he is always taking the world into himself, into his life, his body and mind.

In this sense, we can question — as other characters do in *I Don't Kiss* — whether Pierrot is truly bisexual, or straight, or even (as the film most strongly implies) an asexual narcissist invested in self-love: he could plausibly be all of these at different moments. One of his clients says that Pierrot "doesn't like anything, except clients like me," then asks him, "Is it true that you don't fuck for pleasure?" Pierrot laughs and says that he does not have the time, the joke being that "fucking" is what takes up all his time, anyway. Finally, what one *does* can be separate from who one *is*; this is the most important thing about Pierrot. Narcissistic pride is what remains constant about him, whether he is having sex with men or women. In fact, when he falls in love with the female prostitute Ingrid (Emmanuelle Béart), his pride in his own romantic feelings surges to the fore and makes him incapable of functioning anymore as a hustler. Knowing him as a fellow streetwalker, she assumes he is gay, again mistaking what he does for what he is; when Pierrot asks about her pimp, her first assumption is that Pierrot desires him.

The more Pierrot succeeds as a gay hustler (and the more he is seen as being gay), the more his heterosexual identity — as brought out by Ingrid — seems to matter to him. Is he overcompensating, or does it only seem as though the two sides of him are in competition? Could it be that the sex he has with men enhances his ability to love women, as often happens with bisexual men? It is intriguing, the idea that one's true identity lies buried under a false front which signifies precisely the opposite: one aggressively points away from the direction where one can be found. Pierrot's friend Saïd (Roschdy Zem) confesses that when he first came to Paris he also worked as a hustler, but says, "I closed my eyes and thought of something else. I don't like talking about it. I'm going to marry, have kids." Rather than being seen as interrelated, as a series of changes along a continuum which come together to constitute a single flexible human life, these identities are seen as opposites which can be summoned up to cancel each other out: gay/straight, casual/committed, non-procreative/procreative. Another pair of opposites might be prostitution/love; and yet, as a sexual behavior, prostitution has difficulty locating its exact opposite, since Pierrot slept with Mme. Lebord while she provided him with room and board, yet he vigorously denied trying to exchange money for intimacy in that relationship. Also, when Pierrot sleeps with Ingrid (in an idyll meant to be set apart from their streetwalking lives), it takes place in a hotel room he has had to pay for; he also buys her new clothes. And, as always, sex in all its conceivable forms is only a reflection of already rampant divisions within the self. In *The Witnesses*, Mehdi is filled with internal contradictions beyond the immediately sexual one: he is an Arab man who has been forced to assimilate to French society, and he is also a gung-ho vice squad cop with a reputation for closing down gay bars and arresting prostitutes. He is drawn into his affair with Manu in spite of the fact that he looked upon the boy with mistrust at first, presuming that he was a hustler because he frequented a bar where prostitutes go.

At the end of *The Witnesses*, Adrien brings his new lover Steve (Lorenzo Balducci) to visit Mehdi and Sarah, and we see that the worlds of gay and straight are, idealistically, reconciled. The bisexual Mehdi has helped effect this reconciliation, because of his dual citizenship in both worlds; and yet, he has not automatically brought the gay and straight characters together. In fact, he had threatened to divide them at one point. It falls to Sarah, as the wife, to forgive him for potentially exposing her to AIDS (she is understanding about this), and also for Adrien to forgive him for stealing Manu away (Adrien is less understanding). The world which Téchiné depicts with this ending is

In *The Witnesses* (2007), the teenaged Manu (Johan Libéreau, left) awakens strong and surprising feelings in Mehdi (Sami Bouajila). A married vice squad cop, Mehdi experiences confusion and guilt over his affair with Manu. Mehdi attempts to rationalize their relationship as nothing more than a physical, sexual release, but when his young lover contracts AIDS, Mehdi is emotionally devastated.

one in which the bonds of friendship survive, and are strengthened, by the collective crisis of AIDS, whose dangers, like the bonds themselves, stretch across every line of socio-sexual demarcation. And it is Sarah, as a novelist, who actually "tells the tale" in spite of the fact that this tale is largely gay and male in nature.

When Mehdi and Manu are conducting their sexual affair (they use flying lessons as part of their cover) we are told that the affair is good for them because it teaches them "to fly under the radar." It is the kind of complicated knowledge — useful, life-enhancing, thrillingly illicit, embittering all at once — which all minorities (gays, certainly, but also refugees, immigrants and transplants) must learn at some point. As a bisexual, Mehdi occupies a strange position: he is both under the radar and above it, or more precisely, to the extent that he is an accepted member of straight society (and a vice squad cop), he technically *is* the radar. If there is such a thing as "heterosexual privilege" when it comes to male bisexuality (and Mehdi suffers too greatly, and too openly, from his affair with Manu to be accused of claiming it), it lies more in the fact that male sexual power has the ability to extend itself to other men as an act of hostility and humiliation, rather than an act of love, while nonetheless using the same gestures as those of love. So, *I Don't Kiss* ends with Ingrid's lover and pimp (Christophe Bernard) forcibly sodomizing Pierrot as a brutal way of "putting him back in his place" for daring to love Ingrid. This violent rape is preceded by a vicious beating, and also by a disturbing scene in which the pimp and his henchmen menacingly sing along with a pop love song. There is danger associated in stepping out from behind the conventional, sanctioned labels; once again, the required movement of adaptation is to harsh environmental circumstances, where some camouflage is needed so one will not become available as prey. The bisexual male's risk is to expect the societal camouflage of straight meanings to still protect him even after he has "betrayed" them and revealed their other side, as it were, their gay meanings. Appropriating the social discourse of romance in the form of the love song, the male rape in *I Don't Kiss* is still unmistakably about power and violence, using Pierrot's daring bisexuality against him as it were. This is similar to the way homoeroticism is invoked in David Lynch's *Blue Velvet* (1986), when Frank (Dennis Hopper) is threatening Jeffrey (Kyle MacLachlan) to the strains of Roy Orbison's androgynous singing. The actual meaning of the scene is murderous and homophobic, but at the same time the male intimacy of the scene is dizzying, misleading, and perhaps inadvertently revealing.

The theme of male bisexuality is part of a larger initiative on Téchiné's part to reform "the male" in our culture, to de-patriarchize him, perhaps, while nonetheless retaining his mystique, his allure. Time and again, a man who only plays at being strong is shown to find an even deeper strength in an act of what seems to be "weakness" or surrender: Sami getting attacked by Bilal's dogs in *Changing Times*, Pierrot losing his usual self-control to defend Ingrid in the jail cell in *I Don't Kiss*, Mehdi doing the ailing Manu's soiled laundry in *The Witnesses*. (Even more than this, the world of many Téchiné films is essentially a female one, anchored to and by women; whereas the men pass through, elusive and unknowable, tantalizing and out of reach, provoking feeling, action, and change in others and in themselves.) By this same token, the male drama of adaptation tends to follow the same course — a man who only plays at being strong finds an even deeper strength in what seems to be weakness or surrender — just as Gérard Depardieu was cast as two different men, or two aspects of the same man, in *Barocco* (1976). It does not seem at all coincidental that Téchiné, in that early film, undertook to re-imagine the enigmatic and nightmarish romantic doubling of *Vertigo* (1958) with the genders reversed: a woman (Isabelle Adjani) sees her lover (Depardieu) get murdered, only to come back again. Sometimes, it is death which completes the portrait of a man, the implication being — particularly with young men such as Yvan or Manu — that they will be continuously regenerated through the other lives they have touched. More often, life is revealed to be more difficult and challenging than death; as Serge says in *Wild Reeds*: "There's something even tougher, tougher than war — it's that life goes on." Téchiné allows his male characters, especially the bisexual Mehdi in *The Witnesses*, to go through a process of adaptation (romantic, sexual, cultural) and learn from it an important skill of surviving life's abiding ordeals: how to accept the flawed, unwhole, discontinuous remnants of self and carry on. What they possess, dwelling in the margins of male sexuality, is the skill which the reed boasts about to the oak in the fable recited by François in *Wild Reeds*: the ability to "bend without breaking" and thereby weather the harshest storms of life.

3

Tentative, Tender ... and Trendy? Gregg Araki's Teen Trilogy

> Bisexuality is really really "in" right now. As one of my mentees said to me today: "Even if you aren't bi, it's still like, really cool, you just pretend to be." ... Everyone wants attention, and teens especially do. Hooking up with your same sex friend at a party is sure to grab the attention of other party goers and get people talking about you.[1]

There is a huge and seemingly unintentional irony factor to the quote above. First of all, classifying anything as a "teen trend" is sure to get people's eyes rolling. Nevertheless, many things that have become ubiquitous in our culture — rock and roll, video games — originated as teen trends. But, and this is the crucial point, true bisexuality is not a pretense or pose. In this sense, we have every reason to doubt the seriousness of the "mentee" (I assume this means someone who receives mentorship, though the term itself is new to me). Moreover, doing things to "get people talking about you" is not the point of bisexuality, which, when it does authentically occur in someone, is often a source of shame and an area of discretion.

Gregg Araki, one of the most consistently outspoken voices in gay cinema, has made films which depict the sexuality of contemporary American teens as diverse, painful, fun, rebellious and sometimes even sincere (imagine that). Among his most sincere characters are teenage males exploring the possibility that they might be bisexual, regardless of whether they primarily identify as straight or gay. Araki's "Teen Trilogy" — *Totally F***ed Up* (1993), *The Doom Generation* (1995), and *Nowhere* (1997) — is aesthetically brash, like a graphic novel or an underground 'zine come to life, with bold, snarling close-ups, lurid high-contrast lighting, plots full of sex and violence, and hard-edged dialogue in which young people bicker with a depraved, "I've-done-it-all" bravado. But it would be a mistake to allow the brutalist surface of these films to completely overshadow the wisps of fragile, self-doubting emotion stirring a little deeper below. And, even if a number of Araki's teen characters *have* done it all, the characters who think they might be, or wish they were, bisexual remain somewhat set apart from all the jadedness: tentative and tender, more moony talk than action, more "beautiful dreamer" than teenage Caligula, they are more likely to keep their bisexual urges at least semi-private rather than performing them as party tricks for their social clique. I am thinking of three characters in particular: Andy in *Totally F***ed Up*, Jordan White in *The Doom Generation*, and Dark Smith in *Nowhere*, all of them played by perennial Araki actor James Duval, with his shy, sly grin, long floppy hair, and curious, "sad puppy dog" eyes.

Bisexual fantasy is literalized in the opening scene of *Nowhere*. Araki's camera slowly zooms in on Dark in the shower, his nude body partially hidden by steam. This shot is reminiscent of certain porn films, which open with one of the stars showering, generating the masturbatory lust that will be exercised in acts of sex throughout the rest of the film. Indeed, soon enough, Dark begins to masturbate. In a montage, Araki shows us the permutations of Dark's sexual thoughts, a rapidly shifting orgy of scenarios and roles. The gender of his fantasy objects also shifts. First we see Dark in bed with his girlfriend Mel (Rachel True); she bites his nipple, causing him to yell in pain. Next, Dark and Montgomery (Nathan Bexton) are undressing in a locker room, and Montgomery reaches out and caresses Dark's nipple. Montgomery murmurs: "You have the deepest, blackest eyes I've ever seen. It's like I could just tumble into them, fall forever...." Next, two dominatrixes, Kriss (Chiara Mastroianni) and Kosy (Debi Mazar), tie Dark up and verbally abuse him, calling him a "deviant." Heterosexual disapproval of Dark's gay side is a built-in turn-on within the fantasy: his occasional, or perhaps secondary, attraction to men lends the spice of taboo to his more normalized (albeit S-M-inflected) attraction to women. As Dark's pleasure heightens he returns to Montgomery. Right before the fantasy abruptly ends — interrupted, Oedipally enough, by Dark's mother (Beverly D'Angelo) pounding on the bathroom door — we see his lips slowly moving closer to Montgomery's, about to kiss.

Unlike the racy scenes with the females, Dark's fantasies about Montgomery are not predominantly sexual, or even laden with physical contact. They are, instead, sweetly romantic. Also, the heterosexual fantasies simply occur; the players pop up inside a ready-made mental space and begin to act sexually upon Dark. Only Montgomery seems to arise from a potentially real situation from daily life (changing in a locker room); only Montgomery describes his love to Dark, compliments Dark admiringly, as a preamble to getting close to him. When Montgomery tells Dark he could "fall forever" in his eyes, it is actually a statement of love as much as sexual attraction.

In a nutshell, this is Araki's formulation of young male bisexual experience. Where heterosexual sex is nasty, dirty, and always quickly fulfilled, bisexuality is more yearning, pure and unfulfilled. Where both straight and gay sex are often the stuff of melodramatic interpersonal drama, bisexuality is isolated and calm, a tranquil oasis in the midst of chaos. Both extremes of the scale — pure heterosexuality and pure homosexuality — are normalized within their respective erotic and social zones; their exponents are unchanging, they always do more or less what is expected of them. Bisexuality, on the other hand, is a state of psychical being in flux — we see this with Andy and Jordan as well as Dark. Rather than approach the world in total certainty of who and what they are, these characters struggle to define themselves.

The most original, personal and daring film of the trilogy is *Totally F***ed Up*, which follows six friends, four young gay males and a lesbian couple, as they mope, joke, vent, party, crash and generally ruminate about their alienation. But, for these children of Kinsey and Ecstasy it turns out that their alienation is more real than posturing, reinforced by their daily exposure to extremely disheartening social phenomenon, such as AIDS, gay-bashing, serial killings, parental rejection, dead-end jobs, and homelessness. (Araki made his film specifically in response to the high suicide rate among gay teens.)

Andy (again, played by Duval) stands out among the characters as the most unsure of himself, and the most reticent about sex. "I guess I haven't figured out exactly what it is I like to do yet," he confesses, adding that he thinks anal sex is gross. Andy tells the camera, verité-style:

> I think I'm bisexual. I mean, I never actually boinked a girl or anything. But if it came down to it, I think I could. Like, I've gotten a boner before, making out with one. And I like them, they're soft and pretty. Fun to touch. It's not like I'm afraid of them or anything.

To a certain extent, this reflects contemporary gay male attitudes, in which one affirms one's homosexuality by stating that it is not a reaction against women. Much of what Andy says falls into that pro-gay rationale, except for the disarming moment when he talks about becoming erect when "making out" with a girl. This transcends the realm of politically correct "gay outreach" to the female world. Here we have a predominantly gay male who holds out the option, for himself, to be attracted to women and to even act on that attraction: this is qualitatively no different than the fact that the committed heterosexual Dark in *Nowhere* holds out the option to fall in love or sleep with a man.

But unlike Dark, Andy is pointedly not a romantic. He believes love is a media conspiracy: "Live happily ever after — it's all a load of bullshit propaganda." As a young gay man, Andy seems to view the commodification of emotion as an essentially heterosexual phenomenon; and yet, he is more romantic than he claims to be. He is devastated when his boyfriend Ian (Alan Boyce) cheats on him, a heartbreak which, for all his expressed cynicism, he does not see coming. As a mirror-image of Andy's cynicism, Dark's bisexuality operates within a rather desperate romantic idealism. He always tells Mel that he loves her and wants to marry her: "Sometimes I feel so old-fashioned, like I'm from another planet. It's like I'm half a person without you." He often speaks about wanting to take her far away from everyone else, even leaving the whole planet behind.

For her part Mel tortures Dark with her refusal to be monogamous: "I firmly believe that human beings are built for sex and love, and that we should dole out as much of both as possible before we're old and ugly and no one wants to touch us anymore." In a trope common to numerous bisexual films, the bisexual male's girlfriend is herself bisexual, with a lesbian lover named Lucifer (Kathleen Robertson). Nonetheless, Mel attempts to offer Dark her love, saying that just because she has sex "with other guys and girls" does not mean that her feelings for him are any less. Mel represents bisexuality strictly as a quest for as much and as various pleasure as possible. If true love is Dark's mythic antidote to cruelty and heartache, it is because he understands the prevalence of cruelty and heartache firsthand, like the other disaffected, alienated youths in *Nowhere*, caught up in status symbols and designer drugs. Even though he is ultimately as superficial as everyone around him, and as much given over to negativity, Dark attempts to purify himself through feelings of bisexual love, and to keep these feelings safe from the rest of his life, the rest of his world.

In this sense, male bisexuality takes on the opposite meaning of the "heterosexual privilege" which bisexuals are often attacked for supposedly invoking. "Such attacks were said to come especially from politically active homosexuals who deplored the political fragmentation they saw caused by bisexuals who refused to fight the common enemy of 'heterosexism.' Bisexuals could exercise 'heterosexual privilege'— i.e., they could always revert to a comfortable identity rather than suffer the consequences of standing up for their gay rights."[2] For one thing, this assumes that bisexuality is less natural, and more of a deliberate choice, than either homosexuality or heterosexuality, and this is far from being certain. In Araki's films, bisexuality is about a deeper or more extenuated kind of uncertainty, rather than the certainty that one simply wants more of everything, more sex, more pleasure, more love, more

3. Tentative, Tender ... and Trendy? 55

risk—all things that are at various times sources of ambivalence for Andy, Jordan, and Dark. It isn't so much privilege, then, that motivates Araki's bisexuals as firsthand knowledge of the ruthlessness of a certain kind of (heterosexual) society. This knowledge also provokes the wish to escape from all labels, which perform the equally ruthless function of categorizing, segregating, dehumanizing.

This ruthlessness of heterosexual society is foregrounded in *The Doom Generation*. Araki billed this as "A Heterosexual Movie"—presumably because, atypically for him, none of the characters is gay—but he could have just as easily called it "A Bisexual Movie." The film centers on a trio, emotionally and sexually cathected, made up of two guys and one girl. When the film opens, Jordan White (Duval) and his girlfriend Amy Blue (Rose McGowan) are out on a date and trying to have fun. Jordan is more naïve and contented than the tough, sarcastic, terminally bored Amy. Jordan refuses to have intercourse: "I'm afraid of catching AIDS." "But we're both virgins!" Amy whines hilariously.

They rescue Xavier Red (Jonathon Schaech) from getting beaten by some other teens. Almost instantly, a strange chemistry seems to click between Xavier and Jordan. Jordan happily lets Xavier use his shirt to wipe off the blood on his face. Amy becomes annoyed, perhaps sensing bisexual attraction between the two guys, but the streetwise Xavier stands up to her, showering her in sexist epithets. Amy throws him out of her car: "You're repugnant!" Even though Xavier has christened Jordan with the suggestive nickname "Nutlicker," Jordan urges Amy to be more tolerant of Xavier: "He seemed cool. Kind of strange, maybe."

Xavier then res-

The three protagonists of *The Doom Generation* (1995)—from left, Xavier Red (Jonathon Schaech), Amy Blue (Rose McGowan), and Jordan White (James Duval)—are living pieces of American Pop Art for the 1990s. They become fugitives from the law and, on the road together, Amy sleeps with both Xavier and Jordan. Meanwhile, the two men gradually discover a growing attraction toward each other.

cues Jordan and Amy in a convenience store whose suspicious owner is holding a shotgun on them; in the struggle, Xavier kills the store owner. With this act of pseudo–Oedipal aggression, the teens' crime spree begins, reinforcing their shared sense of difference from the rest of the society, their rebelliousness and their willingness to explore the wild side of life as a trio. What makes *The Doom Generation* much fresher than the outlaw genre whose clichés it mines is precisely the sexual ambiguity at its center, and the uncertain, almost child-like romanticism which Jordan, Amy and Xavier invest in that ambiguity. As the film progresses, Jordan and Xavier share a series of progressively intimate moments, taking place in motels (and finally an abandoned warehouse) where the fugitives stop to sleep. In the first motel scene, Amy is taking a bath; Jordan sits on the floor at the foot of the bed, watching TV, while Xavier sprawls on the bed, letting his head dangle over the edge against Jordan's shoulder. Jordan admires the tribal tattoo on Xavier's bare chest, and the two men's faces seem to be coming together in a kiss, when Jordan suddenly belches to release the tension. He goes into the bathroom and reprises the same look of longing, now in Amy's eyes, but this time without any conflict; he takes off his clothes and gets into the tub with her.

Is Jordan displacing his uncomfortable desire for another man onto his more socially normalized attraction to his girlfriend? Whatever the reason, he consummates sexual relations with Amy for the first time. Instead of their loss of virginity being a "sacred" moment, it is shared with Xavier, who watches everything through the crack of the bathroom door, masturbating. In *The Doom Generation*, the central heterosexual couple, then, is born as a bisexual triangle. (As if to signal his bisexual potential, Xavier licks his own semen from his hand.)

Xavier quickly graduates from voyeurism to participation. That night he climbs into bed between Amy and Jordan. When Amy wakes up, he begins to make love to her. She feels guilty when Jordan finds out that she has had sex with Xavier, but Jordan is completely encouraging: "It doesn't matter.... Whatever, Amy." Again, he defends Xavier, signaling that he does not see the other man as a rival but instead as a friend: "He's sort of like us, lost, like he doesn't fit in." Nonetheless, Amy stays peeved at Xavier for a while, calling him "a life support system for a cock." Both Amy and Jordan project their own needs and desires onto the free-spirited outlaw Xavier.

Their fates now fully intertwined by being on the run from the law, the bisexual connection between Jordan and Xavier begins to strengthen. Jordan is fascinated with Xavier's cowboy belt buckle and begins to play with it; Xavier's cigarette goes straight up in the air between his lips, as if to suggest he is aroused by this. Amy is, as usual, sarcastic: "Jeez, it's his fuckin' belt—

don't turn out over it." In one of Araki's most erotically charged scenes, Xavier is having sex again with Amy, and he asks her what Jordan's penis is like. At first, Amy is suspicious of Xavier's interest; but he becomes playful about his bisexual curiosity in the other man, varying his stroking techniques inside her as he asks what Jordan is like in bed. There is no jealousy within this triangle; in fact, throughout the film, they edge closer and closer to a sexual threesome. Needless to say, it is the more sexually experienced Xavier who broaches the subject and pushes for it:

> *Xavier*: So have you ever done that?
> *Jordan*: You mean, like, hook up with two people at the same time? Naw.
> *Xavier*: It's the best.... You can actually feel his cock through the girl's insides.

This dialogue occurs during a second moment of tentative intimacy between Jordan and Xavier, in yet another motel room, when Amy leaves them together in bed and Jordan plays "itsy bitsy spider" with his fingertips across Xavier's back.

But even though these three have killed people in the course of their road trip, and though the sexual situation among them evolves to the point where both men are regularly sharing Amy (to the fulfillment of all), overcoming the heterosexual taboo against sexual contact between two men proves to be much more difficult. Whenever strong undercurrents of bisexual attraction arise, they summon forth Jordan's defenses; the feelings are apparently real enough to be unnerving to him. In Araki's vision, it is always problematic for a straight male to cross the borderline of same-sex activity. In *Nowhere*, too, Dark bears witness to violence, murder and suicide before he can bring himself to act on his bisexual urges.

When Amy, Jordan and Xavier finally do pile into bed for their threesome, Araki uses dissolves to make their bodies blur and blend into each other. Almost immediately, their pleasure is interrupted by a gang of thugs who have tracked them back to the abandoned warehouse where the three are camping for the night. Xavier is knocked unconscious; Jordan is beaten and restrained; Amy is raped. The ringleader of the bashers castrates Jordan with a pair of garden shears, venting his rage specifically against the part of Jordan that has registered and expressed his increasing bisexual passion throughout the film. Finally, Amy and Xavier rally and kill the ringleader with the same shears. In the last scene, Jordan is dead and Amy and Xavier must take to the road alone.

Is Jordan killed, symbolically, because he has reached the verge of breaking through to a life-changing bisexual liberation? It seems telling that when the three finally give in to the long-simmering fantasy of making love as a trio, they are instantly attacked by representatives of straight society at its most repressive, predatory and conformist. Rather than seeing the element of the threesome that remains heterosexual (both Jordan and Xavier are connected to Amy), the bashers see only the element of the threesome that is potentially homosexual (both men are simultaneously connected to each other). Bisexuality may even seem more threatening to the one-dimensional bashers, who then have to contend with awareness of the fact that even a man who has sex with women (as do they) may simultaneously desire to have sex with men. "Bisexuality is rarely accepted as a valid orientation by heterosexual or homosexual people for their own phobic reasons. Being out as bi is more difficult."[3] Of course, killing males for engaging in bisexual or gay activity is something more likely to be done by straights at their most violently heterosexist. "Relationships with heterosexuals are difficult due to stereotypical judgments on their part."[4]

* * *

In Araki's dog-eat-dog world, heterosexual society punishes everyone. So, in *Nowhere*, it is the heterosexual sex that seems most ugly and depraved. Death-obsessed Shad (Ryan Philippe) cuts his arm with a razor while his girlfriend licks the blood; she performs oral sex on him while he floors the gas pedal of his car, speeding into the night and screaming, "I want to die! Let's all *die*!" In the film's most brutal scene, a popular TV star (Jaason Simmons) sadistically beats and rapes an adoring young female fan, "Egg" (Sarah Lassez), who later kills herself because of the attack.

Straight or gay, love is always something of an illusion in Araki's films, a temporary and makeshift refuge at best (suggesting that Araki himself may identify the most with the views of Andy, that love is essentially a con-job). The fact that love never seems to work out, no matter who attempts it or why, is part of Araki's larger theme, that the generation he is depicting is irremediably lost—the generation which is, as Dark says, "going to witness the end of everything." This theme gives Araki's films their provocative edge, even if it becomes dubious and somewhat navel-gazing as sociology. Moreover, Araki's political sympathies are, if anything, with his young gay characters, who take the brunt of a sex-phobic culture's hatred. Certainly, this is the case in *Totally F***ed Up*. Araki also shows sympathy for would-be tough girls, wounded more easily than they realize they can be: Amy Blue in *The Doom Generation*, "Egg" and even Mel perhaps in *Nowhere*. Still, Araki seems to reserve his deepest sympathies for the bisexual characters he creates for Duval in all three films. They are the repository of a special focus of attention; they are the ones who seem most classically "teen," in that they are still somewhat unsure of themselves, unsure of their ability to get what they want. They are also the true romantics, the ones who dwell in fantasy, and the ones who hold out some hope that an ideal life is even possible. At a wild party in *Nowhere*, in the middle of frantic decadence and violence, Dark finds a kitchen towel with the word HOPE sewn into it. To the extent that they merge the camps of sexual difference, partaking in both the turmoil and triumph of heterosexuality *and* homosexuality, the bisexual male is literally the films' hope for the future. Because they have acknowledged gay feelings in themselves, they presumably understand and champion the gay community more than the heterosexual boys who are frequently depicted as vicious gay-bashers in Araki's films.

It is the quest for an elusive ideal that motivates Andy, Jordan, and Dark. As Mel asks in *Nowhere*, "What would life be without a little mystery?" To a certain extent, teen subcultures are known for their pursuit of "realness," which involves both rigorous honesty and a simultaneous refusal to necessarily define everything that happens: things are just "what they are." In a way, honesty and ambiguity can be natural antagonists; this is another way in which bisexual men often cannot win for trying, so to speak, when they attempt to explore their sexualities against a backdrop of any youthful social scene.

And yet, to a great extent, bisexual exploration often occurs against the backdrop of youth culture, as we see from recent films made by directors other than Araki. For example, *Groove* (2000) follows a set of characters who regularly organize and attend raves in San Francisco. The raves are held in abandoned warehouses, hot-wired for sound and lights; the ravers congregate to dance to the mind-bending music of the DJ's, and to experience the even more mind-bending hallucinogens, acid and ecstasy. These wild parties represent colorful oases of fun in the middle of their dull daily routines. But they also represent a chance at finding real romantic love, connecting with a kind of soul mate.

As the film opens, all of the characters are preparing for a rave to be held later that night. Colin (Denny Kirkwood) has chosen this rave as the special occasion to propose to his girlfriend Harmony (Mackenzie Firgens), even though Colin's brother David (Hamish Linklater) cautions him that he might be moving too fast and impulsively. At first it is David who seems overprotective and overly anxious; but Colin's impulsiveness comes to seem more pronounced, and more problematic, as the rave gets underway and certain aspects of his personality begin to come out under the influence of ecstasy. X, we have been told by one character, promotes "honesty ... like being a kid." Colin makes eye contact with another man, and the significance of this literally sends him reeling to Harmony, whom he hugs and clings to as if for dear life. He seems resolved not to pursue his attraction to the man, but later, Harmony catches Colin kissing the man passionately in a quiet corner of the chill-out room (a place where ravers can go to escape the intensity of the loud music and the dance floor). She tries to play down Colin's betrayal, but she is clearly disturbed, hurt and angry, and runs away to cry in the bathroom.

As the rave begins to break up, the man approaches Colin outside and suggests they exchange phone numbers, presumably so they can get together again. Colin is hostile and shoves him away: "Look," he says, "I really don't do that sort of thing." His earlier avid displays of attraction toward the man belies his words of denial. "I'm not, you know —" Colin says, meaning "gay" but not completing his sentence. "Neither am I," the man says tersely and knowingly as he walks away. Even in a subculture that has seemingly rejected labels as antiquated and meaningless, there is nonetheless a stigma attached to the behaviors themselves.

Colin finds his brother David and clings to him the way he had previously clung to Harmony, telling David that he and Harmony had a fight but that everything will be all right. Harmony finds Colin on the dance floor; she drags him to the chill-out room and, even as he is trying to explain his behavior to her, begins to make love to him. Her indication that she does not require an explanation for his same-sex activity seems to mean that she is willing to offer him the understanding he needs; but all is not truly well. When they are back in their apartment that morning, Colin showers remorsefully while Harmony lies awake in bed, sobbing to herself. Rather than forging a healthy, honest relationship, where Colin's bisexuality is in the open, Harmony and Colin may simply settle in for a bitter war of denial.

Groove is immensely sympathetic to the rave scene. Whether or not dancing and drugging has ever been a genuinely effective way to "change the world," raves are depicted in this film as, if nothing else, promoting a way for sincere and idealistic people to make contact with each other and have fun. But Colin's story is the film's dark side. He is troubled, needy, emotionally unstable. If the designer drugs act like a truth serum, the truth they bring out in him is something which shames him, and which hurts the one he supposedly loves. His girlfriend's very name, "Harmony," is suggestive of the kind of healing balance which he may be seeking as an antidote to his same-sex tendencies. Colin's is a cautionary tale about not being ready for the love he needs because of his inadequate self-knowledge, regarding his gay side.

An even more extreme deconstruction of labels, within the even more extreme youth subculture of skinheads, occurs in Bruce LaBruce's *Skin Gang*

(1999), a provocative and sexually explicit homoeroticization of hypermasculine skinhead iconography. The skinheads talk about gang-raping women, but they mostly have sex with each other, even while strongly denying that they are gay. "No, we're not faggots," they say, ranting about how they'd like to exterminate gay "perverts." Their same-sex activity partly arises from the bizarre aphrodisiac of violence and power. After beating up an effeminate queer (played by LaBruce himself), Dirk (Eden Miller) and Dieter (Steve Masters) begin to make love while standing over their victim's prone body. Partly, too, it is a narcissistic identification with others who share their values and beliefs. Manfred (Daniel Bätscher) masturbates with a girlie magazine and a copy of *Mein Kampf* with Hitler's picture on the cover. They tyrannize women and weaker men as a way of denying any potential weakness in themselves; they could never identify with any man who openly identifies as gay, although at the climax of the film one of their gay victims turns the tables on the skinhead leader by raping him at the point of a gun.

Colin in *Groove* is depicted as a classic bisexual betrayer, hurting his female partner by deceiving her, and becoming hostile toward his male partner when he feels too much pressure from him. Likewise, the bisexual skinheads in *Skin Flick* are heartless and hypocritical predators. By contrast, in Araki's films, one is encouraged to sympathize with the tentative attempts of straight males to realize their bisexual potential. What the Duval characters seek is romanticism; Jordan and Dark find one "special" boy who awakens the homoerotic side of their latent bisexuality: Xavier for Jordan, Montgomery for Dark. This reprises what many actual bisexuals say about falling in love with a specific person rather than a gender.

Not that Araki suggests it is in any way a simple matter to live and love bisexually. He comes closest to presenting a kind of bisexual fulfillment in the final scene of *Nowhere*. Montgomery knocks on the window of Dark's room. Both men are nude, Dark because he has just gotten into bed for the night and Montgomery because he has just escaped from space aliens who abducted him earlier in the film. But their nudity is more a sign of child-like innocence — Adam and Eve before the fall — rather than anything smutty. Montgomery asks if he can "rest here for a while." He lies down on Dark's pillow and then invites a somewhat flustered Dark to join him. In a tight overhead close-up, their faces are side by side and they look into each other's eyes. Montgomery says, "Even though we just met, I like you a lot." "I feel the same about you," Dark finally admits, after some uncomfortable throat-clearing. Montgomery confesses that his thoughts turned to Dark when he as being held captive by the aliens: "If they kill me, I'll never get to see you again. It's retarded and pathetic, but all my life I've been searching for one special person on this stinking planet who I can love, and who loves me for what I am."

Dark nuzzles Montgomery's cheek; he recognizes that Montgomery is speaking the same language of pure, eternal love that Dark has been trying to describe to Mel. The following exchange sums up Dark and Montgomery's tenderness, and can even be paraphrased as a kind of wedding vow:

> *Montgomery*: Is it okay if I spend the night? I really want to sleep next to you.
> *Dark*: Only if you promise to never ever leave me.

But Araki will not permit himself, his heroes, or their generation such a clichéd happy ending. Montgomery and Dark close their eyes and are about to fall asleep when Montgomery begins to cough. This cough becomes a protracted choking spasm, with Dark holding Montgomery and asking him what's wrong. Finally, Montgomery explodes, covering Dark and the walls of his room in blood; Dark is left lying next to a giant cockroach, who rasps, "I'm outta here," and scuttles through the window, leaving the idealistic Dark once more betrayed, disappointed and abandoned.

It is possible to read Araki's painting of Dark's bedroom as blood-stained abattoir as a particularly vivid metaphor for the way bisexual men have been stigmatized as disease carriers, killers, in the AIDS era. "The concept that sperm is a deadly weapon has debilitated our society."[5] (As a potentially lethal body fluid, blood becomes interchangeable with semen and sperm.) Specifically, it has made society less open to engaging in sexual experimentation — and more prone to demonize those who do. The sex that people once turned to for stress-relief as well as trusting, intimate connection has become, in itself, an enormous source of stress and mistrust. "Part of the wonder of life has been a spontaneous eruption of joy in a sexual encounter and we can't allow that anymore."[6] The bisexual male was once the great erotic adventure seeker par excellence. A liaison between gay and straight communities, he suffers now as those communities become more and more divided from each other and placed under more and more stress. "I'm afraid I'm less open to experimentation and flowing with the moment — less open to seeking adventure."[7] "You feel dangerous. But I have to keep it in perspective and hold on to my sexuality in the face of all the horror. I feel like giving it up at times though."[8]

"In the face of all the horror": this could be the same unremitting daily horror that confronts Andy, Jordan, and Dark as they make their shuffling way through a postmodern American landscape of casual violence, bad attitudes, constant simmering rage, and the proverbial war of all against all. All three meet terrible fates: Andy commits suicide by drinking bleach, Jordan is murdered, Dark is left definitively alone. Their inability to embrace their own conflicted sexuality and love themselves — indeed, their very inability to survive — is a problem that has universal implications, just as it stems from society's tendency to scapegoat bisexuality in the first place. Their constant scary temptation is precisely "to give up," whether that means dying quickly from swallowing poison or more slowly from AIDS; but this decision is one they feel driven to, out of hopelessness and despair. As one bisexual male has said, quite poignantly: "It took me a while to realize I had to practice safe sex. I still don't 100 percent of the time. It's because I think no one gives a shit about us anyway — they'd wish we'd all die."[9]

4

Rock Star Bisexuality in Todd Haynes' *Velvet Goldmine*

Meanings are not in things but between them. — Norman O. Brown

Time, places, people — they're all speeding up. So, to cope with this "evolutionary paranoia," strange people are chosen. — Mandy in *Velvet Goldmine*

To the degree that the bisexual male has often reductively equaled "rock star" in the popular imagination (and "British rock star" at that), the early 1970s Age of Explorations taught us something: in the right spotlight, with the right backbeat, the bisexual male could prove attractive to massive numbers of fans, male and female, gay and straight. (Thus, he could be made to make money; for any discussion of pop-culture archetypes must acknowledge that marketability is, unfortunately, the single most crucial element in the culture industry's production-consumption nexus.) Among other things, Todd Haynes' *Velvet Goldmine* (1998), a *roman-à-clef* inspired by the history of glam rock and the life of David Bowie, shows how rock music in the 1980s moved away from its former endorsement of bisexual identity, after AIDS and right-wing politics made sexual experimentation far less marketable. This retreat occurred to the dismay of bisexual and gay fans who had helped create "their" stars in the first place. Depicted as the sad victim of his own opportunism, the character of "Brian Slade" (Jonathan Rhys-Meyers), Haynes' fictionalized composite of Bowie and others, retreats from his own larger-than-life bisexual persona.

In contrast to the bold bisexual males of early 1970s cinema (who were often depicted precisely as rock stars, e.g., *Performance*, *The Rocky Horror Picture Show*, etc.), a very different picture of the bisexual male emerged in

4. Rock Star Bisexuality in Todd Haynes' Velvet Goldmine

cinema of the 1990s. No longer perceived as a bridge between gay and straight communities, but rather as an unguarded point of entry for fatal diseases to pass between the sick and the well, the clean and the unclean, the initiated and the uninitiated, the bisexual male is increasingly presented as a callous villain of one sort or another, implying that the liberation of homoerotic energies has, as its agenda and inevitable consequence, the literal destruction of all who cross its path. The temptation is to eschew any indication that the bisexual male could truly love, could bring pleasure to a variety of partners, and instead to see him as always being bad for at least one of the genders with whom he involves himself. Sleeping with both genders merely gives access to twice the number of "victims."

There is a strain of gay self-hatred, masochism, or internalized homophobia, in which a gay male who attaches himself to a woman is deified as being more attractive or socially powerful than a "full gay," because he is still butch (or disease-free) enough to be able to be with women. It is the mission of much gay activism to exorcise this persistent strain — often the last barrier preventing gay men from truly loving themselves and each other — by stacking the deck against the bisexual male. To an extent, Todd Haynes has done exactly this in *Velvet Goldmine*. Brian Slade's chameleonic nature associates him with the closet and denial; though he succeeds in becoming, for a while anyway, an anarchic bringer of bisexual liberation to the masses, this liberation is severely qualified by the fact that he ends up exposed as an opportunist, a follower rather than a leader, cowardly and out for himself.

In the film's complex hierarchy, there are actually four separate tiers of gay male sexuality, represented by four different characters. Jack Fairy (Micko Westmoreland) is a vision of androgyny, feminine, even wraith-like, always in make-up and drag. Fairy is the most openly and thoroughly gay character, an emblem of gay persecution and ostracism, also an emblem of gay self-will, self-invention and self-empowerment. Haynes suggests that he is, in fact, the reincarnation of Oscar Wilde. Then there is the outspoken Curt Wild (Ewan McGregor): extremely butch and proud, he makes no attempt to hide his homosexuality or even adopt a heterosexual pretense; yet he intimidates people with his antisocialness, his self-destructiveness, his cult of extreme masculinity and his substance abuse. Therefore, unlike Fairy, Curt employs certain crutches to cut into the perceived "sissy factor" of being gay, and help him enact his gayness publicly.

The least famous character (he is not a rock star but a journalist) is also the least "out": Arthur Stuart (Christian Bale) has lived his whole life mainly in the closet. Thrown out of his parents' house as a teenager for masturbating to images of male glam-rock stars, he has half-repressed and half-cherished the memory of a single homoerotic encounter, fatefully enough with Curt Wild himself, star and ardent fan magically getting together after a show. Finally, the film's fourth male, Brian Slade, is the most charismatic and successful of all, the "biggest star," but also the least original, arguably, since he is presented as having concocted his style from a combination of Fairy's androgyny and Curt's punk-ish confrontationalism. Slade is also depicted as the most sexually deceptive and omnivorous, maintaining the cover of a wife while secretly engaging in a gay relationship with Curt.

What complicates Slade is that he is also very publicly "gay" in his image, his delivery, and the content of his song lyrics. He even declares himself to be bisexual at a press conference, which only serves to make him a greater international pop star. However, though he plays with androgyny as far back as his early days as an aspiring folk-singer (wearing long flowing hair and dresses), Slade seems possessed of a kind of pride which is similar to Curt Wild's gay pride but also more conflicted: Slade's pride compels him to frustrate the very expectations he deliberately helps foster, which is to say, the expectations that he is gay, feminine, passive in bed. Topsy-turvy to the usual situation of the gay man forced to come out within the paradigm of heterosexual culture, Slade creates a makeshift but larger-than-life gay ambiance around himself, only to then "come out" as being straight all along. It is a strange syndrome, and one which Haynes, as director, seems eager to deflate by catching Slade again and again *in flagrante homo*, so to speak.

In this sense, Haynes is much harder on Bowie-as-Slade, who is at least publicly supportive of homosexuality for a time, than he is on Bob Dylan in *I'm Not There* (2007). Both films reveal the rock star to be a surrealistic collage of desires and projected desires, a dream begun by an individual but then carried on by the masses of fans who follow him. While it is true that, in *I'm Not There*, Haynes makes highly creative use of Dylan's flirtation with androgyny in the mid–1960s, nonetheless he reverently allows Dylan to retain the ultimate power of his changeling, chameleonic energy, without attempting to hold him, as he does Slade, to one specific example of his many shamanistic transformations. In *Velvet Goldmine*, Haynes seems to be constantly taking a rooting interest in Slade being, secretly and at times not so secretly, a homosexual rather than straight or bi. Slade's abortive affair with Curt is portrayed as the love of his life — while his marriage with Mandy (Toni Collette) remains business-like, indifferent. It is also hinted that Slade's nostalgia for his own repressed past is what he continues to draw on for the part of him that remains poignant and charismatic as a performer. Indeed, even after dwindling into mainstream success and self-parody, becoming his conservative, heterosexual alter ego, "Tommy Stone" (Alastair Cumming), Slade remains, in many ways,

4. Rock Star Bisexuality in Todd Haynes' Velvet Goldmine

Jonathan Rhys-Meyers plays Brian Slade, a fictional rock star from the glam rock era, in Todd Haynes' *Velvet Goldmine* (1998). Here, Slade is onstage, striking a cruciform pose. Although he becomes famous for his androgynous image, Slade is frustrated in his attempt to realize his bisexual desire offstage, in real life.

the strangest of martyrs, one who enacts public spectacles of gayness (for acclaim, prestige and profit no less) while disowning actual gayness in his "real" life.

Is Slade truly bisexual — is his love for Mandy at least as real as his love for Curt? Haynes tends to glorify the male-male drama, while mocking the male-female one. Slade's eyes light up with pulsing neon hearts when he looks at Curt; the two men become, as Mandy says, "Tracy and Hepburn for the 70s." A constant theme throughout *Velvet Goldmine* is the fact that Mandy is generally abandoned by the opportunistic Slade, who abuses her uncommon tolerance and understanding. In a scene that takes place in a gay nightclub, she jokingly wonders out loud what "the piece of flesh between my vagina and my anus" is called, setting herself up for some kind of punch line, and someone jokes back: "No man's land!"[1] After losing Curt, Brian dissolves his marriage, as if a cover of heterosexual propriety were no longer needed, now that there is nothing left to cover up. Mandy finds him in bed, sniffing cocaine from the buttocks of a black transsexual, and presents him with divorce papers. In this scene, she pleads with him one last time to recognize her as his wife;

but her desperate words only send him into gales of helpless mocking laughter, and she runs away, thoroughly scorned and defeated.

If the end of Brian and Mandy's marriage is hellish, the beginning is not much rosier. When he first meets her at a party on New Year's Eve, 1969, his opening question to her is if she can give him a ride home. Later, they have sex, but only after Slade has symbolically seduced Fairy at the party, and, during a passionate kiss, stolen the antique jade brooch which represents Fairy's radical appropriation of femaleness/artifice.[2] In a snowy grove, Slade sings Roxy Music's "Ladytron" to Mandy, reinterpreting Bryan Ferry's lyric about the vicissitudes of romantic illusion into a comment about the unique opportunism of the closeted male, who casts a spell over a woman so that no one will suspect he is actually gay.

Slade is presented as the film's magnetic sexual epicenter, but he always exacts some charge for yielding his services, particularly when he sleeps with someone who is either a woman or an overtly feminized gay man. For all the romanticism in Slade's music, he becomes the unromantic image of a gay man who hates himself and other gay men, a predator who attacks, in others, the feminine weakness he despises in himself. He holds out to gay men the consolation of "understanding," even as he steals their own gayness from them and sells it back to them precisely as this specious consolation. Slade is no different, then, than the street hustler who indulges gay fantasies for a price — in fact, he is this hustler writ large, as a mass-media sensation — and, like the hustler, his sexuality is both more reductive and more perverse than a true bisexual's would be. Haynes presents Slade, alternately, as a heterosexual drawn into the gay lifestyle in order to soullessly cash in on a trend, or as a neurotic gay man who cannot complete his coming-out process — either way, a kind of villain and a scapegoat. As one gay character says, "He was elegance walking hand in hand with a lie," the lie being, presumably, that he has spent his life trying to cover up the reality that he was gay.

Gay histories of popular culture are needed, and it is there, precisely, that *Velvet Goldmine* excels. It is like a secret cultural history as witnessed by a social outsider, watching it from the sidelines and astral-projecting into the stars, linking them to his own marginalized desire and, at bottom, to his own downtrodden humanity. Haynes is skilled at creating moments, often illustrated by dramatic zoom-shots, where we glimpse the candid truth of "behind-the-scenes" reality under the mechanisms of stardom, such as a seemingly candid image of a glammed-up Brian and Curt, surprised with their arms around each other.[3] Another such moment occurs when Slade is waiting in his dressing room to go onstage for his final performance; the manager comes in and says, "Brian — time." At the word "time," Haynes zooms in on

4. Rock Star Bisexuality in Todd Haynes' Velvet Goldmine   69

Slade's expectant face, as if to imply that it is time (in its larger, more abstract meaning) which forces the rock star's hand, causing him to want to "grow up," as it were, and move away from sexual ambiguity. The effect of shots like this in *Velvet Goldmine* is to exemplify what William S. Burroughs referred to as the subversive act of showing/seeing "what is on the end of that long newspaper spoon"—in this case, the fact that media superstars are, in many ways, exactly like us in the audience, in that they desire, love and hurt like us.

We are still within the realm of metaphors here, but metaphors which bear a disarming resemblance to real life, or rather, metaphors which are loved and needed so passionately by so many social outsiders that they become invested with real life. This is Haynes' ultimate comment on glam rock in the 1970s. For whatever reason, Slade was allowed to seize a unique moment in which he could project a bisexual image and become widely beloved for it; and then, for whatever reason, he also reached a point where he could go no further and had to retreat from the ground he himself had broken. Precisely within the lavish context of media superstardom in the Age of Explorations, *Velvet Goldmine*'s bisexual male is forced to narrow his options, to resolve himself as heterosexual—returning to us in all his bisexual glory only in our dusty record collections.

Can the bisexual male's cultural moment come again—or was it, ironically, wholly dependent on a larger pattern of *heterosexual* freedoms and experimentations, i.e., as an adjunct or a side effect of the more general "sexual revolution" of that period? And even in certain decades when bisexuality has seemed "trendy," what does this really mean to the lives of actual bisexual men?

In *Velvet Goldmine*, people often claim that "everyone is bisexual," but this assertion always feels phony, too pat and too insistent, meant either as a deliberate, nervous challenge to the powers-that-be (the scene where a snide glam-rock fan gives a man-on-the-street interview to "Mister BBC") or as an attempt to back-pedal from the public perception that someone may in fact be fully gay (Brian Slade at his press conference, when he sneers in a way that is meant to silence opposition, "I mean, everybody knows most people are bisexual"). Asked about gayness as a trend among his young fans, Curt Wild speaks out, as he often does in the film, from the viewpoint of a certain unabashed, unashamed homosexual purity: "If you're going to claim that you're gay, you're going to have to make love in a gay style, and most of these kids just aren't going to make it. That line—'Everyone is bisexual'—it's a very popular thing to say right now, but personally I think it's meaningless." This remark expresses the dubiousness many gays feel toward men who claim to be bisexual; but this attitude, much like homophobia, only serves to privilege one label over another. By obsessing about the primacy of unambiguous, irreversible acts over what are perceived to be unfounded and unreliable emotional claims, gay distrust of bisexuality upholds the deceptive, reductive mania for "simple truths" which distorts the larger heterosexual society. As if acts themselves could never be ambiguous, and as if emotional claims which someone makes about himself should not be taken seriously, if nothing else then at least as indications of the beliefs which the person holds about himself.

Something that *Velvet Goldmine* makes clear, often poignantly, is that we are wrong to confuse the mass-marketed image of glam rock stars with the private realities of those stars, who were, privately, only as liberated as they could be — i.e., just as inhibited, ashamed and constrained as anyone; just as subject to internalized homophobic strictures to conform. During the brilliant montage of the "Baby's on Fire" sequence, Haynes combines several narratives: in one, Slade mimes oral sex on Curt Wild's guitar while the two men are performing onstage; a photo of this tease ends up in music magazines; an adolescent Arthur is thrown out of his parents' house when he is caught masturbating to this photo; and the real-life Slade and Wild seize the moment to steal away from a heterosexual orgy in their hotel suite in order to furtively consummate their long-simmering attraction to each other. This latter seduction is spied on by the wardrobe mistress, Shannon (Emily Woof), who is reduced to bitter tears at the thought that her famous employer might be gay; one senses that her greatest fear is that this might mean she will soon be out of a job if the rest of the world finds out. Not even within his own entourage, who presumably only exist because of him, and who make money from his expressions of homosexual desire onstage, is Slade free to openly express his homosexual side in his real life.

The rock star crosses boundaries, pushes buttons, awakens dormant, inchoate urges. What makes the greatest rock stars so legendary is the way they offer a natural bisexual appeal: women and men fall in love with them easily, and sex is always a component of that love. But stardom is only the most arbitrary part of the fantasy; the stardom would be hollow without those electrifying elements which the rock star himself provides: skillful musicianship, a certain eloquence, style and ideas, depth of soul. While others project the role of a superman onto him, the rock star is often trying to do something much humbler. Curt says at one point that he and the other glam-rock stars wanted to change the world, but just ended up changing themselves. And, while being taken as a sort of instant guru, the rock star is most likely still trying to figure himself out.

Perhaps we need to think of the rock star more along the lines of a rather

4. Rock Star Bisexuality in Todd Haynes' Velvet Goldmine

flamboyant example of alienated labor: forced to objectify the vagrant moods of his own fantasies in order to sell them on the open market. In this sense, the bisexual rock star finds himself occupying a space of false liberation. He is always a suspect phenomenon, a bastard offspring of capitalism's skill at manipulating desire and fostering trends, rather than an image of authentic liberation for everyone. Being able to become actualized only through a highly mediated fantasy of stardom is equivalent to not being truly able to become actualized at all. To how many of us is the avenue of stardom readily available? The few who do achieve it, and are thereby permitted to play at bisexuality in the public realm, are exceptions which prove the rule; just as the average audience member in the margins of an arena-sized concert crowd is still vulnerable to being attacked and even killed if he attempts to indulge in the same androgynous or bisexual moves of the rock star, shining like a distant light onstage. Does the image of the bisexual rock star ever actually galvanize real changes in peoples' attitudes, or do patriarchal oppressions go on flourishing in spite of, maybe even because, he has momentarily blinded us with the illusion that we can be free, through him, for the price of a record or concert ticket?

Not that Haynes himself is blind to these built-in oppressions. One of the most ingenious set-pieces in *Velvet Goldmine* is the desultory depiction of a mid–1980s straight bar where no one is having any fun at all. The clientele consists of desperately impassive men, trying not to betray any emotion. They cluster around a kind of latter-day Gidget in a football jacket, a young woman who manages to be both perky and menacing at the same time. These heterosexuals consume the Brian Slade songs on the jukebox as trippy nostalgia, completely ignoring the bisexual subtext of the music, which the film has been at pains to excavate and document. In this dystopian vision, *Velvet Goldmine* reveals its true subject: the insidious ways in which heterosexual culture is able to outbid bisexual realities, neutralizing their subversiveness by transforming them not only into commodities but bland, generic heterosexual fictions.

5

For Whom the Bi Tolls: Craig Lucas' *The Dying Gaul* and Ozon's *Water Drops on Burning Rocks*

> [L]ove seems to be the best, most sneaky and effective instrument of social oppression. — Rainer Werner Fassbinder[1]

> As generations of bisexual, gay, and straight literature have shown, desire is often most powerful at its most obsessive, destructive, and doomed.[2]

In true postmodern fashion, cinema is nothing if not self-reflexive: there have been a number of important films, since the 1950s, about filmmakers and the filmmaking process. Hollywood alone has generated an entire subgenre of movies about itself. Like a zone of token resistance within the walls of the citadel, nearly all of these have been markedly cynical and anti-idealistic, almost going out of their way to be self-flagellating and provide a kind of bracing tonic for the dishonesty and materialism on which the industry nonetheless continues to thrive. In spite of the fact that life is as emotionally complicated and problematic in Hollywood as it is in anywhere else, the movies go on reaping the profits from escapist entertainments with simplistic plots and messages, rather than addressing people's actual lives. Picking up on this hypocrisy, Craig Lucas' *The Dying Gaul* (2005) employs Hollywood as the backdrop for a bisexual love triangle involving three lost souls: high-powered producer Jeffrey Tishop (Campbell Scott), his ex-screenwriter wife Elaine (Patricia Clarkson), and his screenwriter boyfriend Robert Sandrich (Peter Sarsgaard).

Bisexuality aside, *The Dying Gaul* is not a complete departure from the Hollywood-on-Hollywood genre; in fact it contains a number of homages to other films about the movies. Like *The Player* (1992) and *The Blackout* (1997), homicide is shown as arising naturally from the omnipotence and greed of the movie business. Like *Sunset Boulevard* (1950), *The Dying Gaul* features a screenwriter whose process of selling out to the industry is reified by the fact that he is also sexually seduced. (Also like *Sunset Boulevard*, a dramatic swimming pool figures into *The Dying Gaul*'s climactic scenes of violence.) What makes *The Dying Gaul* unique and interesting is the way that Lucas makes the movie industry and bisexuality into complementary metaphors for each other: in a predictably negative sense, both are depicted as amoral and unromantic, selling dreams and people to a kind of bottom line of "getting what one wants"; but in a less predictable, even surprising sense, both are also depicted as providing much-needed pleasure and fantasy to the world.

In a scene shot for the film but later deleted, Jeffrey tries to work out his guilt over his bisexual issues with his therapist. He wonders out loud if it even matters what he does with Robert. He haltingly teases out the central theme of his life, and one of the film's central themes: "All I ever do is give people pictures of what they desire, fantasies, for eight dollars. And in turn, if the worst I ever do is hold this man.... If all I ever do is, I mean, love him...?" But is love permitted to someone who deals in fantasies as a business? Or, does the dealer in fantasies, in fact, have a *more* honest, direct and grounded approach to love, since he understands the "formulas" of what will work and what will not? Actually, Jeffrey's life turns out to be less formulaic than either Elaine's or Robert's, both of whom seem far more conventionally sincere and "human" at the beginning of the film (this assumption gets overturned during the course of the narrative). Again, there are two sides: fantasy is both romantic and unromantic, innocent and cynical; it must be both in order to occupy that strange zone occupied by the movies, in which fantasies become real only to become fantasies all over again, in the imaginations of audiences.

In the dense intertwining of all of these metaphors, *The Dying Gaul* suggests that the two sides are, in fact, inseparable: there is no sexual freedom without an inevitable excess, the perception that one has "gone too far" and become cold-blooded. All three of the main characters do become cold-blooded at different points in the film — by the end, all three have revealed their darkest sides. It is only the degree of hypocrisy and self-delusion which truly separates the characters, rather than some abstract, unalterable notion of "good and bad," "predator and victim."

Robert goes to a film studio for a meeting about his script, titled "The Dying Gaul." This script concerns a gay couple, one of whom is dying from

AIDS; the title refers to an ancient Roman statue of a dying Gallic soldier which the couple sees while traveling. The statue was the Romans' tribute to their defeated foes. Appropriately, the relationship between Robert and the producer, Jeffrey, begins as an adversarial one. Jeffrey is interested in buying the script; Robert is pleased and flattered, until Jeffrey brings up the subject of rewriting the script to make it more mainstream: "The idea is to have the broadest appeal, so that we can make money." Specifically, he wants Robert to change the protagonists from a homosexual to a heterosexual couple, where the woman has AIDS. Needless to say, the political implications of this change rub Robert the wrong way.

Jeffrey is disarming in his openness. In general, he stares at Robert intently and somewhat mechanically, and speaks rather strangely: most of the time pontificating sternly about what audiences want to see, but occasionally seeming to drop his guard for moments of seemingly sarcastic candor. "The Dying Gaul," he says, is "a weepy," a genre which is "hard to sell." "They're very hard," he reiterates (lingering on the word "hard" in a way which makes Robert squirm) before placing his hand on his heart and adding: "And they're my *favorite* kind of movie."

Jeffrey's shield of unctuous authority makes him difficult to read. He seems to be turning all of his power of charm and intimidation on Robert, in order to convince him to rewrite the script. Robert, however, stands firm on the fact that his script is an expression of gay pride and especially a *cri de coeur* about AIDS: his gay characters "identify with the Gaul because they're gay and so many of their friends are dying, and they're looking for some kind of response from the enemy." By this, Robert shows his activist spirit: the straight world is the enemy; straights refuse to come to the rescue of gay men and instead help engineer their mass deaths. Jeffrey understands that Robert hopes the film will be a kind of "dying Gaul" for the viewer, a spur to compassion in the public sphere. Robert reveals to Jeffrey that the script is about Malcolm, Robert's ex-lover who has recently died. (Robert himself has remained HIV negative.) "You are an amazing and lovely person, Robert, and you have succeeded in making me feel like a total scumbag," Jeffrey says. "Good," Robert says self-righteously, "I'm glad."

Jeffrey's way of turning up the charm, here, still seems like part of a strategy to get Robert to do what Jeffrey wants. In fact, Robert does agree to sell the script for one million dollars and to rewrite it. That night, Robert calls his ex-wife Kelli (Elizabeth Marvel) to tell her his good news; he is going to set aside a third of the money for their son Mark's college fund. Robert himself has a bisexual history: he left Kelli for Malcolm, her brother, and Kelli cannot forgive him. She hangs up on him while he is saying, "I love you." The complex feelings of this relationship are not further explored by the film, but this scene seems meant to contrast Robert's emotionality and displays of caring with Jeffrey's seemingly cold, stoical lack of feeling. As the film progresses, it becomes clearer and clearer, however, that Robert's busy kindness is motivated by massive guilt.

In subsequent meetings, Jeffrey begins to hit on Robert very directly. "You are very handsome," he says while hugging Robert outside the studio, "and I'm getting a little turned on." Robert stares at him with a blank look, shocked. "You can do anything you want," Jeffrey goes on, "as long as you don't call it what it is. Understand?" On the one hand, Jeffrey is expressing a distaste for narrow labels, perhaps especially the "gay" label. On the other hand, he seems to be offering Robert (unsolicited) advice about the world: one can get away with anything as long as one is discreet about it. One can engage in gay sex, for instance, as long as one doesn't announce it. This logic is sometimes seen in male bisexuality, and it is often viewed by gay activists as regressive, imposing a return to homosexuality's isolated "closet status." At this point in the film, Jeffrey seems to be someone who uses "heterosexual privilege" as a cover for gay activity; we are conditioned to see Jeffrey as dishonest, to say the least. But, as the film later reveals, Jeffrey does not want the demands of abiding by a single identity to become an obstacle to the wide range of possible human romantic and sexual interaction which he could enjoy. For him, the political meaning of identity is less important than the human meaning of what he feels for women and men.

He takes Robert home to meet his wife, Elaine. On the patio of his enormous mansion in the Hills, he tells Robert that he still cannot believe the house, with its panoramic view, is really his: "When is someone gonna march in and demand their keys back?" This may be Jeffrey's way of revealing to Robert how little "at home" he feels in his own skin, and in the heterosexual life he has made for himself; but because he says it in his usual unctuous monotone, it ends up sounding as sarcastic and self-parodying as everything else he says. Elaine brings Robert a vodka, oblivious to the way her husband flirts with Robert whenever her back is turned. Revealing a certain talent for deception, Robert strikes up an instant and mutual friendship with her. She tells him: "Your script is so beautiful. Don't become one of them, all right?" By "one of them," she means "an industry person," but for Elaine — as well as for Robert with his need to pit gay against straight — there is a tendency to divide the world into "us versus them." The extent to which Elaine's "us/them" thinking is motivated by her own regrets and sense of failure, as an ex-screenwriter — as Robert's "us/them" thinking is motivated by guilt — begins to disturb the viewer more and more as the film progresses.

Seeing Robert as a kindred spirit, Elaine engages him in personal conversation. He tells her about Malcolm. They also talk about the gay erotic chat rooms which Robert frequents, partly out of loneliness and partly because he is fascinated by chat rooms themselves. He describes them as disembodied spirit voices, "all this karma colliding out in the middle of nowhere." That night, Elaine steals away from Jeffrey and logs on, looking for Robert. She finds his profile, recognizing it by the Buddhist catchphrases in the tag line. Malcolm taught Robert principles of the Buddhist religion, and now these principles have become bound up in Robert's emotional and sexual life.

Elaine continues to go online to search for Robert. At first, she experiences these moments as something illicit, a secret life she is claiming for herself, almost like a kind of psychological "cheating" on Jeffrey. Finally, she encounters Robert in a chat room and strikes up a conversation, under an anonymous screen name. She pretends to be recently bereaved, and when Robert talks about losing Malcolm, she gets him to talk about his intimate emotional state. He admits that he thinks frequently about suicide, and saw a psychiatrist for a period of time. Instinctually, she asks if he assisted his partner's death. After a long hesitation, Robert confesses to this "stranger" that he did in fact kill Malcolm, by injecting potassium chloride into his IV, because he could not stand to see him suffer. Switching subjects, Elaine, still posing as an anonymous gay male, asks whether Robert would have sex with "him" (she is grinning girlishly as she types this question, suggesting that Elaine is slightly in love with Robert, and is perhaps attracted, more than even she realizes at this point, to males who have a strongly homosexual side). Robert says that he is actually starting a new relationship with his "boss on a project," and then describes this man enough to make her certain that it is her husband. Elaine does not break character, but after signing off, she angrily smashes the laptop.

Robert and Jeffrey do begin a sexual affair, while Elaine launches into an elaborate deception of her own. Paying someone to hack into Robert's computer and raid the files of his ex-psychiatrist, she creates a screen name, ArckAngell1966, and seeks Robert out, leading him to believe that she is Malcolm trying to contact him from beyond the grave. This is where Elaine reveals the dark side behind her own façade of sensitivity and caring. Robert is angered, and believes this to be some kind of practical joke, but cannot figure out who might be behind it; meanwhile, Elaine keeps offering so many specific, detailed secrets from his past that he begins to helplessly believe that it is really Malcolm. The online conversations seem to be building toward a point where she, as Malcolm, will command the increasingly frazzled and guilt-stricken Robert to kill himself— indeed, this specific topic comes up.

"If you tell me to kill myself, I will," Robert types, but Elaine swerves away from this course of vengeance at the last moment, instead reassuring Robert that he should live and continue writing, and that "Malcolm" will always watch over him.

During one sexual encounter, Robert asks Jeffrey if he ever loved Elaine. Jeffrey says that at one time he loved her very much. Robert asks Jeffrey if he thinks about divorcing her, and Jeffrey smirks and implies that, in fact, he thinks about simply killing her. When Robert becomes indignant, Jeffrey gets defensive: "You never fantasized, Mr. Moral? You never fantasized about Malcolm? You never saw him suffering and thought, 'I wish I could put him out of his misery?'" This touches a very raw nerve in Robert, who (hypocritically) denies the instinctual truth his lover has uncovered: "Never," he vehemently swears. Cowed once again by Robert's displays of self-righteous sensitivity, Jeffrey backs down: "Okay, I'm a jerk." Jeffrey's willingness to assume the blame for negative or violent emotions actually speaks to a more conciliatory personality, and a healthier ego in relation to other people. Although a heterosexual husband and father (thereby typified as "normal" by the mendacious standards we apply to such categories), Jeffrey is being revealed, more and more, as the true alien in *The Dying Gaul*, passing through a world that is not truly his, a home that is not truly his, a life that is not truly his, and in the end, unwilling to make any false claims about a sense of security that is not truly his. As befits a maker of films, perhaps, he understands and feels himself to be part of everything human, even things which cause shame and guilt.

Later, Robert goes online and, thinking he is chatting with Malcolm, whom he now thoroughly believes is contacting him like a guardian angel, tells Elaine what Jeffrey said about killing her. This jolts Elaine into a new level of shock and betrayal. "He seemed so guilty and ashamed when he said it," Robert types, as if marveling precisely at Jeffrey's ability to vent these negative emotions openly and, thus, work through them. Elaine signs off and immediately begins making preparations to leave. When Jeffrey comes home, expecting to meet with Robert that evening for a script rewrite, she tells him that she knows, implying that Robert has told her everything. He tries to deny his affair, but she tells him not to lie to her, it will only make things worse. "I'll kill him," Jeffrey says through clenched jaws, swinging his briefcase wildly like a weapon. Elaine sends him away.

Robert comes over while Elaine is packing. She says to him: "Have him, please. Take him. It will help my suit if you're both more open about it." At this point, she can only see Jeffrey, seemingly, as totally "gay," rather than bisexual; her assumption is that he would replace her with Robert. She asks

Robert what unconditional love is like, and Robert, his ego flattered by having seemingly "won" in this affair of the heart, tells her to look within and stop blaming others: "No one is a victim," he smugly tells her, belying his own stance, earlier in the film, of affirming homosexuality as a state of constant victimization by the heterosexual world. Piqued, she tells him point-blank that she was ArckAngell1966 all along. Seething with rage, possibly at the fact that, as one writer to another, Elaine has clearly and handily out-written him in her chat-room channeling of Malcolm, Robert goes out to the garden and digs up a root he has previously identified to her as poisonous. After a half-hearted attempt to chew some of the root and kill himself, he spits it out and instead shaves it into Elaine's salad while she is not looking. Elaine comes back in, takes her bag with the salad, and leaves Robert washing his face in the swimming pool as he sarcastically apologizes and asks for her forgiveness.

Later, Jeffrey arrives at Robert's apartment, angrily accusing Robert of outing him to Elaine. Robert denies this, and tells Jeffrey that she just "figured it out." Pointedly, Jeffrey does not kill Robert, as he swore he would, another instance of him venting a negative emotion and working through it, rather

The bisexual Jeffrey (Campbell Scott) turns out to the most humane character in Craig Lucas' *The Dying Gaul* (2005), although his emotional vulnerability does not emerge until the very end of the film, when he learns that his wife has driven her car into a wall, killing herself and their two children.

than cultivating it or acting on it in a neurotic way. Indeed, Jeffrey's entire position finally becomes clear as he now feels pressured to defend himself. He states:

> Do I seem enshrouded in illusion to you, Robert? Do I seem less real to you? I'm sorry if I don't live up to your standards. The trouble is, I'm bisexual. I like both. You want the truth — but you're lucky to be only one thing. I'm not. I'm not hiding in my marriage! I need my marriage! And not just for business reasons.

In this key speech, the normally unemotional Jeffrey says many heartfelt things. His self-identification as bisexual is important, in that he is not in denial about his gay side. In fact, he claims this non-exclusive identity as the difficult truth which Robert himself searches for (as writer and as human being) but cannot find because he is so deeply invested in the "gay" label. Half-sarcastically, half-sincerely, Jeffrey says that Robert is "lucky to be only one thing." This false security enables Robert to be content with relative truths that are local rather than universal. But the terrible extent of what Jeffrey has risked and lost in the pursuit of his bisexuality is soon revealed, as he gets a call from the police informing him that Elaine has driven her car into a wall, killing herself and the children. Jeffrey collapses on the floor, sobbing, as Robert impassively watches the spectacle of his suffering.

* * *

In the final scene, Jeffrey's speech about the difficulties of being bisexual contradicts the assumption that bisexual males are completely out for indiscriminate pleasure: "anything goes," so to speak, and it doesn't matter what. It is his feelings which lead him in multiple directions in affairs of the heart. This correlates to what actual bisexual males have reported about wishing they had a clearer path, a more defined choice in life, or a label which "fits." No matter what path the bisexual male chooses, the other path continues to beckon, sometimes with greater and greater insistence: "The thought of everyone assuming I was a straight married man began to suffocate me. I told my wife that I had to know that she didn't see me that way and that I needed her support for me to do something outward, positive and constructive with my bisexuality."[3] It is salutary of bisexuality's human outreach that, even when trying to break free of one narrow role (in this case, the heterosexual side), the bisexual male's instinct is to involve and include his heterosexual partner in his embracing of other (homosexual) roles. "Don't invalidate who I am or what that means just because I don't fit your stereotypes."[4]

Suddenly, we realize (if we have not realized before) that nothing about Jeffrey has been "typical," beginning with the fact that Elaine is his wife.

Hardly the kind of trophy wife a powerful movie mogul might be expected to have, Elaine is a complex woman, mature, brainy, literate — as Jeffrey describes her in one scene, "incredibly smart and frustrated and working on herself." She is a Hollywood outsider. Jeffrey apparently sees more in people than what might be immediately gained from falling in love or sleeping with them. Therefore, it is not at all out of keeping for his character that he would also be drawn to Robert. The way Jeffrey is written and played keeps these elements from becoming more obvious — or outbalancing the aspects of his character which seem superficially callous and unfeeling — until the very end of the film. It is a daring choice on Lucas' part, and one which typifies his smart, if sometimes overly ambitious, approach to his material.

For most of the film, there is a schematic implication that Jeffrey is the "bad bisexual" and Robert is the "good bisexual." The miscues begin in the opening shots, before Jeffrey and Robert even meet. Jeffrey and Elaine's kids are running around the kitchen shrieking, so Elaine shrieks back at them; Jeffrey, about to leave for work, joins her in a scream of his own. This quirky domestic playfulness is likely to be read, on a more cynical, probing level, as the symptom of a hostile marriage, a kind of dream-home hell. Meanwhile, Robert awakens from a nap fully dressed in his suit; wiping his face and, oddly, the crotch of his pants, he hurries out the door to be in time for his first meeting at the film studio. Robert's preparedness — concealed behind a rumpled exterior — is, for its part, likely to be misread as near-crippling anxiety. And Lucas continues, for most of the film's early scenes, to play on the natural suspicion we have toward families that seem too good to be true, and the natural sympathy we have toward gay men who have lost friends and lovers to AIDS.

In one of their love scenes, Jeffrey says to Robert, "You are beautiful," and Robert, his low self esteem feeding him lines, counters: "You wouldn't like me if you really knew me." Robert hints, here, that he is aware his sensitivity is a kind of defense mechanism, a learned response to avoid persecution; but Jeffrey, wary of any kind of drama, is content not to delve deeper into the glimpse of self-awareness Robert has shown. He dismisses Robert's survivor guilt with the pragmatic statement, "You lived, he didn't." But it would be a mistake to think that Jeffrey has no feelings, simply because he is able to control (most of) them better than the people around him. And Jeffrey's self-control is, in itself, admirable; although Elaine and Robert cannot stop themselves from acting on their impulses to hurt each other, Jeffrey does not deliberately hurt anyone. The sympathy miscues are also reinforced because Robert shows his emotions more freely, as in the scene where he cries to his ex-wife on the phone and tells her he loves her, and also shrieks and weeps like a baby during orgasm. By contrast, Jeffrey keeps everything inside, and seems to favor sex that is as cut-and-dried as a business deal. But if much of Robert's emotionality is a kind of learned defense, a need to be seen as sincere and caring so that others will extend him sympathy and rights as a gay man, Jeffrey's "closet" permits him to be more stable. Ultimately, he prefers a systematic order (however flawed) to the chaos and hysteria of feelings. And yet, it is Jeffrey who continuously reminds Robert that feelings are universal, whether gay or straight. In fact, Jeffrey's assumption that Robert's script can be "converted" from a gay love story to a heterosexual one is not so much Hollywood squeamishness and hypocrisy, but an acknowledgment of what Jeffrey already feels as a bisexual: that the two orientations *are* interchangeable.

This insight, however fascinating, and however badly articulated by the tight-lipped, peremptory Jeffrey, strikes Robert as a prevarication and drives him, at times, to assert what he believes to be the fundamental differences between gay and straight — differences which Jeffrey, as a bisexual, does not choose to recognize. In another deleted scene, the two men are working on script rewrites, and Robert says, "I can't just change the gender, it doesn't feel the same." "It does to me," Jeffrey says, going on to add: "All human beings feel the same pain." Robert says bitterly, "Yeah, well, people on top always say that." The accusation is that Jeffrey enjoys "heterosexual privilege" because of his marriage and family, partial citizenship in the straight majority. Instead of getting angry, Jeffrey slyly responds, "I like it when you're on top," reaffirming his citizenship in the gay minority as well. But this only frustrates Robert further, who takes it as an indication that the bisexual male is too slippery, too chameleonic, to be reasoned or even argued with. (The two resolve their disagreement in a bout of passionate sex.) To an extent, *The Dying Gaul* seems to say that when anyone feels marginalized, he or she assumes the right to invalidate the experience of "the enemy," whomever that enemy is presumed to be. Elaine does this, too, when she plays her chat rooms games with Robert. Both she and Robert are held back, in different ways, by their resentments, and by their inability to see the other side of things — that human balance which Jeffrey is always striving to achieve, in the movies as well as in his personal life.

But why doesn't Robert also identify as a bisexual, since he was married to a woman and had a child with her, and still loves this heterosexual family of his? After all, some bisexual males who have been married to women and who are fathers still consider themselves to be bi even if they have switched to a predominantly homosexual lifestyle: "And whereas, at this particular point in my life I'm in a committed relationship with a man, I still define myself as a bisexual."⁵ Robert has chosen sides in a way which Jeffrey does not feed the need to do. Jeffrey is the last of the three characters to understand that the other two are at various wars with himself and each other; in spite of his cut-throat tactics as a producer, he is the least warlike, and the least able to see a dark side in someone he loves. Robert experiences guilt over sleeping with Jeffrey, not only because Jeffrey is married to Elaine or because he still misses Malcolm, but because Jeffrey is straight-identified and therefore imposes secrecy on their affair. After Robert begins to sleep with Jeffrey, he has a nightmare in which Malcolm, in the middle of a particularly gruesome medical ordeal, looks at him reprovingly and hisses, "Traitor!" To cultivate self-pride as a gay man is often seen as a matter of rejecting the straight world which does not understand, or which is itself hostile and rejecting. Although this may seem to be an important survival skill in many ways, it pointedly flies in the face of Robert's bisexual experience (which extends to other women beyond his ex-wife). Jeffrey, in many ways, is more of a mirror image of Robert than either man can delineate; like Robert, Jeffrey does not want to simply jettison his family and his heterosexual life, while being as fully invested in gay sex as Robert — in some ways, he is even more direct and demonstrative than Robert. Both men have been in therapy for their sexual issues, Jeffrey specifically trying to work through a sense of shame that sex with a man is morally wrong. A more provocative film might have explored in greater depth this arbitrary assignment of labels, rather than dwelling on the nasty games which people play when placed under emotional pressure. If Elaine were less blind and clueless about her husband's identity, if Robert were not so invested in his gay identity as a guilty tribute to his tragic lover Malcolm, *The Dying Gaul* might have focused more on questioning why it becomes so difficult, in this society, for a man to change sexual identities, or have more than one, or for a woman to be married to a man whose sexual identity is labile. For the title finally applies to all three characters — like the fallen Gallic soldier, stranded in a battleground where love and sex have become locked in to abstract notions of identity, a kind of artificial, fixed allegiance which demands constant fealty and sacrifice.

* * *

The "Good Bisexual-Bad Bisexual" trope also figures into François Ozon's *Gouttes d'Eau sur Pierres Brûlantes* (*Water Drops on Burning Rocks*, 2000), adapted from an early play by Rainer Werner Fassbinder. However, in Ozon's film, the trope is not turned inside out, but presented as a more straightforward metaphor for power differentials in society. Middle-aged businessman Leopold (Bernard Giraudeau) has picked up the teenaged Franz (Malik Zidi) and brought him back to his apartment. "I don't know why I came with you," Franz says. "I had a date, actually." Already we see that Leopold holds inchoate persuasive powers over the young man. "I was supposed to meet Anna tonight," Franz goes on. "It's weird, I really wanted to see her." Leopold stares at Franz without smiling: by bringing up his girlfriend in the middle of what appears to be a gay seduction, Franz seems to indicate that he does not want to explore his interest in Leopold anymore. Indeed, he gets up to go, saying, "Anna and I want to get married" (young heterosexual lust thickening into a respectable domestic future), but he does not leave.

Leopold now brings up *his* ex-girlfriend; the heterosexual future which Franz holds out for himself is seemingly in the past for Leopold. He left her because she was "never satisfied, too complicated.... I really loved her, though." Much like Jeffrey in *The Dying Gaul*, Leopold has a way of saying harsh things, then "redeeming" them, out of the blue, with remarks that are less guarded, even somewhat tender. "Women always ask if we love them," Leopold continues, peevish again. Franz admits he tells Anna he loves her "to get her off my back. Why should I explain my emotions?" The extent to which Franz wants to protect his emotions from the world at large becomes more and more desperate throughout the film; here, however, he inadvertently reveals that the protection of his own ambivalent, private feelings requires an act of distortion or oversimplification, e.g., saying "I love you" to Anna when he does not necessarily mean it. It is precisely through such minor, innocent (self-)deceptions that Franz begins to fall under Leopold's spell. Leopold reveals to the young man that sex is all-important to him, one of the few things in life he takes pleasure in, whereas Franz, in his opinion, seems to "get off" on life itself.

Eager not to seem jejune, perhaps, Franz indulges Leopold by confessing to fantasies of having sex with men, and even performing certain acts with other boys at the boarding school he attended. Aroused, Leopold begins to play on Franz's curiosity. "Well, the ancient Greeks...," Leopold starts to say, as if launching into a pedantic justification of homosexuality, but Franz hilariously cuts him off with the deadpan remark, "Yeah, I know about the ancient Greeks." Unlike Robert in *The Dying Gaul*, Franz does not look to the ancient world for ways to defend his gay feelings; but then again, Franz is not yet aware he will need every defense he can muster against Leopold.

In fact, the two men do have sex, and overnight, Franz's life completely changes. Apparently forgetting Anna, he moves in with Leopold, keeping the house clean while the older man is at work all day. In addition to falling into this domestic routine, the two immediately begin to bicker and fight. Although Franz is sweet and accommodating, Leopold finds fault with everything he says and done; when Franz apologizes to keep the peace, Leopold accuses him of being sarcastic and "always picking a fight." Leopold says he suffers from anxiety; he is also tyrannized by the treadmill of work: "You know I have to work hard or I won't get ahead." The need to get over on his customers and coworkers has seemingly infected Leopold's ability to have intimate, loving relationships. (He talks about having driven a client to suicide after he "cleaned him out with the insurance.") Franz, as a younger man, appears more as a tabula rasa, clay to be molded by Leopold. They both agree that the sex between them is great, and Franz sobs that he does not want women or any other men anymore, he wants to be with Leopold "forever."

Nonetheless, Leopold's constant criticism of Franz does not abate, from telling him he makes too much noise when he walks, to calling him "selfish" when he spiritedly enjoys a recording of the Verdi Requiem with the volume up. It is sad to see Franz becoming ever sadder, beaten down by Leopold's abuse. Having been accused of sarcasm when he was speaking sincerely, he now begins to actually make sneering, sarcastic remarks. Leopold seems to be transforming Franz from a good-natured, innocent boy into a miserable person. When Franz reacts to something personally, Leopold says, as if on cue, "Don't be paranoid." Suddenly wanting to get away from the psychological warfare, Franz packs his suitcase and threatens to leave. At this point, Leopold turns nice to get him to stay, and Ozon cuts to a bewildered, drained Franz stretched out face down on the sofa, his abandoned suitcase nearby. Like Kafka's *The Castle*, but in reverse, Leopold's apartment is a structure which will not seem to let Franz leave, once he has entered it. (In fact, he never does leave it.)

Franz takes to wearing a girlish apron when he cleans, a symbol of his feminization and his increasing malleability at Leopold's hands. And yet, when Anna (Ludavine Sagnier) calls him and says she wants to see him again, he is overjoyed. She comes over while Leopold is away on a business trip: suddenly, it is heterosexuality which must sneak around in the shadow of homosexuality. She finds Franz crying, and is immediately concerned; but he begins to order her around the way Leopold does with him. Telling her to get glasses and a bottle from the kitchen, he drinks a toast with her "to us ... although there is no more 'us.'" She tells him he does not seem happy, and he asks, "Anyway, what is happiness?" She says, "Being satisfied and calm, like we were." He tells her: "We never knew happiness, Anna. We just dreamed of it." Having discovered an intense passion with Leopold, Franz now sees his life before Leopold as being nothing but a dream, or imitation, of real life. Happiness, in Franz's mind, has become an all-or-nothing game, but this game is controlled by Leopold. Nonetheless, he also suggests that Leopold may have been just another dream of happiness. It is as if Franz needs the moments in his emotional life to make sense, to cohere, to add up to a continuous romantic narrative with discernible causes and effects. This need is entirely human and understandable on his part, but human survival often depends on accepting the inevitable presence of chaos and disorder. "I love Leopold, end of story," he tells Anna when she declares that she still loves him. He mocks her feelings, again subjecting her to the same dismissive, bullying treatment which Leopold gives him. But then, as if channeling Leopold's manipulative mood-swings, he says to her that she has become much prettier; taking advantage of her willingness, he kisses her.

They sleep together, and in the morning, Anna decides they will pack Franz's things and leave that day. Franz sees holes in her plan right away, telling her they will need more money than they have. She says he never used to care about money. "You know," he says, "reality is always so different." Anna is, perhaps somewhat surprisingly, completely understanding about the fact that Franz has been having a relationship with a man, and that he still loves this man. "But you know it won't work out in the long run," she says. Anna and Franz spend too long second-guessing themselves, however, and Leopold returns while they are still packing. He laughs at their intention to leave, and sends Franz to the kitchen to make coffee, which Franz dutifully does. While Franz is in the kitchen, Leopold makes advances to Anna, who seems pleasantly surprised that the older man is also interested in women. By the time Franz serves them their coffee, they are giggling together on the couch.

Fortunately for Leopold, sex is the thing in life he enjoys most, for it becomes his weapon of choice in the duration of the film. His ex-girlfriend, the glamorous, quiet Vera (Anna Thomson), appears, and Franz tries to get her on his side, calling her "the woman who put up with Leopold for seven years." Leopold identifies her as a transsexual, and also as a masochist who enjoys being tied down; then he turns to Franz: "You too, huh, Franz?" Franz becomes mad and starts to leave, but now Anna wants to stay, saying that things are getting "exciting." Sadomasochism is the missing piece of Leopold's power puzzle, and it is falling into place. As he orders them around, the women kneel and take off Leopold's boots, then run to the kitchen to make him a snack. Finally, he orders them into the bedroom, which makes them squeal with glee. "You coming?" he asks Franz. Franz says, "You need me?" Leopold corrects him: "*You* need *me*!"

Franz daydreams about shooting Leopold in the middle of the orgy, but instead swallows poison. Feeling left out of the threesome (Leopold likes the young Anna better), Vera comes into the living room and finds Franz lying on the floor in her fur coat. This is a further feminization of Franz. The two rejected characters talk about their situation. She says she could never forget

Leopold: "I'm his creature." They met years ago when Vera was still a young man — Leopold opened up the world of sex to Vera, who felt like she existed for the first time. Then he grew tired of her, and she got a sex change to try to interest him again: "For a while, his desire was renewed.... It was the newness. I deluded myself. Then the desire died again. He made me a whore. Then he left me." Franz stares into space during Vera's tragic monologue, as if discerning that this could have been his own fate. She says she still loves Leopold, and Franz says that he does, too. Politically as well as interpersonally, the masochism of the oppressed is one way in which the oppressor holds onto his power, no matter how much he abuses it. Meanwhile, in the bedroom, Leopold is having furious sex with Anna, training her to enjoy getting spanked and suggesting that she take up work as a prostitute. The cycles repeat. "I'm his creature, too," the dying Franz acknowledges, and the orgy continues, "over Franz's dead body," as it were. Vera tries to open a window, but cannot get it unstuck, and the film's final image is of her as an eternal prisoner, her palms against the glass, her head bowed.

We could say that, in *Water Drops on Burning Rocks*, Franz is the "good bisexual" — sincere, loving, sensitive — while Leopold is the "bad bisexual" — manipulative, predatory, self-centered. Mechanically, as if they were automatons rather than people with actual selves, they never question their roles but simply grind deeper and deeper in the same behavioral grooves. Suicide is Franz's only way out, and the final certification of the fact that he is "more human," somehow, than the other characters. As if Leopold's apartment were some limbo — or, more pointedly, the entire world, divided by issues of power and control — death becomes the only possible escape, since to live at all is to be either controlled or controlling, oppressed or oppressive.

Passive "creatures" transmogrified by their romantic suffering, their martyrdom, Franz and Vera are embryonic versions of the kind of character Fassbinder later specialized in: timid, inarticulate souls invaded by a toxic Great Love, from which they never manage to recover. Psychologically, Fassbinder reminds us that we need to think of imprinting as something which can occur well beyond the developmental stages of infancy and childhood. Young adults, rootless, curious, searching for meaning, can become "imprinted" by charismatic peers and older people, at the point in life where one's romantic and sexual needs are ripe for exploitation. For Franz, bisexuality is part of a general amorphousness, which allows for this imprinting to take place on an epic scale. Fassbinder himself was notably bisexual, and quite liberated in his sexual views (asked once what he liked to do for exercise on a questionnaire from German schoolchildren, he blithely answered, "Faire l'amour"[6]). But he rarely allowed his characters the same sense of liberation, preferring to foreground love's relation to power. In an advanced-capitalist society where people have become consumers, puppets, their desires are manipulated by a central force and turned against them. As a businessman Leopold embodies that central force: for him, bisexuality is the means to extend his control, to create ever more puppets, or "creatures."

* * *

Who controls human emotions? Social victimization of various kinds sometimes promotes a situation in which people defensively identify with their specific group-identity as a way of combating the abuses of power by another, more powerful group. So, in the allegory of *The Dying Gaul*, Elaine seems to stand for Woman, wronged by the men, while Robert stands for Gayness, wronged by heterosexuality. It is not that these minorities do not have legitimate grievances, as do bisexuals as well. But it is also possible to get stuck at this stage where identity becomes a kind of First Cause. It is a difficult thing to realize that sometimes identities and identifications can stand in the way of true human growth, or of giving and receiving love. It takes a certain leap to project outward from one's group-identity and see, as Jeffrey is always mentioning, "the human." He is the only character in Lucas' film who ever mentions "the human" as an indivisible whole, deserving of consideration simply because it *is* human.

Human nature is often shown to be more comfortable with a certain black-and-white thinking, which allows for resentment and blame, self-delusion and self-sabotage. It is not the plain fact of identity that explains human life so much as what one ultimately does, how one behaves toward oneself and others. Franz dies to prove and certify this distinction, as it were. For Fassbinder, of course, fascism was not so much a mode of political thought as it was a primal part of human nature, a destructive instinct that crosses all the lines of social demarcation: socioeconomic, gender, sexual orientation. We might call it "interpersonal fascism." Any human is capable of behaving fascistically toward any other, and anyone is capable of falling for, even welcoming, fascist brutality; this is because love itself can become a means of social control—love and its attendant emotions of shame and fear of rejection. A certain interpersonal fascism wins out when young Franz kills himself, in that the orgy rages on in the next room, undisturbed by his death. In many ways, he commits suicide so as not to become one of the oppressors, like Leopold. To truly love is to reject power over others, even to the extreme extent of consenting to die so as to no longer be part of the predatory societal jungle. False love is the cover for power, and power accrues and grows in any dark, ruthless place that can provide a home for it. It is forever migrating, forever shape-shifting. The power that Jeffrey seems to wield at the start of *The Dying Gaul* gives way to the slashing vengeance of first Elaine, then Robert, the two seemingly disempowered characters. In the end, power metamorphoses far more rapidly, tenaciously, and self-preservingly than any human sexual orientation ever could.

PART 2

Alone and with Others

[E]rotic identity, of all things, is never to be circumscribed simply as itself, can never not be relational, is never to be perceived or known by anyone outside of a structure of transference and countertransference. — Eve Kosofsky Sedgwick

6

Making the Man: The Bisexual Hero

One of the first films to imply bisexual orientation in its hero was Nicholas Ray's *Rebel Without a Cause* (1955). Jim Stark (James Dean) is loved and hero-worshipped by Judy (Natalie Wood) and by John Crawford, nicknamed Plato (Sal Mineo). Their destinies first intermingle in a police station where they have all been separately detained. Jim chivalrously offers to let the shivering Plato wear his jacket. A moment later, Jim's eyes follow Judy as she walks past him, then, less blatantly, Plato as he is taken into another room. In fact, Jim continues to try to get Plato's attention, rapping on the glass and asking, "Why didn't you take my jacket?" as if trying to confront the societal barriers that prevent two men from showing affection.

When Jim sees Plato arriving at school the next day, his head is turned by the sound of Plato's scooter backfiring. Ray cuts to an incongruous shot of the flag being run up a flagpole — discreet visual slang, perhaps, for "getting an erection." Then Ray cuts back to Jim, shuffling his feet and looking down and away from Plato in an embarrassed, somewhat guilty manner.

Of course, all of the overt romance in the film is heterosexual and takes place between Jim and Judy. And yet, their romance is constantly mirrored, echoed and expanded upon by the feelings between Jim and Plato — also, to some extent, Judy and Plato. Judy first really notices Jim when she sees the way Plato looks at him at the "chicken run," and when she hears Plato extol Jim's sincerity. In other words, Judy learns to admire Jim from watching the way another man admires him. Plato offers to take Jim to a deserted mansion in the hills, presumably to be alone with him; it is this mansion where Jim later goes with Judy and where Plato joins them. Rather than shutting Plato out to be alone with Judy, Jim lets Plato into the hide-out, and they immediately form a natural trio, completing each other: Judy's presence on Jim's arm completes Plato's image of Jim as a father-figure, while Plato's adoration in turn completes Judy and Jim's image of themselves as a couple. The dynamic is a bisexual one, in that sexual appreciation from both genders is needed. In a touching moment, Jim lounges with his head on Judy's lap and with Plato's head at Jim's elbow, but only for an almost furtive moment before Plato sprawls on the floor at Judy's feet like a child or a family dog. Judy and Jim's conclusion is that Plato needs Jim as much as Judy does — i.e., sexually, romantically, although this is not stated. Although clearly the trio are in some ways trying to construct their own nuclear family — their families of origin being so fraught and traumatic for all of them — it is somewhat unconvincing when Jim determines that this was all Plato wanted. "He wanted us to be his—" he tries to explain to Judy, but cannot finish the line, cannot say "parents," a hateful and difficult word by this point in the film. And perhaps it was Dean himself, as an actor, who could not bring himself to utter the obvious falsehood, since the action of the entire film demands that new attachments be formed to replace the unfulfilling, obligatory love of parents, so that the line should read, "He wanted us to be his lovers."

When Plato is shot and killed by the police (restorers of sexual law), it is clear that Jim loves both girl and boy. The very fact that Plato must die suggests that his connection to Jim is stronger than friendship, stronger, therefore, than can be allowed. Because Plato threatens the balance of things, heterosexual society itself arises to kill him off and, along with him, the possibility of Jim's bisexuality.

Rebel is a noteworthy instance of how movie stars' sexual glamour and reputations seep over to make their onscreen roles more resonant and mythic. An "intimate" James Dean biographer writes: "Nick Ray was not averse to using Jimmy's bisexuality to good purpose. The director knew that Sal was homosexual, and encouraged him to explore that part of him that would love Jimmy. At the same time, according to Ray, Jimmy fell in love with Sal."[1] In this sense, there has always been a fluid interplay of mythos and backstage innuendo in the movies. Attractive male actors spoke to, and helped awaken, bisexual and homosexual feelings in their male viewers, who responded by enshrining the stars in an enduring sexual celebrity that was part "gaydar" (the ability of gay men to detect fellow gay men), rumor and wishful fantasy. "All great stars are bisexual in the performative mode."[2] *Rebel* was not the first time, nor would it be the last, that the movies engendered, or helped define, an essentially bisexual way of looking at the screen, which is also to say, looking at the world.

However, the bisexual subtext of Ray's film would have to wait before it could be revisited more explicitly. There still are not many films centered around bisexual heroes. For one thing, we tend to assume that a hero is heterosexual. Furthermore, even with heterosexual heroes, we assume that sex is not what makes him heroic in the first place, so his important public exploits are segregated from any sex life he might happen to enjoy. Indeed, one looks mostly in vain for films — even the few that do have openly bisexual heroes — where some kind of bridge is built between a man's public and private personas: where who he is "in the world" is directly informed by who he is "behind closed doors."

This suggests one of the reasons why bisexuality is often not discussed in daily life any more than it is portrayed in films: as human beings, we generally prefer to establish an individual's sexual category once and for all, so that we can then discreetly forget it and go on to view him in non-sexual ways. It is one of the great strange ironies of interpersonal consciousness that, if X's sexuality is undefined, we can only, helplessly, brood about it, speculate about it, and consume ourselves with wonder at "what X is"; whereas, as soon as the mystery is solved, the entire sexual component can be deleted from our thinking about X. This is why so many great stars have been bisexual, gender-bending, or sexually ambiguous: the lack of certainty fosters an obsession in the minds of fans. Surely an element of projection is always present in contemplating the sexuality of others, which we can only understand in relation to how well we understand our own.

Even in biographical films about famous people, it is unusual to find much emphasis placed on the private recesses of sexuality (unless sex is being dealt with precisely as a "problem"). Why is there so little room for the sexual fantasizing that heroes and famous people must surely do? Wherever this does occur, it is usually laughed off as comic interlude. The idea of dwelling on any man's sexuality (past the all-important point of initial identification) would doubtlessly seem distasteful to the puritanical; it might also signal that the film is meant to be "a treatment of sex" rather than a human story of general interest. As if sex itself were not part of humanity, and as if the fulfillment of his complex sexual needs what might not be part of what makes a man a hero in the first place.

Criminal Lovers

François Ozon has suggested that bisexuality is entirely healthy, even necessary to psychosexual development; this was the theme of his landmark short film, *A Summer Dress*, and it returns in his feature film *Criminal Lovers*, albeit in a much darker and more disturbing way. What makes *A Summer*

Dress unique is that no one suffers in it, in spite of people freely trading off partners and genders; it is atypically sunny and upbeat in its depiction of sexual balance, while *Criminal Lovers* is a descent into sexual madness. Only in the last moments of *Criminal Lovers* is a sense of bisexual love finally wrested free from a thicket of depravity and perversion, and even so, this love is not innocent; it is blood-stained and doomed. Yet, the young hero's bisexual experience, no matter how problematized, is nonetheless presented as a demystification of sex, a heightening of sexual awareness, and an unlocking of emotional potential, helping him formulate a fuller picture of himself and his emerging sexuality.

As in *A Summer Dress*, the hero of *Criminal Lovers* is an adolescent named Luc (Jérémie Renier). Luc's girlfriend Alice (Natacha Regnier) is obsessed with Saïd (Salim Kechiouch), an Arab boy who has been pursuing her sexually. After writing a detailed, erotically charged description of Saïd's mouth in her diary, she recounts a conversation in which the cocky Saïd asked her if she had "decided" yet whether to sleep with him or not. "I'll fuck you, asshole," she says, her tone laden with menace. A shy virgin, Luc is the carnal opposite of Saïd. If Saïd is able to touch a nerve in Alice and throw her off-balance, causing her to despise him, it is Alice who dominates and manipulates the hapless Luc. In the film's opening scene, we are shown her propensity to lie to Luc, and to control him sexually. Luc is wearing a blindfold while we hear Alice, offscreen, describing herself undressing; when Ozon cuts to her, we see that she has not actually removed any of her clothes. In a further twist Ozon cross-cuts this scene of Alice and Luc with a scene in which Said is in his bedroom with his buddy; Saïd brushes his hair in the mirror somewhat narcissistically while telling his buddy that Alice approached him sexually. Cut back to Alice climbing on top of Luc as he lays supine, passive, still blindfolded. Cut back to Saïd caressing his buddy's shoulder and chest to demonstrate where Alice touched him, before the two boys explode in laughter, wrestling and mock accusations of being "a fag." Finally, Alice laughs at Luc and snaps a picture of his exposed penis, threatening to send it to his mother. Luc is hurt. "It was just for fun," Alice says, "and to turn you on a little." Here, Ozon shows heterosexuality as being not natural but mediated, constructed from objects (blindfolds, mirrors, photographs) and situations (once-removed descriptions, jokes). Ozon also establishes the bisexual triangulation of desire that will be an essential theme of *Criminal Lovers*. Alice is the absent third point of reference in the mock-sexual contact between Saïd and his buddy; likewise, Saïd will become the absent third point of reference between Alice and Luc.

Conceiving an evil plan, Alice tells Luc a story about Saïd that later turns out to be a fabrication: she says Saïd dragged her into a basement and began to rape her; then four of his friends, wearing ski-masks, appeared out of nowhere and gang-raped her while Saïd watched and took photos. Alice tells Luc that she wants to kill Saïd, for revenge and ostensibly to get the humiliating photos back. She asks Luc to help her. In the shower room of a deserted gym at night, Alice seduces Saïd. Luc waits in the doorway, watching them have sex. It appears as though Alice is enjoying herself, giving herself freely to Saïd, but when she notices Luc watching, she turns steely and ice-cold. She rolls on top of Saïd, pinning him, and Luc rushes in to stab him repeatedly.

As Alice and Luc drag Saïd's shrouded body to the trunk of their car, they are watched by an older man through the glass door of the gym, another instance of triangulation, the motif of two-men-and-a-woman (usually overlaid with guilt) which becomes constant in Alice and Luc's relationship throughout the film. Later, when they bury Saïd's body in the woods, they

After they murder an Arab student, Luc (Jérémie Renier) and his girlfriend Alice (Natacha Regnier) take a shower together in François Ozon's *Criminal Lovers* (1999). Alice dominates Luc, and throughout the film, their relationship is triangulated by other male figures. It is not until Luc discovers his bisexuality, by having sex with the woodsman, that he and Alice can break through to a new level of equality and intimacy in their lovemaking.

are watched again; we see a hand pulling down the branch of a tree to get an unobstructed view (the camera's view) of them. This turns out to be the woodsman (Miki Manojlovic), a figure of threatening adult male sexuality, but also of all-important sexual knowledge. Luc finds the woodsman's cabin and spies on him as the woodsman bathes, standing naked in a tub. When the woodsman captures Luc and Alice and imprisons them in his basement dungeon, he takes a special interest in Luc; he sniffs Luc out, examines his teeth. Luc cowers in bewildered, disgusted fear, but in the next scene he himself is bathing the woodsman, joining as a participant in the erotic scene he had only witnessed before as a spy.

During his captivity Luc joins the woodsman more and more in a series of rituals: they go out hunting rabbits, the woodsman leading Luc on a collar and leash; they eat rabbit stew together. In yet another triangulation, Alice watches the two men through the ajar trapdoor. We soon learn why the woodsman has allowed Luc to "come out" of the dungeon, but not Alice. The woodsman is a cannibal, and he has different methods of preparing male and female "meat." In a sexualized comment that begins to awaken Luc's own bisexuality, the woodsman explains: "I like my girls dry, with just muscle and skin on their bones. Whereas I like my boys nice and plump." For the sexually skittish, bashful Luc, sex requires an initial act of going-too-far, an absolute horror from which mere sex can then emerge as a less threatening option. With Luc and Alice, it is the murder of Saïd; with Luc and the woodsman, it is the revelation of cannibalism (bisexualized cannibalism, no less). These extreme transgressions help Luc to focus his own sexual instincts. Inviting Luc into his bed, the woodsman masturbates the boy ("Let it happen!" he yells when Luc tries to fight off his hand), and later penetrates Luc anally, a deflowering that is, naturally, watched by Alice through the trapdoor.

Fearing for their lives, Luc and Alice eventually contrive to escape from the cabin. Alice wants to stab the sleeping woodsman, but Luc does not allow her to do this. Is this a sign that Luc now feels love for the woodsman? Before Luc leaves, he looks back at the woodsman, who opens his eyes, revealing that he has only been pretending to be asleep and is, in fact, allowing the couple to escape. Is this a sign of his love for Luc? Wandering in the woods, Alice taunts Luc with this possibility: "You liked it when he fucked you!" It is the only time Luc shows physical rage toward Alice, shouting at her to shut up and shoving her down to the ground. Alice softens, acknowledging that Luc's sexual capitulation to the woodsman is the reason why they are both still alive.

Alice and Luc bathe together under a waterfall and finally make love on a rock; like the heterosexual encounter in *A Summer Dress*, Alice and Luc's lovemaking coincides with the great outdoors, with the natural world. Foxes and rabbits, the kind of small furry creatures that Luc once stuffed as a taxidermist, now circle around the couple, curious, bristling with life. In an image of submission to Luc's newly found male power, a hedgehog crawls around Luc's feet as he grinds on top of Alice. But the police arrive before Luc can consummate. As in *Rebel Without a Cause*, the police are representatives of repressive society, come to punish and destroy the fantasy of bisexual idyll. Luc and Alice must run, dressing quickly as they go. Luc is caught in a bear trap; Alice is cornered and shot. Under arrest, Luc witnesses the woodsman also being led away in handcuffs and beaten. Luc tries to defend the woodsman, yelling: "He didn't do anything! Please! Let him go! Please!" Lying on the ground, the woodsman smiles up at Luc, and Luc and the woodsman make eye contact one last time before Luc is thrown into a police wagon and driven away.

Ozon tells most of his story through flashbacks. Here is where bisexuality, as a human option, begins to inform narrative logic. The bisexual may not experience his sexual life as a direct line from Point A to Point B, "first I was this, then I was that, and I stayed that"; on the contrary, there may be simultaneous movements in two directions at once, a process of overlapping and circularity. This is the complex narrative structure of Ozon's film, and it becomes a fascinating mimetic substitute for bisexuality itself—a sexuality that is non-linear, discursive, able to re-evaluate its own direction and priorities at any given moment. Indeed, like a dream or a barely registered movement of the unconscious, *Criminal Lovers* pieces itself together from the drift of moments, from interludes, moods, fleeting glimpses, and fleeting awarenesses. When we see from Luc's viewpoint, especially, his agonizingly deferred and displaced sexuality invites us to read into it, to help complete it and bring it to light, as in the scene where he watches a shirtless Saïd, skin glistening with sweat, sparring in the boxing ring. Is this Luc zeroing in on his target, focusing the anger toward Saïd that Alice has instilled in him, or is this Luc showing his helpless fascination at the other boy's attractive physicality? Luc prepares Alice for her lethal seduction of Saïd by painting her nails, applying her lipstick, choosing her necklace, as if displacing his own secret desire to be feminized, to offer himself to Saïd, onto Alice as a kind of living sexual doll. These are strong hints of Luc's latent bisexual potential.

This potential emerges throughout Luc's ordeal of "training" at the woodsman's hands. He still responds with tenderness toward Alice, sneaking food to her while the woodsman sleeps. But he also defends the woodsman from Alice, when the two are escaping and Alice wants to kill him. Luc had already experienced a moment where he held the knife to the sleeping woodsman but withdrew it at the last minute. In one of the film's most delirious metaphors for repressed sexuality, the refusal or inability to murder denotes an acceptance of one's own sexual attraction. It is when one denies one's attraction that one kills (rejection being, psychically perhaps, equivalent to murder). The men achieve a strange tenderness toward each other: the woodsman, initially fattening Luc for the slaughter, eventually lets him escape; Luc spares the woodsman and, most significantly, expresses sorrow at seeing him arrested and beaten by the police. The periodic eye contact between Luc and the woodsman is the only sign of unguarded human tenderness in *Criminal Lovers*, since lust usually turns violent and every other kind of eye contact (Saïd winking at Alice; Alice dominating Luc with her stare) is associated with a certain glassy manipulativeness, keeping feelings at bay through a suppression of the weakness that reveals itself through gazing.

In true bisexual fashion, both Alice and the woodsman hold the psychical keys to Luc. The woodsman's key is literalized, as the one that locks Luc inside the cabin; as well as the key to the bondage collar which the woodsman has fastened around Luc's neck, and which remains a glaring reminder of Luc's connection to the woodsman even when Luc is having sex with Alice. Just as they share Luc's body, Alice and the woodsman are the same in their brutality: they have made their own peace with the world, and with their own perversity. Much more than Luc, Alice has journeyed into the adult world where people do what they want and must, even though it might harm others and create isolation from the herd. By contrast, Luc is vulnerable, kin to the darting, quivering rabbits in the woods, and the ones hanging skinned in the woodsman's cabin (the woodsman even calls Luc "my little rabbit"). Even though Luc's character goes the farthest as a bisexual, his is an embryonic sexuality in that he remains passive, self-sacrificing, generally averse to hurting other people.

Alice is easily more complex and frightening, more charismatic, than any of the males. (In one memorable scene she even channels Rimbaud.) Because of this, and because she is beautiful, she exercises a powerful heterosexual hold over the males — but what is Alice's sexuality? She triangulates everything, pitting Luc against Saïd and then requiring contact between her two male sexual objects — violent, rather than loving, contact. It is Luc, and Luc's knife, that Alice finally uses to rape Saïd. The choreography of the murder is like a kind of bisexual threesome, with Alice and Luc ministering to different areas of Saïd's prone, naked body. "Dark red blood spurts like sperm," Alice muses in voiceover, sexualizing the penetration of the knife and the paroxysms of death itself. Later, in the woodsman's dungeon, she dreams that she is watching the woodsman seduce, then strangle Saïd; in the dream she masturbates by grinding against a giant tree trunk. She seems as equally fascinated by male sexual power as she is disturbed and angered by it. She may be in a state of denial that she herself wishes to commit the penetration in sex. Is she a heterosexual woman who wishes to be a homosexual male and thereby penetrate other males? It is the males' power to penetrate her that makes her despise them. Her ultimate reason for wanting Saïd dead is the chilling assertion, "He wanted to fuck me. He deserved it." By Alice's logic, love is kill or be killed, a logic which the film rigorously follows to the end: after she finally surrenders to her feelings for Luc by making love with him, she herself is killed, ecstatically, orgasmically, in a hail of police gunfire.

Luc's cruelest fate is to be used by the larger agency of repressive society to punish both his female and male lovers. Throughout the film, Luc has been searching for his masculinity — in having an attractive girlfriend like Alice, in killing Saïd to defend her, in submitting to the woodsman, finally in having sex with Alice. But he does not actually find his masculine self until the very end, in the helpless pain of losing both partners; because it is the nature of masculinity to be inadequate before the ultimate test — which is to say, death, the omnipresence of death that manifests itself in daily uncertainty, in the tendency of meanings and circumstances to change, and of truths to become relative, unreliable. Therefore, to posit one's masculinity outside of oneself (in often meaningless rituals) is to continuously risk losing it. The film ends with an anguished close-up of Luc in the seeming realization of what he had, and the simultaneous realization that he no longer has it. Unable to keep either of his loves, Luc finds no cause for celebration in the discovery of who he is. Indeed, the revelation of his bisexuality is finally the failure of even bisexual all-inclusiveness to protect a man from loneliness, punishment and death.

Bi-opic

Bill Condon's *Kinsey* does several things very well. First, it clearly establishes why there was a need for Kinsey to launch his public conversation about human sexual behavior. The film documents the widespread superstition, religious repression, misinformation, folklore and puritanical shame that crippled the sexual development of many Americans prior to the latter half of the twentieth century. Women were perhaps the greatest victims of this societal blindness. In Condon's film, Dr. Kinsey (Liam Neeson) treats a young married couple where the wife cannot achieve vaginal orgasm and the husband refuses to perform oral sex because his older brother told him it can make a woman sterile (this schoolyard rumor turns out to have been published in a pseudo-scientific marriage manual). Kinsey also receives a poignant letter from a young woman whose father beat her vagina whenever she got her period; after years of this abuse, the woman became infertile. We see that Kinsey's main battle is with the misguided belief that pleasure is unhealthy, pathological, an enemy of life, when just the opposite is the case: punishment, rigid denial and violence have always been the real enemies of life.

Secondly, the film treats the complexities of Kinsey himself. He is never without his scientific rigor, which his wife Mac (Laura Linney) and his colleagues find difficult at times to apply to the messy passions of sexuality. He is drawn to sex research partly because of his own demons and inner conflicts. Kinsey's growing understanding and acceptance of an enormously wide variety of sexual inclinations, proclivities and orientations helps him discover the truth about himself: he falls somewhere in the bisexual "gray area" of his famous scale.

The son of a fire-and-brimstone preacher, Kinsey was a virgin on his wedding night, as was his wife. Kinsey's marriage is the film's central relationship, as it is his main source of personal strength. However, there are hints of bisexual stirrings in Eden — indeed, they first arise literally in a garden. Working outdoors with his young research assistant Clyde Martin (Peter Sarsgaard), Kinsey instructs him on how to use the right muscles for digging and planting; both men are shirtless. In a moment of bisexual triangulation, Mac appears in the garden path with a tray of lemonade; she stops in her tracks at a distance and surreptitiously watches the two men with an ambiguous reaction. Is she curious, suspicious, aroused, or all of the above? Mrs. Kinsey's curiosity here, and the fact that she is the one who suddenly seems out of place, signify the scene's bisexual subtext: again, as in *Criminal Lovers*, it is the presence of a third point of reference which lends an erotic charge.

Kinsey and his staff become an intimate brotherhood. In the best scientific tradition, theory feeds into daily practice, and vice versa. Compensating for the prudishness of the often hostile outside world, Kinsey's staff learn to announce their sexual arousal openly. At a get-together, one of the research assistants, Pomeroy (Chris O'Donnell), wraps his arms around his giggling bride Martha (Heather Goldenhersh) and says to the group: "And since my third leg keeps hittin' me in the face, I think it's time for a tumble." This is presented neither as a tasteless joke, nor a moment of exhibitionistic titillation, but as evidence of utopian matter-of-factness and lack of public shame in Kinsey's new world of sexual transparency. Not only do the researchers freely discuss their own sex lives, Kinsey films Pomeroy having sex with a multi-orgasmic woman. Also, the bisexual undertones of Kinsey and Clyde planting their garden soon bear fruit, when the two men use their own placement on the Kinsey scale as a way of declaring their mutual attraction, with Kinsey saying that he always admitted to being a 1 or a 2 and now feels like a 3; Clyde has always been a solid 3.

Mac is aware of her husband's bisexuality. She says she has often observed "a look, a gesture — the pet student who suddenly becomes a member of the family, then disappears just as suddenly when you tire of him." Nonetheless, she is not all philosophical acceptance; her human emotions of betrayal and jealousy naturally surge to the fore. Condon has commented on the way the film cuts from Kinsey and Clyde's first kiss to a close-up of Mac in tears as Kinsey talks to her, almost in a spirit of scientific inquiry, about his bisexual explorations: "In a way, there's the whole movie in that cut. You've got Kinsey, who's exploring sex in all its various forms as his work, and then you see the way it affects his life, the fact that there aren't just two people involved in that kiss, there are three."[3]

It does not take long, however, for all the points of the triangle to grow comfortable and cozy with each other. Spending time as a trio, Mac and Clyde discover how much they both instinctively care for Kinsey, when they both reach out to catch the sandwich he is about to distractedly drop from his hand. In fact, a relay of probing, reassuring looks begins to connect Mac and Clyde, and cause the erotic energy of the triangle to shift. Mac and Clyde talk about their sharing of Kinsey, one of numerous liberated conversations which the script of the film is able to make wholly natural as well as informative and epochal. "Most women would have had me murdered," Clyde says, acknowledging Mac's right to be angry. "Oh, I considered it," she says, but goes on to admit "there have been benefits. It certainly sparked things up sexually." Here, again, we see that a bisexual male's relationship with a woman can be enhanced by his simultaneous relationship with a man, and vice versa.

The outcome of this is that Clyde, acting on a natural attraction, initiates an affair with Mac as well. Kinsey is no hypocrite: though he cannot suppress some irritation at having to share Mac (or having to share Clyde), he accepts the situation less as quid pro quo (biblical vengeance has no place in Kinsey's pleasure-centered view of life) than as the proof of his ultimate theory, that human sexuality is infinitely varied in its responses, a vast untapped potential. The idea of the student teaching the teacher — Clyde is the aggressor in all of his sex scenes[4] — is a buried subtext of *Kinsey*, suggestive of the ways in which youth would lead the way toward the sexual revolution.

It is society that infects its members with debilitating shame when their natural urges seem to go against the expectations of the herd. In a chorus of overlapping voices, many of Kinsey's interview subjects ask if they are "normal." "From a sexual standpoint," Kinsey argues at one point, "it's hard to say what's common or rare because we know so little about what people do. This leaves people feeling anxious or guilty." Nonetheless, Condon seems to want to orient his film around some concept of sexual and social "normalcy." One of the centerpieces of the film is a long interview with a particularly forthcoming and experienced subject, Kenneth Braun (William Sadler), who becomes a walking, talking personification of sexual pathology. Haggard and raspy-voiced, he boasts of having had sex with over nine thousand people, including thirty-three family members. He also lists zoophilia and pedophilia among his "tastes." Pomeroy is disgusted and storms out of the room; here is where Kinsey is allowed to abandon his laissez-faire outlook, to draw a firm line between consensual sex and any activity that harms others. "I didn't realize you were so square," Braun drawls.

Braun is a gimmick, of course — he exists in the film so that legitimate objection can be raised against the idea of "going too far" sexually. He is there precisely to show that even the tolerant Kinsey has limits, and to soften the audience's potential prejudices against Kinsey (still criticized by some for supposedly enshrining "perversion" in a holy mantle of science). This is what we might call, by the skittish logic of Hollywood covering its bases and hedging its bets, the trope of the "Bad Monster–Worse Monster," familiar from decades of horror films, and deployed effectively in Jonathan Demme's *The Silence of the Lambs* (1991). In *The Silence of the Lambs* Buffalo Bill's function — as a terrifying and seemingly unstoppable serial killer on the loose, abducting, torturing and murdering young women — is to create sympathy for Hannibal Lecter, whose crimes are certainly grisly but largely in the past (or carried out against his prison tormentors). However, serial killer films deal in moral issues by definition; in a film like *Kinsey*, the "Bad Monster–Worse Monster" trope looks like pandering. The fact that Condon even feels the need to make Kinsey appear "normalized" implies the precarious state of bisexual issues in our time, as well as how deeply ingrained it is to view everything from the standpoint of good and evil (itself a primal western dualism, like male and female or gay and straight). Perhaps sexual liberation is the only cause that must be cautiously qualified even as it is being championed.

In general, Condon's film is a nuanced, sensitive treatment of Kinsey's personal odyssey, balanced with a portrait of the era itself, even if one cannot help but imagine the far more provocative film that could have been made, had Condon stayed with the daring awakening of bisexual feeling. After their dual involvements with Clyde, Kinsey and Mac revert to a more or less staid, well-entrenched married life, and the film ends with a return to marriage as the basic building block of a successful life: Kinsey and Mac stroll in an ancient forest, admiring the inspiration of the natural world and its eternal reproductions. Procreation is given the last word. To be fair, this is often what happens in individual bisexual lives, since the pressures of maintaining an unstructured life, of braving social discrimination and abuse, often cause people to choose in favor of something more traditional.

"Can't you see how guilty I feel?" The Matador

We are somewhat accustomed to thinking of artists and thinkers as prone to bisexual inclinations (to sexual experimentation in general). But what about the traditional action movie hero, tough, violent, rough and ready — could a man like that ever be depicted as bi? This dubious boundary was crossed with *The Matador* (2005). Julian Noble (Pierce Brosnan) is a world-class assassin who takes his assignments from a secretive agency (his boss goes by the suggestive rubric, Mr. Stick). Julian is also a colorful, hard-drinking bisexual.

There are two ways of looking at the fact of Noble's bisexuality. One is that it is "bad for bisexual men," since it associates bisexuality with a cluster of anti-social and dysfunctional traits (mercenary killing not least among them); Julian's sexuality is part of what puts him "beyond the pale," and contrasts him with the other main characters, who are from the "straight world" (in both senses of this term: non-criminal and non-homosexual). Another way is to acknowledge *The Matador*'s rather careful attempts to identify Julian's sexuality as his redeeming grace: in his insistent visibility as a bearer of bisexual desire, his constant self-outing seems to compensate for the darker secrets he keeps hidden in his killer's briefcase. Time and again, the awkward Julian calls attention to himself, stumbling drunkenly like a bisexual bull in a heterosexual china-shop, helplessly making an "incriminating" display of his bisexual needs.

Indeed, the biggest risk that *The Matador* takes is in presenting an action hero who is not a "cool cucumber" when it comes to sex. The action hero is generally assumed to be heterosexual in a de facto way that does not need to be examined. Except in Bond films, where James Bond's heterosexuality is constantly on heightened display, often to show that he brings the same steely self-discipline and resolve to seduction that he does to catching bad guys, action movie heroes are often portrayed as being able to easily master their own sexual impulses. It is a failure of *love* which usually defines the action hero: single, divorced, widowed, "gun-shy" when it comes to women; his mission to defeat the bad guy parallels a psychological quest to find the right woman and break his losing record in affairs of the heart. There might be a likely candidate for this Miss Right role, an ex-wife or female friend, usually undeveloped and provisional, taking a back seat to all the fist fight scenes and exploding cars. So, we get the cliché of the hero's woman, kidnapped by the bad guys at a strategic moment to force the hero to submit: this moment actually forces a showdown on both of the action film's narrative fronts, the conflict of good and evil as well as the hero's psychological acceptance of love. Otherwise, action movies transpire in an often virtually sexless realm, where violent action substitutes for pent-up sexual release. In *The Matador*, not only does the hero constantly talk about, and act on, his sexual desires, but these sexual desires are strongly implied to flow toward both men and women; for this reason the film achieves something which even the most hard-bitten, cynical action movies pointedly do not: it largely drains any residual sexual thrill from the violent action itself. "My business is my pleasure," Julian leers in one of his many double entendres, and we understand that this is true, though not in the expected way: his main purpose in life is finding sexual pleasure; while his work of killing people is "just a job."

Certainly, Julian insists upon the mixing of sex with his work wherever possible. In one scene Julian discusses an upcoming hit with his contact (Philip Baker Hall) while simultaneously waving and flirting to three schoolgirls on a nearby park bench. Asked if he studied the assignment, Julian says, "No. I shredded the assignment, then I humped the bell boy on the room service cart." His contact refuses to be shocked. And indeed, such campy, half-joking, half-revealing pronouncements abound from Julian until they no longer *are* shocking, if they ever might have been. "I wouldn't know how to get a mortgage for all the teenage twat in Thailand." "I look like a Bangkok hooker on Sunday morning after the Navy left town." "I'm as serious as an erection problem." (Whose erection, and whose problem?) Barthes had a clever term for this sort of cultural act of neutralizing a taboo by exposing the public to controlled doses of it: "Operation Margarine." Ultimately, the effect of Julian's inappropriate comments is that their potentially subversive impact is nullified: they become part of who Julian is, accepted, even doted on, by anyone who knows him. "Just consider me the best cocktail party story you ever met," he says to his heterosexual sidekick Danny Wright (Greg Kinnear). (But whose cock, and whose tail?)

In a central scene, milked by the scriptwriters to create ongoing suspense about whether Julian has ever had sex with Danny, Julian knocks on Danny's hotel room door late at night, drunkenly apologizing for his off-color behavior: "Can't you see how guilty I feel?" It is Julian's character—perhaps his truth as a bisexual who cannot help but hide his feelings—to want or expect the world to see his inner turmoil in everything he does. Hence the gaudy externalizations, the acting out, the one-liners. Julian presents himself—out of some sense of guilt perhaps—as walking bi entertainment for the delectation of square straights and wannabes. In another scene he stalks, drunk again, through a hotel lobby in nothing but dark glasses, black speedos, and motorcycle boots, and walks right into the deep end of the swimming pool where, still holding his drink, he notices that there is a shark under the surface of the water: typically literal in everything he does, Julian must swim with an actual shark to demonstrate that swimming with sharks is precisely what he does, as hit man and globe-trotting sexual adventurer.

We might read this as generic Hollywood sexual guilt, what any sexually unconventional character is expected to feel, the puritanical inverse of too much sexual pleasure emerging in Julian's reflexive need to court disaster-through-openness. But *The Matador* does not judge Julian sexually: it is not guilt at being bi that weighs on him, but at the murders he commits. This is why he must be a hit man as well as a bisexual, so that the bisexuality will seem completely life-affirming by contrast. At first Julian finds it harder to come out to Danny as a hit man than as a bisexual. The two "guilty" identities feed into each other: reifying the tendency of people to sometimes disbelieve or discount bisexuality itself, Danny laughs off Julian's admission that he is a hired gun, and calls Julian "the best bullshit artist" he's ever met. "I don't believe you for a second." As if to clear up an issue of sexual ignorance, Danny asks Julian to prove it to him by showing him how it's done. The only scene in which Julian's assassin-work is sexualized is this one, in which he initiates Danny into his trade. We might compare great things to small by saying that this scene is like the thief's apprenticeship in Bresson's *Pickpocket* (1959), where criminal training substitutes for forbidden and covert sexual knowledge. In this exclusively male scene of criminal activity, the characters are both sexually charged and hyper-masculine with each other: "Show and tell is for sissies," Julian says, "and a sissy I'm not." Randomly choosing a man in the crowd, Julian shows Danny how to stalk him; when some random police officers pass by, he spontaneously leads Danny in impersonating a gay couple, so as to throw off these officers. If bisexuality is sometimes demonized as a cover for undisclosed gayness, here gay identity is cheekily used as a cover for unlabeled, sexualized male bonding that occupies a gray area between gay and straight.

Julian and Danny follow their target through a subterranean corridor where the tile walls and floor are shiny and damp, as if slick with body fluids; in this uterine setting, Julian and Danny's male bonding is completed, not without some unwillingness on the panicked Danny's part. Julian must threaten him with a phallic knife to force him to enter the men's room where they will presumably kill their quarry. Unconsciously (or perhaps in a calculating way), this moment of threat taps into the idea that a bisexual man who is predominantly straight might have fantasies in which he is coerced into exploring his gay side through an act of rape. But the entire killing is unconsummated: Julian bursts in on the startled man in his toilet stall, only to apologize suavely and close the door again. He wanted to demonstrate how he *could* do it for Danny, not actually do it, a distinction which preserves the "integrity" of the two men's non-sexual friendship. "I might be psychopathic, but I'm not psychotic," Julian says, distantly echoing the logic of what some view as the "heterosexual privilege" of bisexual identity: "You're safe with me; I may be bi, but I'm certainly not *gay!*"

In its depiction of two men gleefully bonding by breaking laws, this sequence is kind of sexy in its way, and suggests the extent to which bisexual fantasy might originate within a larger homosocial context (also a fantasy): to be a masculine man and become close to another masculine man in the course of an adventure that requires ingenuity, street smarts, strength. One's own masculinity is reinforced in the mirror of another man's: the latent bisexual subtext of *every* buddy action film and western. In this sense, the homoerotic side of bisexuality may ultimately serve once again to reinforce heterosexuality. It also reinforces heterosexuality by providing a safety-valve to relieve the pressure of commitment. Just as Julian shows Danny how to use misleading distraction (of the police, of by-standers) to carry out a murder in public, so bisexuality functions as a distraction in the carrying-out of heterosexuality — or more precisely, since no one sexual proclivity may be the anchored one, the option of being-all-things-at-once (bisexual) distracts from the responsibility that comes with having to be only-one-thing-all-the-time. Bisexual males often speak of their heterosexual marriages improving when they are able to engage in affairs with men on the side. "There was a good part of me going unexpressed, and this led me to build up hostility towards her."[5] "We have a better marriage than we ever had. The one major factor is that I no longer have this big dark secret to hide."[6]

In the world of mainstream cinema, this "bisexual option" cannot be made to appear too wonderful, however: it must be approached a little grimly, tolerated rather than actively embraced. In the logic of *The Matador*, bisexual sex is compared to a founding crime, the concealed, even repressed "spilling of blood" which enables something worthwhile to grow. As Danny says, "Don't people, successful people, always live with blood on their hands?" But if bisexuality represents passage into the scary adult world, where having a secret to hide is the price of membership, it also represents the (equally scary) world of childhood helplessness invading adult security. When Julian begins to lose his edge as a hit man, he starts to see himself cowering in the crosshairs of his own rifle; then he has a vision of one of his targets turning into himself as a child. This vision causes him to faint. Has he killed off the child within?

Is the adult world of sin, sex and death the ultimate betrayal of the innocent child-self? Or is the child-self coming in as a reminder of the pure bisexual urges which are life-affirming and which constitute the "noble" part of Julian. (Julian's family name is, allegorically enough, "Noble.") After all, Freud believed it is precisely in childhood that we are allowed to experience equal yearning for "love objects" of either sex, namely one's parents.

The psychoanalytic idea of bisexuality as a need to have rapprochement with both man and woman, as substitutes for father and mother, is conveyed in the scene where Julian visits Danny and Danny's wife Bean (Hope Davis) in the middle of the night, needing a place to hide from the vengeful Mr. Stick after bungling one job too many. From the very start this scene seems to be edging rapidly toward a sexual threesome. Bean wants to get to know Julian, whom she has heard so much about from her husband, and proposes that they all drink whiskey. Julian suggests a toast "to a stranger arriving in the middle of the night," and Danny says, almost as an admission of something much deeper between the two men, "You're not a stranger." Here, the script is still playing its suspense card: did they or didn't they have sex? Rather than getting jealous, Bean (her very name is tellingly asexual, genderless) seems eager to explore the possibilities. At one point, wide-eyed with excitement, she asks Julian to show her his gun, almost as if asking to see his penis. "Bean knows a lot of things about a lot of things," Danny assures Julian, denoting not only that she might know "about them," but that she is generally worldly. Yet, in the end, after a romantic dance with Bean, Julian sublimates the epochal encounter into heartfelt conversation, turning to the couple for emotional succor, confessing his recent failures as a hit man the way a son might turn to parents for advice.

What is most refreshing about *The Matador* is that Julian is not doomed: the worlds of bisexuality and the heterosexual family can overlap without anyone being converted in either direction, and without the bisexual needing to die to expiate his supposed "sins." If anything, the bisexual man and the heterosexual man enhance each other's existence, define each other by offering a mirror of what the other is not. "That's why I like you," Julian tells Danny. "You're the exact opposite of me." The homoerotic innuendo turns out to be harmless to the straight characters, which probably means it is not particularly effective as homoerotic innuendo goes: Operation Margarine again. Ultimately, *The Matador* offers a world in which everyone is free to go as far as he wishes, or as far as he can — like the innuendo, which can be interpreted in exactly as "decadent" or "gay" a light as the viewer decides for himself. But perhaps that is in keeping with the essential possibilities opened up by the bisexual male, as it were: the freedom to explore, or not to explore.

7

Illegible Patriarchies: Bisexualizing the Family

Male bisexuality bears a strange and challenging relationship to the family structure, particularly the traditional patriarchal family. In concept if not always in reality, families are organized around hegemonic desire, one husband and one wife loving each other heterosexually (and exclusively) and producing children from this union. When male bisexuality enters this neatly framed picture, it can threaten the entire order of things; it can change the fixed roles which, in many ways, make up the very definition of a family, everything within a family being defined in terms of gender and procreation (father/mother; son/daughter; ancestor/offspring; etc.). Families are less rigid in their codes today than they once were: single-parent households are commonplace, as well as extended living arrangements among more distant relatives and even non-related persons. Nonetheless, bisexuality remains deeply subversive to the whole idea of family, in that it often takes place outside the bonds of monogamy. And to the extent that patriarchy derives its power from its heterosexuality, male bisexuality can throw patriarchy into question, rendering it artificial, unpredictable, illegible.

However, there is also an aspect of male bisexuality which could be accused of deriving from "patriarchal privilege," in the sense that the bisexual husband/father feels entitled to have relations (with other men) outside the home. A feminist argument could be made that male bisexuality is an extension of "chattel rights" to other males as well as the wife and children. This would be particularly true in situations where a male is exploitative or abusive. Yet (and this is reflected in numerous films), the position of the bisexual male is a precarious one: he gains less than he potentially loses by experimenting sexually with another man. Rather than cruelly augmenting his "power," he may feel helpless in the face of unfamiliar, risky desires; he may also feel guilty about cheating on his wife and abandoning his children, and confused about being torn between sexual identities. Plus, there is the fact that, by loving another man, he experiences something of the "woman's role"—by which I mean any of a wide range of experiences: romantic, emotional, domestic, sexual. Because of this, there is the possibility that the bisexual male represents a more sensitized male, willing to abdicate the purism of patriarchal power for something more uncertain, but which enables him to grow more as a person, and leaves him open to that wider spectrum of experiences. I do not mean that the man will become "feminized" or effeminate; I am suggesting that it will enhance the man's potential for empathy, helping him identify with other kinds of people (people, in fact, who have traditionally been subjugated to patriarchal domination: women, gays, children) and thereby undermining patterns of sexist, male-dominated thinking. As one bisexual male has stated: "As bisexual men, we can take some of the insight we gain from the experience of loving and being attracted to other men, and use that to be more effective lovers, partners, companions to women."[1]

No matter how much the look and composition of a "normal family" may be changing, the basic idea of family still remains conservative, tradition-bound, and hostile to sexual experimentation. People still raise families for reasons that have to do with wanting stability and security, wanting to pass along lineage and traditions, and wanting to celebrate a state of "normalization" in their lives. (Even for gay couples who marry and adopt, this is true; these decisions generally accompany a sense of being ready to undertake the enormous commitment, being settled and mature.) This is not to say, however, that an actively bisexual male may not want a family, or that the lure of "normal" family life does not occur in the lives of many bisexual men. It is deeply ingrained in the human instinct to seek consolation and ameliorate loneliness in communities based on shared identity, the most intimate of which is, of course, the family. Also, as a simple matter of fact, bisexual men fall in love with women and have children with them, while nonetheless remaining bisexual. Others discover they are bisexual during the course of married life. If families are difficult places to diverge from heterosexual conformity, they are also inevitable testing grounds for such divergences. Ultimately, both stability *and* personal freedom are needed for balance and happiness in individual lives.

A family can be defined as any group of people who live together for their own nurturing and happiness, and for the welfare of any children they bring into the world. "What counts is how we interact with each other."[2] It will be the task of filmmakers and other artists to begin to imagine and depict what "bisexual families" might look like. Would they automatically be any more (or less) dysfunctional than traditional heterosexual families? There may be benefits for children being raised by parents who have accomplished the difficult task of working through an unconventional sexual orientation and having the integrity and courage to acknowledge it as part of themselves. As one bisexual father states: "I think the way that I've compensated is to really want my children to have an openness and tolerance about other's lifestyles and to understand, also, why I need to be honest about my own."[3] If it is true, as it is often said, that "one is only as sick as one's secrets," then perhaps a bisexualized family which is open and honest should logically be much healthier than a nuclear heterosexual family which is in some form of denial.

Some of these questions and issues are raised by the French film *In Extremis* (*To the Extreme*, 2000). Thomas (Sébastien Roch) is a hedonistic young bisexual male who lives every aspect of his life intensely: when presented with a birthday cake, he does not blow out the candles but simply smashes the whole cake in with his fist. Sexually, he is involved in a long-time relationship with Caroline (Christine Boisson), an older widow with a thirteen-year-old son named Greg (Jérémy Sanguinetti). Thomas reserves the right to come and go in Caroline's life, though she wishes he would settle down with her: "It's hard to accept not being with you all the time," she says. "Too much happiness depresses me," he says, indicating that he is not ready for a family: "to go on vacation, to be a father." The distance he imposes is not necessarily what he would prefer, but seemingly a psychological necessity: he tells her, "It's hard for me, too. You don't seem to understand that." In spite of not wanting to be a father, he gets along well with Greg, playfully reading him sex scenes from erotic novels. Caroline says she thinks the novel is "too old" for Greg, but takes a basically laissez-faire attitude toward Thomas' interaction with Greg. For his part, the precocious Greg says, "Don't patronize me, I'm not a baby anymore," and generally seems to regard Thomas as a surrogate father.

Sex is a kind of power constantly flowing through Thomas. We see him swagger down the street in dark glasses, smoking, with the neon word GOD reflected in a storefront window. He has recently picked up high-school student Vincent (Aurélien Wiik), with whom he has begun a lusty affair. He is also still semi-involved with his ex-girlfriend Anne (Julie Depardieu), a hooker who lives with another hooker, Géraldine (Candice Hugo). In a torrid threesome, Thomas avidly makes love to both Vincent and Anne. But as the sexual configurations pile up, Thomas' swagger becomes more like a weary trudge from one assignation to the next, and at times he expresses the need to get away from everyone in order to clear his head.

The delicate balance of Thomas' life is upset when Caroline is suddenly killed in an accident. Mourning for her, he finds himself wanting to take care of Greg. Greg would like to live with Thomas, but the court system will not grant Thomas custody. Greg is placed in an orphanage pending adoption, but he runs away to see Thomas. Suddenly having doubts about the situation, Thomas tries to discourage Greg: "I'm not a good guy. It's not me who can make you happy."

The film becomes increasingly complicated. On some level, we are meant to see the court and the other social institutions as cold, unfeeling and prejudicial: they do not understand that, on a basic human level, Thomas and Greg already have a kind of natural father-son rapport. Greg describes the orphanage: "It's like a prison here.... No one cares about me." Both Thomas and Greg, after all, loved and miss Caroline. All of the characters reserve the right to lead their lives as they choose — even young Greg, though this decision is not up to him. However, as much as he cares about Greg, Thomas himself is torn about whether he wants to give up his sexual lifestyle to become Greg's father. Indeed, wherever there is overlap between Thomas' bisexual partying and his innocent relationship with Greg, it feels both extremely natural and also a source of unconscious strain. Thomas never conceals his bisexuality from Greg, nor does he conceal Greg from Vincent, Anne and his other friends. But it's clear that something is about to break in Thomas' veneer of defensive pride when he ducks into a nightclub bathroom during a rave and spits at himself in the mirror.

Cinematically, faster editing accompanies all of the scenes in which Thomas parties and has sex (at times the cutting is almost dizzying), while longer, more solemn takes characterize the scenes in which he grapples with love and family life. He is making a conscious effort to slow down his lifestyle, and the film's pace slows as well. A film, like life, has a certain pulse, and in bisexual life, it is suggested, there may be periods when activities move more quickly, or with greater simultaneity, and other periods in which a more traditional stability might be pursued.

One night, Thomas makes the desperate decision to take Greg from the orphanage. Greg stays with Anne and Géraldine; in a cute scene, he displays a natural curiosity, as a pubescent boy would, about what they do at night, and they are circumspect about letting him know very much. In fact, Greg likes being treated like an adult; it is Thomas who begins to regress and fall apart under the pressure of being responsible for the child. (Actual bisexual fathers have stated as much: "Childrearing forced me to face the ways I had not been trained to nurture."[4]) Anne reassures Greg that Thomas really does love him, even though he has begun to stay away for weeks at a time: "He's kind of wild and crazy right now, but he'll get it together." Thomas has further to fall, however: he descends more and more into promiscuous sex and male prostitution; both Vincent and Anne worry about him. The breaking point comes when he invites Greg to a late-night sex party. Entering the noisy, crowded club, Greg brushes past nude, decadent bodies, staring at all of the sex acts with wide-eyed horror. Finally, he comes upon Thomas, in make-up, being anally penetrated, and a look of cold, disappointed disgust comes over Greg's face.

In a frenzy, Thomas rushes from the party with Greg and throws himself into a public fountain. Splashing in the water, he seems at first to be trying to drown himself, but soon he rises from the fountain as if from a kind of baptism, a rebirth. Soaking wet, he clings to Greg and asks: "How is this going to end?" "I don't know," the astonished Greg replies. Momentarily, the father becomes the dependent child toward the son he is supposed to be raising; but the admission of his own weakness is a powerful catalyst for Thomas to change. He flies with Greg to his abandoned family home in Ibiza, and the two of them homestead in the empty mansion. Thomas gets rid of Vincent, saying, "You know I can't give you what you want," and Vincent immediately disappears into the crowded street, as if he had never even existed in Thomas' life. Thomas returns to Anne, and they rekindle their sexual relationship; but the police, searching for Greg, begin to place pressure on her. She arranges to meet Thomas and Greg in Spain, but policemen surprise them at the rendezvous. Anne is killed and Greg is forced to flee in a motorboat alone. Thomas escapes to Switzerland and freezes to death in a snowy wasteland.

In many ways Thomas is an archetypal bisexual male, although his same-sex attachments are given somewhat short-shrift. They are presented as less intense and long-lasting than his relationships with women. We are constantly reminded that he has only known Vincent for a short time. There is a theme of the two men lighting cigarettes which they never get to finish — cigarettes, like ephemeral passions, burn up quickly. Although they claim to love each other, Thomas says at one point that intimacy works differently with Vincent than it does with other people: instead of feeling closer to Vincent the more time he spends with him, Thomas feels he knows him less and less. Sphinx-like, Vincent merely smiles at this, his enigmatic and inadequate reaction underscoring the emotional truth of Thomas' judgment. Finally, Vincent has no part in helping to take care of Greg, but is only employed as an alibi for Thomas when the police come knocking on the door: when Vincent attests that he and Thomas have been making love all night (and now want to be left alone to make love some more), the suspicious cops cannot accuse Thomas of taking Greg from the orphanage on the night in question. Existing outside of even the most makeshift family life, homosexual activity — or rather, the gay side of Thomas' bisexuality — is only legible as something deceptive, mechanical, excessive, skin-deep.

Greg seems to want Thomas and Anne to form a couple. Anne explains to Greg that her relationship with Thomas is complicated: "Sometimes, even if you really love someone, you can't live with the person." She goes on to say to Greg, "You're going to be stronger than us." Seemingly, bisexualized families place more faith in the next, up-and-coming generation, that it will grow, adapt, and find ways of surviving which have eluded the previous generations. If traditional heterosexual families often stay mired in a ritualized, endlessly reified obeisance to the past, then bisexualized families are about living in and for the future — and making the future livable in the present.

Water is highly significant in *To the Extreme*. It is the symbol of ever-changing, ever-fluid life energy, and it is generally associated with revelatory moments or moments of bliss. There is the scene of rebirth/baptism in the Paris fountain. Later, when Thomas and Greg are in Ibiza, they spend a great deal of time in water, swimming in the ocean or the pool at Thomas' family home. Water is acceptance, porousness; it is maleness breaking through narrowly confining boundaries, coming closer to femaleness. For this reason, it is also a dangerous, forbidden zone. The Ibiza police begin to track Thomas and Greg because of a motorboat they have borrowed from the neighbors, thinking it abandoned; as a vehicle which enables people to cross the fluid medium of water, a "stolen" boat is like a symbol of subversion, an illegal shortcut. Finally, Thomas freezes to death in snow, which is frozen water: the medium of change and fluidity has been rendered dense, an impediment, as has the possibility of bisexual life itself.

Thomas, like so many bisexual male characters in films, is depicted as having had a ruined childhood. In movie terms, orphans, survivors of childhood sexual abuse, and products of broken homes and divorce are all likely to act out bisexually. In Thomas' case, both his parents died when he was young. To a certain extent, this sort of internal conflict "works" dramatically, but it is questionable as pop psychology on several levels. The most egregious aspect of this stereotyping is that it tends to pathologize bisexuality, by couching it in blatantly Freudian terms, which can often be judgmental: the bisexual man is searching for a hopeless rapprochement with father and mother, both the paternal and maternal love which he was denied. His mere existence is both a reproach to the parents' heterosexual marriage, and a possible guilty reason for why the marriage did not work. Therefore, he is doomed to undermine stable relationships wherever possible.

The film implies connections between Thomas' adult sexuality and his childhood. During sex with Caroline, he flashes on the image of a woman's face; this turns out to be his memory of his mother. As visual objects, films are often required to render subconscious processes in all too blatantly obvious terms; even if we accept that sublimation occurs to whatever extent, it is never a conscious process. And yet, bisexuality involves love for a man and a woman, and this synchronizes, however schematically, with that other situation in which a male feels love for a man and a woman: his early childhood love of father and mother. In this sense, bisexual attachments become symptomatic of a neurotic repetition-fixation: *I needed my father and my mother; I now need a man and a woman.*

By this logic, however, bisexuality could never simply be a positive attribute in a person, the outcome of a sexual development which simply finds a natural attraction and pleasure in both genders. But in a deeper sense, this need to use male bisexuality to validate the Oedipus complex — as an example of when sublimation fails — raises problematic questions about the Oedipus complex itself, and about sublimation. After all, what if bisexuality really is the solution to the son's unresolved jealousy, hatred and fear of the father? Even in psychoanalytic theory, there was always the possibility of a psychical remainder, what is left over after the conflicted boy transitions to normalized manhood; this remainder is the psychical dust swept under the rug so to speak, and is often characterized as a lack: repression, inadequacy, failure. A shift in thinking could turn this remainder, however, into new, life-giving energy within the individual's psychosexual economy. One man's neurosis could be another's panacea.

The Freudian Oedipus complex privileges patriarchy in the sense that heterosexual society perpetuates itself by each male generation consenting, at some point, to become exactly like the father rather than continue to fight against him: an infinite line of readymade patriarchs stretching toward the vanishing point, so to speak. But male bisexuality presents a third option, neither to fight against the father nor to become exactly like him, but to sublimate the need for his love into sex with other men, just as a (heterosexual) man supposedly sublimates his need for his mother into sex with women. In a way, male bisexuality inadvertently proves the Oedipal complex even as it subverts its patriarchal implications: today much more than in Freud's time, we recognize that father-son relationships should not be authoritarian and competitive, but as loving and nurturing as mother-son relationships. Therefore, if sublimation is good for the goose, so to speak, as the son learns to love and be loved, it must also be good for the gander.

Thomas cannot quite clear the chasm that separates him from his goal — in part, the goal must be made impossible in order to preserve the artificial strictures which define the patriarchal world and its given roles. He dies in a quest for wholeness, but the odds have been stacked against him from the beginning: the faceless, uniformed cops who pursue him are foot-soldiers of a patriarchal order that would rather return Greg to no father at all than to a surrogate father who has subverted the masculine role through androgyny and bisexuality.

Bisexualized Patriarchs: The Trio *and* Dry Cleaning

Two films by female directors — Hermine Huntgeburth's *Das Trio* (*The Trio*, 1998) and Anne Fontaine's *Nettoyage à Sec* (*Dry Cleaning*, 1997) — offer contrasting visions of bisexualized families. Both employ elements of black comedy as they investigate the conflicts created by male bisexual desire within family units; in both, the inner coherence and strength of family life ultimately win out.

In *The Trio*, it is the patriarch, Zobel (Götz George), who is bisexual. He presides with a somewhat iron fist over an extended family of grifters and pickpockets, including his daughter Lizzi (Jeanette Hain) and his male lover Karl (Christian Redl). They live in a mobile home, symbol of the family in constant state of flux. In the opening scene, Karl is the victim of a young thief at a carnival. Zobel is not one for turning the other cheek: he and Karl corner the thief, Rudolf (Felix Eitner), on a Ferris wheel, and not only recover the stolen money, but make the young man strip. Down below, Lizzi catches Rudolf's clothes as they fall piece by piece, and steals his wallet. Zobel berates Karl for getting old, being too distracted, losing his touch — problems which begin to carry over in their criminal activities, in which Karl becomes an increasing liability. On one job, Karl is accidentally hit by a car and ends up in the hospital.

Scouting for a replacement, Lizzi spots Rudolf at the garage where he works as an auto mechanic. She follows him home; he is wary of letting her in, and when he does, she wanders around his messy apartment, stealing small personal items and snooping into his papers. "But I know you," she wheedles. He says, "How? You'd be the first," implying some mystery or secret in his life. However, they begin to bond when she makes friends with his pet snake, an emblem of Rudolf's soon-to-be discovered affinity for the phallic (and the reptilian). Although tensions seem to be looming from the start, Lizzi and Zobel bring Rudolf in on their three-man operation, teaching him the art of picking pockets. In a way similar to Bresson's *Pickpocket* (1959), albeit far less solemn and profound, pickpocketing is eroticized in the casual brushing against stranger's bodies, the illicit taking place in plain sight, as it were.

Zobel and Rudolf also begin to bond around an easy masculine physicality, mock-fighting and wrestling. Zobel puts Rudolf in a headlock, taking advantage of the situation to kiss him on the head. Lizzi tells Rudolf to hit Zobel in the balls, which he does. The two "subservient" members of the family have to gang up on the patriarch to keep him from abusing his power over them. We see that this subservience also extends to the division of labor and money within the group. Karl had already accused Zobel of letting him and Lizzi do all the work and take all the risks. Zobel gives Lizzi and Rudolf an "allowance" (the term is redolent of parents doling out monies to their children) while keeping the rest in a strongbox under his bed.

Rudolf moves into the mobile home, and not long after that, a bisexual love triangle evolves. Rudolf takes off his shirt and washes up in the kitchen sink, while both Lizzi and Zobel watch him, then pretend not to notice. Lizzi seduces Rudolf first. But then Karl dies from his injuries; while Lizzi is asleep, Rudolf tries to comfort the mourning Zobel, and the two men end up making love. After that, both Zobel and Lizzi try to get rid of each other at every opportunity so they can be alone with Rudolf. Father and daughter sharing the same lover is a somewhat unsavory premise, but it highlights Zobel's patriarchal control; he does not respect his daughter's feelings. Meanwhile, Rudolf somewhat opportunistically leads both of them on, trying to make time for "quickies" with each of them while the other is briefly away. Here, we see that the love triangle operates around a certain principle of blindness, one or more of the members not seeing what is really going on, or looking the other way, so to speak; this blindness is reified, and literalized, in the trio's pickpocketing scheme, which involves one of them pretending to be blind in order to bump into people.

Eventually, in a scene where the increasingly harried Rudolf is caught between a naked Zobel in the shower and a seductive Lizzi in his bed, the triangle is exposed. Lizzi is furious at her father's betrayal: "You fuck the love of my life and all you can say is 'I'm sorry.'" She accuses him of using her to procure younger men for him, now that he is growing older. She runs off. Realizing that he is losing hold over his domain, Zobel threatens Rudolf: "Bring her back to me, or I'll kill you!" Rudolf chases after Lizzi, and they end up getting on a bus together. Left alone, Zobel becomes stagnant, a kind of shiftless displaced patriarch, a king in exile. For their part, Lizzi and Rudolf live together, but their relationship deteriorates into recriminations, silences, and tearful scenes. The parts of the triangle cease to work when disengaged from the others, probably because family ties are so deeply embedded within this triangle.

Lizzi and Rudolf return to Zobel, and give him an ultimatum: they will run things now, planning their heists and dividing up the money. They also make Zobel sleep in the front seat of the van while they share the bed. Sulky and discontented at having his authority usurped by the younger man, and possibly at having lost his sexual connection to Rudolf, Zobel steals a train conductor's wallet and tries to frame Rudolf; but when Rudolf turns the tables and accuses Zobel, the police find the wallet in his coat and Zobel goes to prison. Rudolf and Lizzi visit him during family visiting hours; again, the family bonds persist and transcend the destructive desires and crimes within the family itself—indeed, this family is based upon precisely those destructive desires and crimes, and as such, it continues to grow. At the end of the film, when Zobel is released from prison, Rudolf and Lizzi have had a little girl, whom they have already taught to pickpocket—the patriarchal imprinting of the father's vocation passing itself along to the next generation. As they all walk away, Zobel briefly takes Rudolf's hand, suggesting that sexual tension between the two men, and fights for possession of him between father and daughter, might in fact continue.

Zobel represents male bisexuality as patriarchal privilege. His relationships with men are self-serving and lack any sense of trust (even though he once said to Karl, "Friendship means you trust someone else completely"). He often picks up young hustlers, in a kind of exploitation of others' vulnerability. He berated Karl for being fat and inept, and also berated Lizzi when she attempted to defend him. Liking Rudolf and sensing an attraction between the young man and Lizzi, Zobel lays down an impromptu rule of their working relations, "no exchange of bodily fluids" between members of the team, a rule which he himself is prepared to break with Rudolf. "I'm still the one who says who plays with whom," Zobel states, asserting the double standard as part of his privilege.

Rudolf is, in some ways, a younger, more clean-cut version of Zobel; he displays a certain wide-eyed innocence at first, but soon enough decides to exploit the situation in which he finds himself. His opportunism is similar to Zobel's. Visiting Karl in the hospital, Rudolf steals from another patient's meal tray, because he is hungry. Later, he casually describes his sex with Zobel as satisfying a similar kind of momentary "hunger": "It just happened. Our bodies need it sometimes, right?" At the same time, there are moments of tenderness and affection between the two men; in fact, for most of the film it appears as if Rudolf is more "in love" with Zobel than he is with Lizzi. In spite of the fact that all of the sex scenes are filmed in a somewhat stiff and un-sensual manner, the film seems to argue that, qualitatively, there is little difference between heterosexual and homosexual romance: both are passionate, emotional, and satisfying of a certain human need. Indeed, to be able to satisfy their needs is what drives all of the characters, who often speak of knowing how to "get by" in life. Simple survival is the only thing that matters.

Nevertheless, these shifting configurations of relatives and lovers really do constitute a family. Though Karl and Zobel bicker constantly, Lizzi acknowledges it as a kind of foreplay — the kind of quirky behavior which a family allows for. When Karl dies, both Zobel and Lizzi mourn, shedding tears. Zobel burns Karl's drag outfits because he does not want anyone else to wear them: a family is exclusive if nothing else. Zobel blames himself for Karl's death: "It's all my fault." Accompanying patriarchal power is the sense of paternalistic responsibility for "the flock"— but even this, while seeming to represent tender weakness, only serves to augment and certify Zobel's power-status all the more strongly: just as he expects to take all the credit for the family's successes, so Zobel accepts blame for its failures and losses. Rudolf is accepted into the family, not so much as a replacement for Karl but as a new member, whose unique influence brings about a new chapter in the family's story.

Writer-director Huntgeburth has said, "I have a special affinity for family stories. For me, the father-daughter conflict is very interesting and that is why I made this movie like this."[5] Indeed, it is intriguing that *The Trio* was written and directed by a woman, and that it has, at its heart, a daughter's conflict with patriarchal authority. Her father's authority is so boundless that he will make even her boyfriend into his "chattel." When her boyfriend becomes as distant, and as power-hungry, as her father, she must face the same battle of authority all over again, so as to prevent Rudolf from becoming Zobel. Female desire must assert itself in opposition to a male desire which is identified as surplus, overflowing its "natural" bounds. Zobel, bisexual patriarch, and Rudolf, bisexual patriarch-in-training, must both be brought in line around heterosexual female desire, and the birthing of the next (female) generation.

If *The Trio* represents male bisexuality as patriarchal privilege run amok, then Anne Fontaine's *Dry Cleaning* presents a different way of bisexualizing the family and throwing patriarchy into crisis (sexual crisis, crisis of authority). Patriarchy still has the last word — indeed, violently so. But here, the patriarch is not the bisexual figure; rather, a young man enters the family unit as an outsider and attempts to reorganize it around *his* bisexual desire. To a vague extent, this plot is reminiscent of Pier Paolo Pasolini's *Theorem*, a key work in the history of films about male bisexuality. In *Theorem*, "God" (Terence Stamp), in the form of a handsome young man, seduces the members of a wealthy Italian family in turn, males and females alike, causing the family itself to implode. Pasolini employs male bisexuality as a complex metaphor for miraculous religious purity and Marxist socioeconomic equality: the supernatural energy is so purely and honestly loving that it tears away the family members' artificial defenses and their petty, mercenary values. Fontaine's film is very different: it does depict the bisexual outsider as a powerful, nearly irresistible force, but nonetheless wholly human, even somewhat bedraggled and helpless; in the end, he fails to "convert" the family's patriarch, and in fact becomes a martyr to the institution of the family with its thoroughgoing capacity for denial and shame.

In the small French town of Belfort, Jean-Marie Kunstler (Charles Berling) and his wife Nicole (Miou-Miou) are frustrated with the pressures of running their dry-cleaning business and catering to their customers. They take the evening off to unwind at a nightclub. There, they watch with delight and fascination as two women, "The Queens of the Night," perform a slow, sensual dance, including simulated sex. The Queens of the Night are actually a brother and sister act, with the brother in drag. The brother, Loïc (Stanislas Merhar), happens to come into the Kunstlers' store, needing one of his dresses cleaned. He chats them up, even flirting rather broadly with Nicole, inviting her to come back to the club. Later, she expresses surprise to Jean-Marie that Loïc is not at all effeminate. Nevertheless, Jean-Marie expresses reservations: "Don't tell me a drag artist is just like you and me."

The Kunstlers return to the club. This time, they also meet the sister, Marilyn (Mathilde Seigner). She proposes that they all go back to the apartment she shares with Loïc and have "a foursome" for the price of 800 francs. During the drunken night, Jean-Marie suddenly changes his mind; he pushes the amorous Marilyn away from him, and angrily breaks up his wife's lovemaking with Loïc. There is an incongruous cut from the interrupted orgy to a scene of a children's birthday party at the Kunstlers'— they have a young son, Pierre (Noé Pflieger). It is an arresting visual reminder that the worlds of illicit desire and domesticity are about to collide. (Fontaine might also be suggesting that the drag world and the sex games are actually extensions of the childlike world of play, repressed in the adult routines of work and married life.)

Nicole is feeling dissatisfied with her life, "cleaning other people's shit," as she puts it. Jean-Marie asserts, "All I want is for you to be happy," but she is not sure what she wants. Impulsively, he suggests they take a weekend trip to Basel, where Loïc and Marilyn told them they would be. "Maybe we'll bump into the Queens of the Night." This thought seems to make both of the Kunstlers happy. In Basel, they find the brother and sister performing in a gay bar, and they all go out for drinks. That night, Loïc has a drunken falling out with Marilyn, and ends up staying with the Kunstlers in their hotel room. Jean-Marie and Nicole spend the rest of their weekend with him before going home to Belfort on the train.

On his own now, the drag act over, Loïc turns up at the dry-cleaning shop. Jean-Marie invites him to stay for dinner, and then to stay with them, sleeping on their sofa-bed. Because Loïc needs a job, Jean-Marie begins to train him in dry cleaning. Family problems arise almost immediately. Training Loïc leaves Jean-Marie no time to attend Pierre's basketball game. Jean-Marie's elderly mother (Nanou Meister), who lives with the Kunstlers, takes an instant distrust to the newcomer. And Loïc has kissed Nicole, a kiss to which she briefly surrendered before pulling away.

It turns out that Loïc excels at dry cleaning. He also initiates sex with Nicole in the basement of the shop. Fontaine cuts from this sex to a shot of Loïc ice-skating with Pierre, as if he is replacing Jean-Marie as both husband and father. Family life seems attractive to Loïc, who is an orphan; he says to Nicole: "I feel good with you two. It's like having a family." At this point, the film seems to be becoming a sort of "housewife" romance fantasy of the bored woman who gets to have it all: stable husband and sexy young lover. But then, the narrative takes an unusual departure. Loïc goes to stay at a hotel when the mother finds his gun while snooping through his bags. A few days later, Jean-Marie visits Loïc in his hotel room, asking him to come back for a permanent job and a share in the store's profits. Suddenly, Loïc makes an unexpected pass at Jean-Marie: "You make me hard." He insists that he knows Jean-Marie wants him. "I should clobber you," Jean-Marie says and storms out.

Is Loïc projecting his own bisexual desire onto the hapless Jean-Marie? Or is Loïc right—is Jean-Marie hiding something? In terms of personality, Jean-Marie seems wrapped very tightly; he grumbles, mumbles and generally speaks in gruff, low monotones, as if terrified of letting some

In *Dry Cleaning* (1997), Stanislas Merhar plays Loïc, an orphan and a drifter who begins an affair with a married woman, then comes to realize he has a strong attraction toward her husband as well. Merhar is frequently unclothed in the film, a way of highlighting not only his attractiveness but also his vulnerability.

security wall crumble inside him. "You never smile in photographs," Nicole observes at one point, while looking at their wedding album. At one point Loïc says to him, "I can read guys' faces. I've done it for money. But it's different with you."

Loïc does come back to work, and continues his affair with Nicole; in fact, they make less and less effort to hide it. Jean-Marie angrily leaves a meeting of local business owners when someone suggests to him that it is bad for the image of his dry-cleaning shop to allow Loïc live with his family. "Cleaning other people's shit," as an enterprise, must presumably keep up a certain image of propriety and integrity. What Jean-Marie does not tell Nicole is that Loïc continues to make advances toward him whenever the two men are alone. The film increasingly becomes a power struggle (only partly acknowledged) between Loïc's liberated bisexuality and Jean-Marie's fragile, loosening grip on his position as head of the Kunstler household. Eventually, desperate for an end to the situation, Jean-Marie announces sweeping changes to their lives: the mother is going into a nursing home ("the Golden Age Club"), Pierre is going to basketball camp, and the Kunstlers are moving to Canada for a "change of scene." Jean-Marie has already purchased the travel tickets.

At first, Nicole is excited about this, but when she learns that he intends to leave Loïc behind, she becomes upset. "I'm afraid we can't go on like this," he tells her, adding: "It's my fault for letting him move in." As with *The Trio*, the patriarch accepts blame for disappointment and loss, all the better to augment his absolute control over everything that happens in the family: the affair is only happening because Jean-Marie has allowed and even encouraged it. Loïc is also upset when Jean-Marie tells him they will be closing shop soon and moving to another country. Both Nicole and Loïc, separately, ask Jean-Marie, "What did I do wrong?" His decisive actions bring about the return of his patriarch status, according him the power to approve and disapprove, to pass judgment.

But Nicole rallies for a last-ditch attack on Jean-Marie's authority and a defense of her own happiness. For her, there is no future without Loïc, only a past she does not wish to repeat: calling Loïc the first good thing that has happened in their lives, she says, "I warn you, I'm not going back." She makes up her mind to follow Loïc: "If Loïc goes, I go with him." Jean-Marie is working late in the shop when Loïc comes in and begins to stare at him. "I want you," he says to Jean-Marie, moving behind him and placing his hands on Jean-Marie's crotch. "Don't," Jean-Marie gasps, "please." "I know you're hard. See? You can't fool me." In males, it is often said that physical arousal "never lies," but even if this were true, it does little good if the complex psyche of the owner of the erection is unwilling to accept it as the "truth."

Loïc pulls down the shuddering Jean-Marie's pants and, bending him over the ironing board, begins to penetrate him anally. Jean-Marie seems to be either in paroxysms of pleasure or sheer panic. Loïc tells him: "What were you scared of? Looking like a fag? Say you love me. Say it!" Suddenly, Jean-Marie lashes out at Loïc, striking him in the head with the iron. Loïc dies. Deeply shaken, Jean-Marie appeals to Nicole, who rushes to the body. Almost immediately, she undertakes to hide Loïc's corpse and to scrub his blood stains from the floor, going in a flash from Loïc's lover to accomplice in her husband's murder of him.

Throughout the film, cleaning is used as a metaphor for a sometimes conscious, sometimes unconscious act of repressing what is sexually taboo and forbidden. After the scene where the Kunstlers first see the Queens of the Night, there is a cut to the hiss of an iron steaming a garment. Later, Fontaine cuts from Nicole looking at the sleeping Jean-Marie on the train back from Basel, to a close-up of clothes cycling in the round window of a dryer. Routine, order, and above all, the removal of stains follow upon those moments when the husband and wife tentatively try to break free from what is socially and sexually expected of them. When Loïc first comes to the shop, he already flirts, a bit obliquely, with Jean-Marie, cheekily asking him if semen stains on the clothes ever "bug" him. Jean-Marie does not take the sexual bait, insisting instead: "I keep going till it's perfect." "Cheers," Loïc says and turns away, happier, at this point, to generate the stains than to clean them. After one of the scenes in which Loïc propositions Jean-Marie (he has caressed his thigh in the front seat of the Kunstler delivery truck), we see Jean-Marie in a car wash, shivering with his hand over his mouth as the sudsy water rains down on the truck from all sides. Again, "cleaning other people's shit" is how Nicole characterizes her crisis of dissatisfaction with the life she has chosen; it turns out she does not feel she was cut out for such work. Yet, her ultimate act—which must then be counted not only as a betrayal of Loïc, but a self-betrayal, performed for the sake of her husband and family—is to get down on her hands and knees and clean away all traces of Loïc's blood from the floor of the shop.

Fontaine ends the film with a strange, disconnected shot of Jean-Marie and Nicole striding with determination, side by side, down a road somewhere. They have chillingly closed ranks and are marching toward whatever future awaits them, an echo, perhaps, of Buñuel's discreetly charming bourgeoisie. And if that comparison seems grandiose, *Dry Cleaning* is a kind of allegory of two different lifestyles at total war with each other: thus, the nuclear family itself marches onward, never looking back at the unconventional sexualities which it eternally tries to exclude.

An Extreme Case: The Pillow Book

A film as disturbing as it is brilliantly made, Peter Greenaway's *The Pillow Book* (1996) bases its critique of patriarchy not on the fact that it is too straight but that it contains an element of "bisexual weakness." Greenaway's film ultimately upholds the idea of a core family unit that is traditional and heterosexual, but one that is matriarchal and matrilineal as opposed to patriarchal and patrilineal. Specifically an examination of male bisexuality from the viewpoint of a scorned and vengeful heterosexual woman, *The Pillow Book* establishes its matriarchal family literally over the dead bodies of bisexual and homosexual men.

Hitherto, the films I have written about have tended to feature young female characters who are supportive of their bisexual male friends and partners; even when they admit to not understanding, they at least live and let live. Not so with *The Pillow Book*, which places a Japanese woman, Nagiko (Vivian Wu), directly on a course of war against the homoerotic aspect of bisexuality, since it takes from her what she feels should be hers (the bodies and hearts of men), and since it also brings back painful memories of her much-adored and much-eroticized father (Ken Ogata).

On her fateful birthday as a little girl, Nagiko's father inaugurated the family ritual of painting her face. As he daubs calligraphic characters on her cheeks, forehead, mouth and chin, he utters the words of a creation myth: "When God made the first clay model of a human being, he painted in the eyes, the lips and the sex. Then he painted in each person's name, lest the owner should ever forget it." According to this ritual, then, one's first loyalty, what one must never forget, overlook, or leave behind, is to one's name, as given, patronymically, by the father; this emphasizes the little girl's bond with her father, which will drive her actions as an adult woman throughout the film.

The climax of the ritual is to paint his own name on the back of Nagiko's neck: "If he approved of his creation, he brought the clay model into life by signing his own name." This is the patriarch as creator, life-giver, avatar of God himself, his authority forged from the bonds of ownership, cultural tradition, linguistic appropriation, and, lest we should forget, blood. Indeed, Greenaway heightens the red of the father's ink so that it glows like freshly spilled blood on young Nagiko's flesh.

What taints this ritual, and makes the otherwise highly legible role of the father illegible, is the fact that when young Nagiko witnesses the primal scene, it is not her father having sex with her mother, but with another man, her father's publisher (Yoshi Oida). Does this make Nagiko born, as it were, to love bisexual men — or to detest them? She says in voiceover that she knew it would take her many years to understand the meaning of what she has seen.

As a young woman, equally filled with hate for the publisher as with profound erotic longing for the act of having a man write on her body, she leaves home. She has decided, in a way that the film itself can never verify, that the publisher was blackmailing her father into having sex with him for all those years, presumably in exchange for agreeing to publish his books. In other words, Nagiko determines, or rationalizes, that the gay sex must have happened against her father's will — and simultaneously, that her father was not a good enough writer to be published without acquiescing to sexual blackmail. This plants the seeds not only of Nagiko's fetishization of and hatred for bisexuality, but the way in which she will seek to supplant her father, in a female version of the Oedipal complex which will eventually divert patriarchy into matriarchy. To believe that her father may have simply been bisexual is apparently beyond her capacities. She discovers that her beloved patriarchy only comes alive when a man writes upon her flesh. Which is also to say, the beloved patriarchy only comes alive when she, a woman, worships it into existence; when she engineers its triumph within the space of a private, semi-public, or public act of exhibitionistic love. She tries out a series of calligraphic lovers, and what she relishes most, it seems, is taking a shy, nervous older man, and coaching his inner paternal authority to come out, via the calligrapher's brush: "Some of the great Japanese calligraphers were very modest and unassuming men, humble clerks by day, daring and poised by night." Patience, steadiness, delicacy of touch, intuitiveness, love of written words, art and language: these are some of the virtues she seeks in a lover, and needless to say, they are not macho ones. The only thing that could explain the initial family ritual is that her father was always already sexually metamorphic in the first place, at least to some degree — though this is impossible for Nagiko to admit to herself— and indeed, the pieces of her strange puzzle do not begin to fit into place until she meets Jerome (Ewan McGregor).

Jerome is bisexual, so he gives the lie to Nagiko's assertion that male bisexuality must necessarily be coerced. He is also a skilled translator; being polyglot is a sly implication of sexual polymorphism (just as so many conventions of writing, reading, and printing will become increasingly sexualized in the course of the film). But Nagiko's true agenda immediately begins to emerge, to her initial dismay. She asks him to write on her, and he obliges by writing the Yiddish word "Brusten" in big block letters on her breasts, like a schoolboy with a vocabulary exercise. She becomes dismissive: "You're not a writer. This is not writing, it's scribbling." If the power of the real God (the real Father, the real Creator) is to come up with names where none existed before, then what Jerome is doing, as a late 20th century son, is merely following in the footsteps, memorizing the names that have already been given, passing them along (as a translator) while creating nothing. To reify what has already been named is a patriarchal dead-end, even an abdication of patriarchy, and it is this perceived sterility which Nagiko reacts against.

At the same time, the emotionally impacted Nagiko does not yet understand that her battle is against the patriarchy itself, here symbolized not by her kindly and sexually ambiguous father, but by the harsh, homosexually acquisitive publisher. Jerome's bisexual body will soon become the canvas on which she goes head to head with the publisher in an epic power struggle. As a passive conduit, Jerome will sacrifice himself more and more, thereby becoming more and more like Nagiko's beloved father, but thereby reifying more and more her father's despised bisexuality. As we see at the end of Nagisa Oshima's *Ai No Corrida* (*In the Realm of the Senses*, 1977), performing calligraphy upon a lover's body (in death) is the ultimate sign of ownership of that body. In *The Pillow Book*, under Nagiko's tutelage, control of male bodies will revert from the males themselves and from other males, to female hands. "In the name of the father," to celebrate her father's patriarchy, and redeem him from his own bisexuality, she will force male bisexuality to declare itself a lie.

Nagiko decides to become a writer herself: again, we see elements of Oedipal usurpation within the father-daughter relationship. Looking to slay the biggest Oedipal dragon (and inadvertently revealing just how deeply her fixation runs), she applies first to her father's publisher, who rejects her out of hand. She goes to the publisher's offices, seemingly more as a spy than in any official capacity, and there she finds out that Jerome is also the publisher's lover. Nagiko stiffens, but must obey the logic of the primal scene. In becoming the publisher's lover, Jerome has become her father. "If I could not seduce the publisher," she says, "then perhaps I could seduce the publisher's lover." This is a sentence that needs to be considered alongside Freud's examples of the linguistic coils which homosexual panic takes (I do not love him, I hate him; I do not love him, she loves him; etc.). What Nagiko is really implying, unconsciously, is this: If I cannot have my father sexually, I can have the man who most reminds me of my father — i.e. the one who is bisexually sleeping with the same gay man my father slept with. To replicate itself, the triangle divides.

And seduce Jerome she does. Their sex is genuine, lustful, passionate, intense — and very sexy. As a passive instrument for Nagiko to use in her crusade to destroy the patriarchy by revealing it once and for all as her own construction of assumed desire, the bisexual Jerome is perfect. In a move that can only be explained as the father-figure acquiescing in his own usurpation, Jerome offers to place himself at Nagiko's service as her blank page to write upon. Significantly, Nagiko teaches Jerome the family face-painting ritual so central to her erotic life, her selfhood and her mission to reclaim her father as a whole man, a man whose love was hers rather than for another man.

Jerome offers to go to the publisher as her living manuscript, with her words written all over his irresistible body. "A sacrifice," she sneers acidly, "but not without pleasure for you." Already it is the specter of Jerome's bisexuality — a reminder of the unthinkable possibility that her father invited and enjoyed the publisher's sexual attentions — which Nagiko fears and despises. She does not tell Jerome that the publisher was also her father's lover, and that this new triangle only reifies the primal one which she carries around as psychic baggage, and which consumes her with constant thoughts of jealousy and vengeance. But as if following a pre-ordained logic, she covers Jerome with her writing — not before shaving his body very closely, however, a further act of feminizing and de-patriarchizing Jerome, in preparation for her eventual matriarchal usurpation.

In a stylized sex scene, Jerome strips for the publisher and stands like a waxworks doll; the publisher sniffs his skin, kissing and licking certain words as he reads. After a few seconds, he claps for a female amanuensis to come into the room and transcribe the body. Women are presented here as handmaidens of this patriarchal literary culture, the peripheral witnesses to an exchange in which one male evaluates the strength of another male; but the seeds of the destruction of this patriarchal order have already been planted, even if the destruction will be wrought for the "wrong" reason: not because the publisher is particularly sexist, but merely because he loves men and invites their love.

Watching Jerome and the publisher carry on as a happy couple touches too deep a nerve for Nagiko. Following them down the street in a van, she calls Jerome over and upbraids him: "You're enjoying it too much!" This is precisely the kind of evidence of authentic bisexuality which she seeks to repress from her memories of her father, who must be cast as unwilling victim of gay desire, not enthusiastic participant in it. In general, wherever a world of men seeks to close ranks in front of Nagiko, she is reminded of the primal scene and grows moody, despondent, violent. "But with your permission — and only according to the quality of the writing," Jerome counters, reminding her that she, the woman, controls the gay sex albeit from a distance. The two men are allowed to enjoy their power only through her.

But this is cold comfort to the suffering Nagiko, who threatens to replace Jerome in a fit of pique. Trying to escape the emotionally impacted stalemate which keeps her tied to her father, she writes on two men whom she picks up in a restaurant, and sends them to the publisher as the next two "books." With this kind of casual, even semi-anonymous "sex" (for calligraphy and sex are now thoroughly cathected in the film), she seeks to tear at the patriarchy even more, punishing Jerome for his bisexual infidelity to her and insulting the publisher by insinuating that he will take anything — in other words, his desire for Jerome is not special but can be satisfied by any attractive male body. (This strategy of Nagiko's becomes more and more acute throughout the film, and of course, the publisher proves her right.)

Jerome is suitably chastened. Heart-broken, he swallows an overdose of pills and dies naked in Nagiko's bed with her pillow book covering his genitals. She is finally ready to confess to his corpse what she has been hiding: "You deceived me with the man I detest, with the man who blackmailed my father." And, again like the ending of *In the Realm of the Senses*, she takes ultimate possession of her lover's body by writing on it.

But the publisher has the same idea, of laying claim to Jerome's dead body as reading matter. After the publisher learns that Jerome is dead, the film becomes a war between straight woman and gay man for the bisexual male body. He has Jerome's body dug up and the skin cut into paper from which the publisher makes a pillow book of his own. (The organs, including the heart, are tossed into a slop basket like so much offal.) Once more displaying bad faith toward the gay side of bisexual experience, Greenaway depicts the publisher's interest in Jerome as being only skin-deep, superficial, not a profound or sacred love but a kind of objectification or covetousness. The publisher revels in his pillow book, smelling and kissing the flesh-pages, rubbing them on his own bare torso in a way that is reminiscent of Nagiko's fetishization of calligraphy and flesh. But while Nagiko's attempt is always seen as poignant in its sense of longing for childhood, the publisher's "act of sacrilege" is seen as greedy consumption, the ruthless, all-powerful conqueror wallowing in his ill-gotten spoils.

Striking a bargain to get the Jerome-book back, Nagiko agrees to complete her own work, sending the final books to the publisher on a series of indifferent hustlers. Again, she insults the publisher's gay desire, implying that Jerome was not special to him. The men become cheaper, more and more parlous. One man-book shrieks with demented, half-wit repetition: "I have a deal to make." The deal now is that the publisher must not only publish Nagiko's writing, but have sex with the bodies on which it is written. Nagiko wants to degrade gay desire prior to destroying it and eradicating it utterly. These bodies erase desire even as they reify it over and over again. They become cockier in trapping the publisher in an uncomfortable awareness, that the sex means more to him than the writing itself. A young man comes in from the rain soaking wet; the ink has run all over his skin, but when he offers his naked body to the publisher in lieu of the book, the publisher sends the scribes out of the room presumably to take the sexual deal. Nagiko wants to expose the publisher as not having "high literary art" in mind, but tawdry sex; the bodies, once used as bait, have become the entire *raison d'être*.

Gay desire "procreates" (in the form of books) but begets only an increasingly arid idea of desire: indeed, an *idée fixe*. Meanwhile, Nagiko is pregnant with Jerome's child, a daughter who will complete the switch from patrilineal to matrilineal dynasty. Heterosexuality represents devotion, commitment, stability, honor, respect, the family; while homosexuality represents pathological compulsion, obsessiveness, using up each anonymous body as part of an abstract search for delusional meaning, never finding the ultimate meaning but always moving on to the next provisional substitute-meaning, and the next one after that. If the bisexual male partakes of both heterosexual and homosexual eroticism, Jerome, as a bisexual who dies for love of the woman, implicitly makes a false choice of heterosexuality over homosexuality, in life and in death.

The final book (ominously enough, the Thirteenth) comes written on an impassive, imperious sumo wrestler. After the publisher has read his body from head to toe, the wrestler pulls a razor from his ceremonial hair-bun and slits the publisher's throat. The publisher seems to offer himself as a willing sacrifice, murdered by an avatar of his own desire for male flesh, male beauty, and the (literal) language of the male body — here presented at its most "straight" and therefore unattainable, in the body of a purified warrior. We see again that Nagiko — as woman, emissary of the dominant heterosexual culture — has always controlled the gay sex, which she has now steered toward the homosexual's death.

Nagiko accuses the publisher of having stolen, violated and desecrated all the men in her life. It is the implacable fury of the woman who feels herself confronted with the reality of male-male relations, from which she is excluded. Bisexual male bodies are what gay men and straight women share; they are the mediation of the two worlds of desire. It is through these bodies, literally, that gay man and straight woman attempt to communicate in the film: she by writing words, he by reading, validating, disseminating. Yet the communication is in bad faith from the beginning. She wants to shame and destroy the gay man; she turns the bodies away from love and toward an indifferent, venal prostitution, ending in sordid sexual murder. But whose love is automatically purer and nobler? Nagiko's usurpation of patriarchal power is treated as a heroic quest, whereas the publisher's delight in participating in female culture by making his own pillow book is invalidated as pathological, grotesque, "an act of sacrilege." Again and again, Greenaway stacks the deck against the gay man, but even then cannot avoid depicting moments of true happiness and erotic tenderness between the publisher and Jerome, moments which seem to belie Nagiko's vengeance even as they effectively whet her jealousy.

In the end, Nagiko's revenge is complete, but what version of the patriarchy has she destroyed, the truly oppressive one, or only the already anti-patriarchal one in which two men can freely love one another? And she has destroyed it in the name of her father, who may have been more acquiescent to the sexual demands of his publisher than Nagiko was able to admit. The film raises the question of what constitutes a family in the first place: a nexus of fetishized rituals, or a constellation of living passions? Finally, what new power structure — matriarchal perhaps, but modeled on the patriarchal in its consolidation of power — has she erected? The final image of the silk flowers "planted" in the ceremonial urn that holds Jerome's paper-and-ink remains can be read as a mocking image of bisexual manhood: his transitory role in procreation fulfilled, Jerome is laid to rest, not in the natural world but one that is definitively decorative and sterile. Also laid to rest is the father's troublesome bisexual experience, now expunged, resolved in favor of unbroken procreative heterosexuality. *The Pillow Book*'s conclusion implies that a female world which excludes males is somehow very different in meaning and tone — certainly not as painful or damning — as a male world which excludes females; but this misses the inclusive point of bisexuality itself.

The Other Side of Machismo

A recent film from Spain, *Azuloscurocasinegro* (*Dark Blue Almost Black*, 2006), employs male bisexuality specifically to critique the macho codes which support the patriarchal family. A politically correct social comedy, *Dark Blue Almost Black* deconstructs machismo wherever it finds it: the hero, Jorge (Quim Guttiérrez), is carefully portrayed as a sensitive, non-macho male, but more virile and sexually potent than his extremely macho older brother Antonio (Antonio de la Torre), who is sterile. Two patriarchs appear in the film, one wheelchair-bound and suffering from dementia in the wake of a stroke, and the other sexually ambiguous.

The latter is of interest to us here, especially in terms of the impact which his bisexual lifestyle has on his son Sean (Raúl Arévalo). A kind of young slacker, Sean takes blackmail photos of a masseur who performs sexual favors for his male clients. One afternoon, Sean sees his own father naked on the masseur's table. This revelation of his father's bisexuality is difficult for Sean; however, because this is a comedy (and an often funny one at that), Sean's anxiety is not treated as a crisis but as a source of offbeat humor. For one thing, he immediately begins to anonymously blackmail his father for money, which he turns around and uses to buy the van his father is selling.

At the same time, Sean does question himself, wondering if having a "gay father" makes him gay, too. He reminisces to his friend Jorge how he once masturbated to a copy of *Playgirl* when he was fifteen. "Then it disappeared.... Shit, my dad must have stolen it, the fucker." Sean, who dresses like the Euro-equivalent of an urban American "gang-banger" and who displays sexist attitudes toward women, goes through a process of emotional growth as he explores his own potential bisexuality. (Like father, like son, as it were.) In fact, he starts to steal his father's appointment times with the masseur, whose erotic services Sean comes to enjoy much more than he ever thought he could.

But if *Dark Blue Almost Black* seems to regard it as healthy for males to explore their gay sides, it resists placing the kind of labels on Sean or the father which might necessitate a complete reevaluation of their family life. This is not from Sean's lack of trying. Frustrated with the lack of honesty in his household, and with his own growing insecurities, Sean confronts his father, who denies that he is either gay or bi. "I won't explain myself to you," the father says, exercising his patriarchal dominance over his son even after being exposed as participating in sex with other men. (Sean's father frequently belittles him throughout the film.)

Sean rebels against living "in a house where everything is a fucking lie." This moment evokes James Dean's anger at his parents in *Rebel Without a Cause*, but now the subtext of the son's (and father's) sexual confusion can be fully spelled out. However, when Sean angrily exposes his father's secret to his mother, he gets a surprising reaction from her. Instead of becoming mad at her husband, she becomes mad at Sean; she knew all along that the father was bisexual. "This sucks," Sean says, defeated. The mother says: "No. It sucked before, when your dad was always bitter and made my life hell.... He's learned to live with it. And so have I." The implication is that, not only have the husband and wife learned to live with the husband's bisexuality in their own ways, but that her love for him has helped him come to terms with it. The mother tolerantly defines the family — speaking for the progressive views of the film itself— as any configuration of people who come together to love and nurture each other. As if to underscore the fact that his parents' marriage works successfully, Sean later overhears them having loud, passionate sex.

But *Dark Blue Almost Black* has one more ironic twist to its premise of a father and son sharing the same hustler. Both men show up outside the masseur's building at the same time, and the father becomes contrite: "If you stop coming, so will I." "I have a better idea," Sean says with deadpan comic timing. "You get even days, I get odd." The film has achieved its happy end: the son has brought honesty to the family; the father retains his patriarchal control; the family unit remains intact and contented in spite of absorbing potentially subversive, unconventional bisexualities. This is because, for all its winning political correctness, *Dark Blue Almost Black* does not wish to completely sunder the bonds of social institution, just make them elastic enough to include sexual minorities. Far more genuinely radical is Pedro Almodóvar's masterpiece, *Todo Sobre Mi Madre* (*All About My Mother*, 1999), in which patriarchy is eradicated in favor of a makeshift but powerful extended family of soulful, liberated women who find that they do not need men at all.

Except, of course, for purposes of procreation: this immutable biological fact never changes, no matter what else does within a family's structure. Two of the women in Almodóvar's film become impregnated, at different times, by the same man. That man is a transsexual named Lola (Toni Cantó), who prostitutes herself to men and who is dying of AIDS. Back when he was still male, he met and married Manuela (Cecilia Roth) in Barcelona, but during the course of their marriage, he decided to get surgery to become a woman. Manuela says that because he was still much the same as before, "apart from the tits," she went on trying to live with him, but left for Madrid when she became pregnant by him. She became a nurse and raised their son Esteban alone; Esteban was christened after Lola's male birth-name. When Esteban is tragically killed on his eighteenth birthday, Manuela journeys back to Barcelona to find Lola. Instead, she meets a young nun, Hermana Rosa (Penélope Cruz), who has slept with Lola and also become pregnant by him. Manuela becomes enraged at this (she calls Lola "that lousy, fucking bitch!"), almost jealously, as if she had thought that she might have been Lola's last female partner. It turns out that Lola has given Rosa AIDS, and Manuela begins to take care for her. Rosa dies in childbirth; her son survives and is also named Esteban — the third generation of Estebans — according to Rosa's wishes.

Lola's sexual power over women is chalked up to a certain romantic masochism on their part. There is also a pragmatic aspect to their seemingly unlikely love for Lola. Manuela says, self-deprecatingly: "Women will do anything to avoid being alone." Several possible reasons are implied for Rosa's attraction to Lola, all of them dependent on her vulnerability: her youthfulness, her Viridiana-like need to "save the world," her painfully broken relation to her parents, even latent lesbianism.

Lola is an absent presence for most of the film, existing as a malleable if also implacable creature of myth, legend, rumor and memory. Late in the film, he finally appears, at Rosa's funeral. He stands high on the ramparts of an ancient building, his gaunt, shrouded figure surreally recalling Murnau's Nosferatu, an angel of death, or even Jack Fairy, that "shipwreck of the streets," both swaggering and ethereal in the opening credit sequence of *Velvet Goldmine*. Manuela confronts him. He is patriarchy on the way out: "I was always excessive. And I'm very tired. Manuela, I'm dying." She finally tells him that she gave birth to his son eighteen years ago. He rejoices at the news ("I always dreamed of having a son") and pleads with her to be allowed to see him, from a distance if nothing else. She tells him that he died, and they both weep together.

Against the wishes of Rosa's conservative mother (Rosa María Sardà), Manuela takes Rosa's baby to see Lola. (The mother calls Lola "that monster ... who killed my daughter.") Manuela allows Lola to hold the infant Esteban: "You're with Dad," he says, expressing regret at having possibly passed on the AIDS virus to the next generation. Manuela gives him a photograph of the deceased adolescent Esteban. Again, as with his appearance at Rosa's funeral, Lola makes for a somewhat surreal image: a mannish-looking transsexual, dolled up in highly feminine attire, sobbing as he holds the infant son he has just had with Rosa and also the photo of his other son with Manuela. But it is in keeping with Almodóvar's passionately nonjudgmental view of outrageousness that the moment is presented not only as highly poignant and even strangely beautiful, but also somewhat matter-of-factly indicative of a world in which narrow categories are breaking down, intermingling with each other, giving birth to "mutated" figures and giving way to greater openness. Lola literalizes, and takes to extremes, the space-between which the bisexual male often inhabits, as a perfect (or rather perfectly imperfect — since we are meant to see all the obvious bifurcations on display) blending of masculine and feminine personalities, anatomical genders, and heterosexual and homosexual sex drives. Lola is, to use a crude linguistic formula which nonetheless expresses her self-implosion as a sexual sign, the father-fucker as well as the father-fucked; and since the film is "all about [the] mother," she is motherfucker as well, and mother-fucked. She is perhaps the most illegible patriarch in all of cinema.

And a patriarch she remains, for Lola also functions as a blatant critique of machismo, all the more so for being misbegotten, partly female. Almodóvar has said: "The Latin male has a lot of limitation at the moment of his present self, because, you know, a 'macho' is just to be one side only."[6] Women have more sides, more sensitivity, more emotional depth. And yet, although Lola has become something of a woman (and, as a prostitute, an abject one at that), he nonetheless continues to hold macho values associated with patriarchal birthright. He has seduced, impregnated, then abandoned two different women, spreading his seed while taking no responsibility for the women or children. He also prizes the fact that the children he has fathered are males. His machismo has emerged in other ways, too. Manuela relates the fact that, after he got his sex change, he spent all his time on the beach "in a tiny bikini, screwing everything he could," while possessively demanding that she dress demurely. "How could someone act so macho," she says, "with a pair of tits like that?" They first met in an amateur theater group production of *A Streetcar Named Desire*, while he was still a male; she played Stella, and he played the ultimate macho, Stanley Kowalski. Machismo is like a disease even more tenacious than AIDS; in fact, Manuela tells him, "You are not a human being, Lola. You're an epidemic!"

As Almodóvar shows us Lola gazing longingly at the photograph of his adolescent son, the director creates a dizzying image of patriarchy turned inside out, its viscera exposed. Does Lola weep for the boy with his masculine side, as a proud, grieving father? Is he weeping for a patriarchal lineage cut short? Or is he weeping with his feminine side, for a good-looking youth whom he possibly would have, under different circumstances, initiated into sex? (He kisses the photo of Esteban on the lips.) In fact, it must be both, since Lola is nothing if not a person of "halves" — just as Esteban once called him the missing half of his life. "Lola's got," Manuela says, "the worst of a man and the worst of a woman."

Like Jerome in Greenaway's *The Pillow Book*, Lola must die after fulfilling her (male) role as progenitor of children and thereby allowing an all-female family to rise up on the ashes of now thoroughly illegible patriarchies. But somehow, *All About My Mother* does not play as much like unremitting war between the heterosexual female characters and the bisexual/gay male ones. Still, both *Dark Blue Almost Black* and *All About My Mother* valorize the roles of women over the roles of men; the men aspire either to be women (Lola's sex change; Esteban's adoration of Bette Davis and other actresses), or to be as sensitive as the women in their lives (Jorge in *Dark Blue Almost Black*). The idea that women are kinder and more tolerant reflects what actual bisexual males have spoken of as the relative ease in forming relationships with women as opposed to with men, whether because there was greater social support for their relations with women or because the women themselves were perceived as more selfless and loving. "The sex [with men] was neither satisfying nor relaxing and I was always searching for ... emotions.... I started to miss sex with women. I caught myself eyeing couples kissing and hugging in the street."[7] The need for affection (and public displays of it) is certainly an innate human need, regardless of gender or orientation; the fact that boys and girls are still usually socialized along opposite lines (rewarding tough, stoical, competitive behavior in boys, and cooperation and emotional transparency in girls), as well as the fact that society encourages heterosexual activity and discourages same-sex activity, become projected onto women themselves as oases of sanctuary and redemption in a hostile, "all-male" world. But it is easier to see through this societal hypocrisy than it is to make peace with it or find a way around it; and the idea that men and women simply "get along better" recurs often enough in the testimony of bisexual men to suggest that it is a key factor in how they think of themselves and their relationships. "It's easier for a male and female to bond — men and women don't have to create a ritual, men and men have to build a bridge."[8] While this statement may smack of a certain complacency — received rituals do not always make for healthy relationships, marriages and families, while the work of building bridges might in fact be essential to any understanding we may gain about each other — there is some natural biological evidence to support the idea that men and women do complement each other and "fit" together. "With women I feel more able to talk about things that trouble me, to reveal weakness."[9] Partly this is not necessarily strictly biological at all, but again, a result of learned codes of machismo, which require men to behave in colder and more brutal ways. As posited by *Dark Blue Almost Black* and *All About My Mother*, male bisexuality is one of the "evolutionary" cures of this machismo.

"Gonna take a miracle": A Home at the End of the World

Is it ever possible for the procreative family to include male bisexual desire? About this question, the films I have examined in this chapter emerge as being mostly pessimistic. What we tend to see in these films is that the family structure tolerates nothing ambiguous, nothing undefined; in fact, its members derive their meanings from their preordained roles in the family, and any members who resist these narrow roles (father, mother, son, etc.) often find themselves exiled, physically or psychologically, from the protective confines of the family itself.

Also, in all of these films, patriarchs have been highly conspicuous and powerful, sometimes especially where they have seemed most absent. A family is generally structured around a charismatic leader and his followers — even if this power is benign, and even if the leader is not a patriarch per se. Therefore, although bisexuality often constitutes a decentralization of patriarchal control through a greater inclusivity of male and female peers, it becomes subject to the iron laws of the family when it attempts to participate in family life; even when it attempts to construct a new and radicalized family of its own. Thus, the Ur-bisexual triangle in *Rebel Without a Cause*, which we looked at in the last chapter: fleeing the rigid, stultified or loveless structures of their own home lives, Jim, Judy and Plato try to recreate a kind of family, but their basic roles are never given the chance to change — Jim, the closest thing to a patriarch, must be strong and protective; Plato must remain needy and impulsive like a child; etc. The family has a way of overtaking even the most wayward tendency and imposing a generic frame upon it. This occurs in Michael Mayer's *A Home at the End of the World*, in which a young bisexual man, a young gay man, and a young heterosexual woman strive to create a family among themselves, offering each other unconditional acceptance and protection from past childhood traumas. They coexist for a while as a "family of children," so to speak, only to break apart when they themselves become parents and the woman feels compelled to choose between their unconventional, bisexual living arrangement and something more traditional.

The story begins in 1967. Bobby Morrow loses his older brother and his mother at a young age; when his father dies, he is taken in by the Glovers, the family of his high-school friend Jonathan. This friendship includes getting stoned — in a triumphant scene which manages to be uncomfortable, joyous and poignant all at once, Bobby introduces Jonathan's mother Alice (Sissy Spacek) to her first joint while all three dance to Laura Nyro's "Gonna Take a Miracle" — and, later, mutual masturbation between the boys.

Caught at this sex act one night by Alice, Jonathan's ties with his mother are partly sundered, and he decides to move away right after high school. However, somewhat surprisingly, the bond between Alice and Bobby only deepens. He stays on in the Glover household as a surrogate son. In fact, Bobby stays into his adulthood, until the Glovers retire to Arizona and he is forced to find another home. Not surprisingly, the hapless Bobby (Colin Farrell) journeys to New York to relocate Jonathan (Dallas Roberts), who is living in the East Village with Claire (Robin Wright Penn). Jonathan is a gay man, but he and Claire share an intense relationship which they both characterize as love. However, Claire falls in love with Bobby and takes his heterosexual virginity. She becomes pregnant by him, and the three main characters make an attempt to live as a family, moving to a secluded house in Woodstock to raise their new daughter. Over time, Claire becomes jealous of the attention Bobby gives to Jonathan (who has discovered, in a rather low-key subplot, that he has contracted AIDS). Giving up on her hope of having a more conventional married life with Bobby, and acknowledging that the two men are the loves of each other's lives, Claire takes the baby and leaves.

In the film's final shot, Jonathan and Bobby are walking together toward their house; Jonathan goes into the house first, while Bobby lingers outside for a minute or so, staring at the landscape, before finally following Jonathan into the house. This slightly awkward, choreographed delay is meant to suggest Bobby's bisexual nature, divided, in this case, between the part of him that wants to remain with Jonathan and the part of him that is still very much tied to Claire and their daughter. It is only with a sense of resignation that he goes on as a couple (with Jonathan) rather than the idyllic, if now impossible, trio (with Jonathan and Claire). Bobby, one feels, will always hold out for the regeneration of that bisexual idyll.

Mayer has said: "These three characters are completely in love with each other. The other two sort of make up the perfect partner for the one in the whole triangle. So it's quite moving to see them trying so hard to make a life together."[10] To emphasize their triangulated love, Mayer often films all three of them grouped together in medium and long shot, such as one scene where they have a group hug against the backdrop of a vast landscape, and another where they all crowd into the frame to peer down at Claire's newborn. Jonathan and Claire declare love for each other and even talk about having a baby when Bobby first moves in with them, but it is Bobby, not Jonathan, who is, in his childlike openness and neediness, the film's bisexual fulcrum. Actually, Bobby resists labeling. "Why are all the good ones gay?" Claire moans, typically homophile, while watching Bobby thrash around on the dance floor of a punk rock club. "Bobby's not gay," Jonathan says, adding: "Well, it's hard to say exactly *what* Bobby is." It was a stroke of genius to have the chiseled, classically masculine Colin Farrell play Bobby. Farrell's handsomeness and sex appeal tempt viewers to read Bobby in a more strictly heterosexual light, and make it all the more startling whenever he reveals his tenderness for Jonathan. Particularly disarming is the sequence in which Bobby weeps, soulfully and joyously, while Claire devirginizes him, then later wanders fully nude into Jonathan's bed to fall asleep beside him.

Of all the characters, it is Claire who, in one of her frustrated moods, attempts to express their nebulous, shifting love as a bisexual narrative, giving up even as she attempts the impossible work of trying to making the intangible tangible: "How pathetic is *that*, me in love with you [Jonathan], and then Bobby comes along and I fall in love with this one, and then I think that *we*, that the three of us, maybe we — Oh, fuck it!" The kind of loving, three-way marriage she is trying to define cannot be put into words; there is simply no (non-pejorative) word for it in our language.

7. *Illegible Patriarchies* 137

In *A Home at the End of the World* (2004), Bobby (Colin Farrell, left), Jonathan (Dallas Roberts, middle), and Claire (Robin Wright Penn, right) attempt to forge an unconventional family based on the strength of their strong three-way bond. To emphasize how fragile and doomed their quest is, director Michael Mayer films them against vast, inhuman landscapes.

Pain is the biggest motivator of sexuality and elective affinities in *A Home at the End of the World*. Claire endured an abusive relationship with a drug-addicted male; this seems to influence her search for security with Bobby and Jonathan. Bobby's pain — his early childhood losses — have made him extremely passive and amorphous, even somewhat asexual. Even as a teenager he sees himself as doomed to a state of aloneness: "So that's it, man, I'm like the last of my kind now," he cries to Jonathan after his father dies. As a witness to Bobby's lonely, beleaguered boyhood, Jonathan understands the fractured emotional truth behind Bobby's boy-next-door exterior. He understands that Bobby's sexuality is, in some ways, most thoroughly invested with the adult care-givers he had as a child, especially Jonathan's mother. Bobby's intimacy with Alice verges on being disturbingly incestuous in an emotional-psychological way, and though it is not intended to be harmful or negative, Jonathan often winces at how Bobby has displaced him in his own mother's affections. (This is Jonathan's great pain.)

As a sort of perpetual child, Bobby is able to show physical affection toward Jonathan as an extension of the family life in which Bobby's childhood took place. Sexual contact between men is normalized as the extraordinary and special activity of two pseudo-brothers who cling to each other within a nexus of family dysfunction. Bobby is so child-like that sex itself does not even seem to mean to him what it means to others. Bobby's romantic contact with Jonathan is mainly physical cuddling in bed, impulsive kissing ("a little kiss between brothers," Bobby says, "nothing wrong with that"), and in two very poignant scenes, moments of slow dancing. Bobby takes this kind of closeness exactly at face value. For Jonathan, however, these glimpses of Bobby become a kind of golden ideal which he vainly seeks in more prosaic sex with strangers.

But in this drama of projections and surrogates, even Jonathan is a substitute for the beloved older brother who turned Bobby on to rock and roll, fed him his first tab of acid at age nine, and who died at a party running through a sliding glass door. Early in their friendship, Bobby gives Jonathan his brother's jacket to wear. If Plato conceived all material things as copies of ideal forms, then a similar mimesis obtains in the way people learn to form attachments: a male lover is an imitation of a foster brother, who is a further imitation of a real brother, who was himself a substitute for an actual father. ("My son, this is your inheritance," Bobby's brother tells the boy when he takes him to his favorite "stoner spot" in the cemetery.) Like the wheelchair-bound father in *Dark Blue Almost Black*, fathers are infirm in *A Home at the End of the World*: Bobby's father is shown only as a man passed out in bed, a prefigurement of the corpse he will soon become; Jonathan's father has been wasting away for decades. Having a weak, sickly or, indeed, dead father seems to promote the idea that the next generation will be more free to experiment sexually, and that they will elect one of their own (the sexiest, most charismatic male) as surrogate patriarch.

So Bobby, in some ways, comes to replace Jonathan's father, even while still a teenager, not only through his sway over Jonathan but, in a further cathection, through his strong bond with Jonathan's mother. This bond all but forces Jonathan out of his own family when his sexual shame of being gay is revealed. Bobby understands that his presence has awakened Jonathan's gay desire; but when Bobby attempts to leave the house to smooth things over, Jonathan's mother Alice makes her surprising choice of wanting Bobby to stay. A secondary bisexual triangle (without actual sex) forms among Alice, Bobby and Jonathan, with Alice using her affection for Bobby to express her loneliness within her marriage, and perhaps some unconscious hostility toward her gay son and her weak husband. Jonathan's pain of having his first sexual awakening with Bobby witnessed by his mother, and then having this first love psychologically stolen by her, is perhaps what fuels his inability to truly become close to anyone as an adult: the sex he has with men is promiscuous and anonymous, and he is hesitant (perhaps rightly so) to allow Bobby to fully charm his way back into his heart. Jonathan experiences patriarchy's Saturnian command to all its sons: to die, to sacrifice themselves that the father might live; and die he does. The specter of patriarchy — or more precisely, Freudian Oedipalization — hangs over these characters even when they have nominally divested themselves of father-figures as such. Rather, "fatherness" (as bringer of shame, as rival threat, as stealer of maternal affection) migrates from one character to the next at different times. It is through other brother-figures that a diffuse patriarchy is eternally passed on, learned and unlearned and learned all over again. To grow up in a family (as nearly all of us do) is to be inculcated with a yearning for family structure, even a yearning for the scars that structure inflicts. It is as a final capitulation to the yearning for their family of origin that Bobby and Jonathan reach their final decision (not without intense heartache) of remaining together as a male couple without Claire and the baby. We have no reason to think that this decision is in any way motivated by sex, but rather by ongoing desire for the consolation of displaced or depleted family bonds.

Actress Robin Wright Penn has said: "We're all born with that need to have family or a home."[11] This need for family is certainly borne out in the experience of bisexual males. "It would be easier to swim in the same direction as the rest of the fish. There are moments that it would be neat to have marriage and a house with a white picket fence."[12] The bisexual couple that forms between Bobby and Jonathan can be read as a metaphor for the need of bisexual and gay men to be able to form families, or to fit more comfortably into their heterosexual families of origin, even if, in the case of Bobby and Jonathan, their love is basically a celebration of their family of origin. It is a case of exceptional bisexuality, dependent wholly on Bobby's need to remain a child-man, with Jonathan being the magic ingredient in this, since he represents childhood. Another film which examines the same type of exceptional bisexuality, albeit more from the standpoint of twisted comedy, is *Chuck & Buck* (2000). The child-like Buck (Mike White) reenters the life of his childhood friend Chuck (Chris Weitz) in order to rekindle their "best friendship," which included experimental sex games. For the gawky, grinning, unworldly Buck, his fixation on these sex games represents recapturing a lost spirit of innocent fun (what Buck calls "the good old days" of backyard camp-outs and make-believe games), but Chuck, now working in the music business in L.A. and living with his fiancée Carlyn (Beth Colt), would like nothing more than to repress that spirit, since it does not fit in with the competitive adult world he aspires to conquer. "He's not a very sentimental guy," Chuck's fiancée says about him. It becomes Buck's mission to recall his friend to that childhood state where affection is possible and not shameful.

Based on his sexual experiences with Buck, Chuck qualifies as bisexual, though the film establishes that he would never respond in such a powerful and intimate way to any other man besides the one who represents "childhood" to him. Both *A Home at the End of the World* and *Chuck & Buck* allow for certain characters to behave like children disguised as adults, so to speak. Buck is even more regressed than Bobby (he is always playing with toys), but his *Kindermenschheit* functions in a similar way, to neutralize the more subversive aspects of his sexual contact with Chuck. Oral gratification is conflated with the many lollipops and other sweet treats which Buck moons over and devours throughout the film. Nonetheless, both films suggest that in the adult world of stress and loss, men need some way of recapturing their sense of childhood play, and of getting their needs for reassuring intimacies met; and that bisexuality can be a way of doing this. Chuck, and the rest of the straight world, are made to seem heartless and cruel for outgrowing their natural bisexual tendencies.

Because they are trying to stubbornly hammer out some kind of family to right all the wrongs of their lives, the trio in *A Home at the End of the World* never outgrow each other. On the contrary, they keep trying to make things work out among them. Similar to Luc's tragic recognition, in Ozon's *Criminal Lovers*, that not even his all-inclusive bisexual experience can protect himself or his loved ones from harm, Bobby, too, must accept that he cannot "save the world," in spite of his own big-hearted bisexual wish to do precisely that. Claire, perhaps because she is an outsider to Bobby and Jonathan's childhood loves and traumas, is the one who comes to feel that the triangle is untenable, and is unable to stay in the relationship. Becoming a mother redefines her as someone intolerant of unconventional sexuality. (Much like Alice, in fact, she ends up trying to take Bobby away from Jonathan, in order to have Bobby all for herself.) This pessimistic choice for Claire is, perhaps, short-sightedness on the part of Mayer and Michael Cunningham (who adapted the screenplay from his own novel); one is reminded of how Téchiné ends *The Witnesses* with a mélange of straight, gay and bisexual characters coming together to raise the new baby, the next generation. One of Claire's first real moments of unease around Bobby and Jonathan is in watching them tenderly playing with her newborn daughter; not only does she feel left out of their co-fathering ("Daddy One and Daddy Two," Jonathan jokingly calls them), but she seems to experience the sight of male intimacy as wrong in and of itself.

Claire embodies Hollywood's fraught and often thankless vision of the Bisexual Male's Girlfriend: the assumption is often that there must be something wrong with her, or something unnatural. Like Mandy in *Velvet Goldmine*, Claire is very much an artificially constructed woman. She is given to outlandish, fashion-victim hairstyles. After watching Bobby and Jonathan in one of their intimate dances, she questions her own ability to stay in this unconventional triangle: "You know, I think maybe I'm not this unusual. I think maybe it's just my hair." When Bobby first shows up at the apartment she shares with Jonathan, she is in the middle of putting on her elaborate make-up: one eye is heavily painted and the other is bare. "Okay, I'll just put on my other eye," she says, "and we're out of here." This rather obviously suggests the character's part-time blindness. As a woman who chooses to love both a gay male and a bisexual male, and have a baby with the bisexual male, the implication is that she sees only what she chooses to see. Again, she must be presented, by Hollywood's standards, as blind, freakish, unnatural. "She's quite lost," Wright Penn says of Claire, but goes on to defend her character with a classic valorization of bisexual activity, as a healthy alternative to the social norms of love: "You know, you can't find everything in one person, nor will you ever; it's the sadness of love, and [Claire] realizes that — that dream that is so 'what society plays on your heart,' she wants it but it's not her."[13]

8

Fazes and Mazes: Inside the Triangle

> Touching a reality beyond words, the bloody ground has become a sweet, sad bed sheet of reconciliation. Three bodies are conjoined, I in a woman, a man in me. Am I still clinging to my mother while trying to win my father's withheld love? Is my life a revised replay of the primal scene I witnessed as a child, I possessing both my mother and father? If true, then my bisexuality can play with even these neuroses and make them life-affirming.[1]

In films, male bisexuality is almost always dramatized as a twist on the classic love triangle: a man is in love or sexually involved with two different people at once, but instead of the heterosexual model of one man plus two women, it is now one man plus one woman and one man. From a dramatic standpoint, this "works" to encapsulate and intensify the bisexual male's ongoing dilemma: *whom do I love; what do I like about each gender; do I prefer one over another; can I have both?* It also sometimes distorts the actual reality of bisexual lives. But where bisexuality remains encoded at the level of thought, emotion or desire, it often remains too subtle, too evanescent, for the camera to capture. Films are behavioralist in nature; they ask us to observe characters in given situations and to consider the truth of these characters and situations as arising from what the characters actually do. Therefore, the love triangle — already enshrined as a convention of the romantic-dramatic and romantic-comic genre — becomes identical with being able to identify a male as bisexual: *he loves two, therefore he exists.*

Structurally, there are a few constant, nearly unchanging elements of the bisexual love triangle, no matter how much the details or circumstances or settings might change. These elements reflect powerful, primal emotions, life-changing moments, and psychologically "typical" reactions. Again, there are inevitable distortions in many films, inevitable assumptions of what would be, even under the fairly atypical conditions of bisexual relationships (atypical by definition), the way people go about things, the way they handle themselves, the way they respond. Most mainstream films are still constructed in slavish devotion to what an audience is presumed to "want" to see — or what it is presumed it will tolerate or recognize. When the subject of bisexuality is taken up by the mainstream, these laws of averages are applied to it as they are to every other subject. And yet, by its very nature, bisexuality challenges the assumptions of precisely what most people want, see, and recognize. This is why male bisexuality is increasingly employed as a "twist" on the conventional love triangle (by a movie industry whose essential meaning hinges on a contradiction in terms: always give the audience something new, but always rely on the tried and true, the surefire, the bankable) while reifying the primacy of the convention itself.

The first distinct element of the bisexual love triangle, the foundational element, is, therefore, the bisexual male's dilemma of being torn between loving women and men. In Gerardo Vera's *Segunda Piel* (*Second Skin*, 1999), Alberto (Jordi Mollà) is more or less happily married to Elena (Ariadna Gil) and simultaneously engaged in a passionate, semi-public love affair with Diego (Javier Bardem). He goes back and forth between them with an almost blind ability to compartmentalize his feelings. His feelings, nonetheless, are strong; he tells both that he loves them on a regular basis. Indeed, he does not seem able to disappoint either one of them, as though being able to be there for both of them is part of what he wants, as well. For Elena as well as the slightly effeminate, sexually passive Diego, Alberto is the masculine "anchor" in their lives. He demonstrates masculinity as a performance, to be enacted equally with a woman as with a man. Conducting this performance causes him to defer, or refuse to identify, his own needs. He cries when he admits to Diego that he has never actually done anything in life that he truly wanted to do: "I've spent my entire life passing everyone else's tests." Part of the drama of bisexuality is that it causes masculine men, stoical, closed-off emotionally, to unlock those internal feelings which they keep under tight rein, segregated from the rational system of their lives. He also cries with Elena, when she tells him she is leaving him: he throws himself into her arms and sobs, "Please help me."

But for Alberto, the stakes are too high. He speaks of a game he played as a boy, running into the ocean as far as he could, until the waves nearly swept him away and his mother worried for his safety. Is Elena the mother, whom he defies by running into the "ocean" of his love for Diego? Or is the ocean simply an image for the infinite waters of emotional life itself, with Alberto seeing how far he can go and still remain afloat? He is upset at the thought that people might think he is gay — "I know people don't care," he says, "but I'm not like that" — and when things with Diego threaten to become too public, too intense, he lashes out by sleeping with one of Diego's female friends. He is so used to lying, to being partly alone even in his most intimate relationships, that keeping a distance becomes second nature. It isn't only to maintain his one major sexual secret, but to keep to himself what he calls "the shit we all carry inside." Even love does not seem to allow him to let down his guard. He fights with Diego, who says, "I just want you to understand me, the real me," to which Alberto, nearly beside himself with frustration and heartache, shouts, "You could do the same!"

This last point is crucial. The bisexual male characters in these films usually do not begin with an agenda, or even a fixed pattern of response. They fall in love with women and men based on impulse and the feelings which these people inspire in them, not because they are this or that gender, or this or that "type." In keeping with the fact that he understands himself to be complex and perhaps flawed, the bisexual male seems to accept his partners, for the most part, for their own complexities and flaws. The bisexual male never tries to change anyone: Alberto wants his wife to be a straight woman; wants Diego to be a gay man. But, in *Second Skin* and other films, the partners do not accept the bisexual man's complexity, wanting to be able to rely on him as a single sexual dimension, rather than allowing him to be who he is.

To a certain extent, this is because Alberto, again, plays such a masculine role for his partners: protective, tough, charming, supportive. By itself, with either Elena and Diego, this masculinity would be ideal. But its perceived strength is undermined by the fact that he needs both and cannot choose between them. Both Elena and Diego are so caught up in the pain that Alberto's bisexuality causes them, that they cannot see the real him, cannot see his pain. Several times in the film, Alberto smacks himself in the face, as if to dramatize his inner turmoil and to punish himself. At its deepest level, his pain is that of not knowing who he is. "If I'm not *that* Alberto," he wonders, meaning the Alberto who has gone through life meeting others' expectations and enacting the role of husband and father, "then who am I?" He has tried to create a situation in which he can have it all, but what he actually needs remains elusive, since it is tied to how he feels about himself. He can have uninhibited, fulfilling sex with Diego, but cannot stand beside him at a cocktail party. He can have a loving domestic marriage with Elena, but still thinks about, as he confesses to her in one scene, sleeping with someone else.

The "I" whom Alberto cannot accept is the bisexual "I," the deepest and most challenging realization for a bisexual male. Tragically, Alberto cannot ever make the parts of his life add up, and in a rash moment, commits suicide by crashing his motorcycle. He needed his deceptions and self-delusions more than anyone realized, and when he lost the ability to lie to himself, to lie to his loved ones, and to keep the different parts of his psyche separate, he lost everything. While equally existential, the dilemma of Carlos in the bisexual sequence of *Possible Loves* is not as unbalanced and all-consuming. Carlos is torn between his lingering love for his ex-wife Julia, and intense love for Pedro, the man whom he left her for. With Julia, he can be close to their son Lucas, and have a family life; Pedro cannot give him this. He says: "Gays can't have kids. Cats at most. And I hate cats." Carlos, like many bisexual males, has fallen in love with a man (Pedro) but not with the gay lifestyle; this side of his identity is still an uneasy fit. In some ways, he feels more natural with Julia: "You were the woman of my life," he tells her. At the same time, he calls Pedro "the only one I trust." Like Alberto, Carlos is reluctant to let go of any intense feeling he conceives for someone, and almost sees it as part of being a man — a good man — to be there for those who love him, Julia and Pedro alike.

Carlos' son Lucas is wise beyond his age, and, seeing his father going back and forth between relationships, asks him: "Do you like mom or Pedro?" His question is posed with all the common-sense innocence in the world, and it strikes at the core of Carlos' identity. He answers his son seriously and honestly: "Both of them, son, in different ways. If only I could have them both." "Can't you?" Lucas asks, a poignant question: not least of all because Carlos has been trying and failing to do exactly this throughout the film, but also because Lucas now sounds more like the child he is, assuming that there would be nothing "impossible" about such a situation. Is bisexuality, in part, a kind of childlike thinking, the belief that love and gratification can never be bad or harmful, and that adult problems and responsibilities can be indefinitely deferred? Lucas is too young to understand sexuality yet, but *Possible Loves* implies that in the future (represented by Lucas, the next generation) such loves may be even more "possible," as people evolve into a state of placing fewer and fewer limitations on their emotional lives.

But regardless of what the future holds for society, male bisexual flexibility remains problematic for some in the present. In *Leaving Metropolis* (2002), Matt (Vince Corazza) runs a diner with his wife Violet (Cherilee Taylor), and begins to feel attracted to David (Troy Ruptash), a gay painter who works for them as a waiter. Like Alberto in *Second Skin*, Matt prides himself on his strength: in a running theme of the film, he identifies with the comic book hero, Superman. He finds himself restless in the routine of his marriage, and feeling the powerful attraction which David arouses in him. He tells David: "I like women, I've always liked women, I've never wanted to do anything like this before." He says that he is drawn to David partly because of his artistic talent: "I like talent — talented people." He also says that David makes him "feel": "There's something about you." Still, when the two men kiss for the first time, Matt pulls away at first to insist on reminding David: "I'm straight." Matt will not permit his activity with David labeled as part of a larger identity or syndrome; for him, it is sui generis. Yet it is also real. Matt's reiteration of his straight identity is not to prevent sex from happening with David, but rather to impose a condition on how the openly gay David will have to regard their intimacy. This is like Jeffrey's comment to Robert in *The Dying Gaul*: "You can do anything you want as long as you don't call it what it is."

Matt is only beginning to come to some kind of bisexual awareness. He finds that he enjoys being with both Violet and David. In a montage, we see him "fertilizing" both of his lovers at one time: the film cuts back and forth between him having sex with Violet, giving her an orgasm, and David alone in his studio, breaking his creative block by painting a nude, erotic portrait of Matt. In another scene, Matt substitutes David for Violet in his imagination while she is performing oral sex on him. The need for both a male and female lover becomes stronger and stronger in Matt, but so does his denial. When his secret threatens to be made public, Matt wants to end the relationship with David: "I don't love you. I lied." At the same time, he continues to want both Violet and David in his life, perhaps out of unwillingness to let either of them down, or perhaps because the need to be adored (like his idol, Superman) is intrinsic to Matt's selfhood. In the end, he takes the brave step of revealing his affair with David to Violet, telling her that he has always loved her and still does. This protestation that he really does love both the woman and the man is merely an expression of who Matt is, as a bisexual; yet it cannot help feeling duplicitous at times to the partners who must share him — like the kind of "line" a guilty husband uses when seeking forgiveness. Indeed, Matt loses both Violet and David.

Matt liked the way he appeared in David's paintings: a muscle-bound, boyish caped crusader, wise and soulful and sexy. "I never saw him like that," Violet says when she finally sees the paintings herself. For Violet, David is part of her doll-house existence: she collects dolls, not for their camp value but out of a sincere affinity for them. She says, "I just like a doll's life — it's perfect, you know." Part of this existence is that David fulfills her expectations of the perfect doll-like husband, always coming home on time and never forgetting to put the toilet seat down. Neither Violet nor David can understand Matt the way the other one sees him, and ultimately neither of them can accept his or her own vision of Matt after they have seen each other's. It is a complicated psychological and emotional moment, in which the bisexual man is knocked from his pedestal, so to speak, for the "crime" of inspiring different kinds of love in different people. Again, like Alberto in *Second Skin*, he is not allowed, by dint of his masculine role, to be as complex as he himself allows his female partner and his gay partner to be.

What Alberto, Carlos and Matt all share is a powerful and consuming sense of guilt at needing love from more than one person, and more than one gender. This is why the bisexual male seldom appears self-righteous about being bisexual — not only because bisexuality lacks the political clout which feminism has largely won for women, and which the gay rights movement has won, to a lesser degree, for gay men, but because the bisexual male approaches his partner from a position of wanting to have certain intimacy needs met. These needs may seem duplicitous, even hurtful, but they are no less genuine for that. The bisexual male tends to accept those who meet his needs for who they are, at face value, as it were, in the hope, perhaps, that they would accept him in the same way.

* * *

Another structural element of the triangle involves the reactions of the bisexual male's two partners, the woman and the man. Often, these partners come to represent, not particular individuals, but representatives of their entire gender or sexual orientation. The woman involved with the bisexual male becomes all of womankind, or all of heterosexuality. For the bisexual male to love her, or to betray, reject and move away from her, implies his feelings about womankind and heterosexuality. Likewise, the gay male partner comes to represent all of homosexuality. Even when the triangle is not directly depicted as a contest, the audience is often hard pressed not to keep a kind of running score of the bisexual male's conquests and attachments: "one for this side," "one for the other side," and so on.

These may seem like dramatic oversimplifications, but they may not be entirely inaccurate from a psychological standpoint. A woman who loves a man, believing him to be exclusively straight and finding out that he is actually bisexual, may feel as though the part of him that does love her has died, so to speak; that he is no longer hers in any way, shape or form. The gay man who "turns" a bisexual man away from his female partner may believe that he has successfully converted a straight man, and may feel proud of this, as a kind of undermining or direct assault upon heterosexual hegemony. Unfortunately, neither of these reactions is commensurable with the actual feelings of the bisexual male, who remains attracted to both. The bisexual love triangle is a constant reminder that, in cases of intersubjective response, we can never see things exclusively from our own given viewpoint: where others are concerned, our viewpoint is a false one, distorted by allegiances to self as well as to group identifications. What the bisexual male struggles with — the central question deterritorializing his identity — must be passed on to the two partners, who must learn to accept that they, too, are relative rather than absolute.

These lessons are difficult to absorb, of course, in a context of passionate romantic love and sexuality, in which we enter a world of absolutes by definition. Love is mainly an internal illusion, even where it is fulfilled and untroubled by external contingencies. We magnify what we admire most in someone, minimize whatever bothers us. We tell ourselves, "*It must be*," and thereby extend a feeling — fleeting by definition, rippling on the stream of consciousness — into the central, immutable fact of that consciousness. This is what is called "commitment." Love is always a house built on water. Commitment is the insistence that the water is actually land.

Needless to say, then, the two partners often have strong, instinctual reactions to the bisexual male. They not only seek to defend their existential territory but to reclaim that wholeness of absolute identity which they view as defining them. The bisexual male begins with the difficult attempt to love people rather than categories, specific moments rather than "lifetimes," pleasures and bodies rather than genders; put otherwise, to escape from destiny and determination. But he ends up stuck in a situation where the "objects" of his love refuse to be anything but examples of their respective categories. Enraged and embittered after Carlos leaves her for Pedro in *Possible Loves*, Julia cuts her hair extremely short and begins to dress boyishly, as if she could no longer be a woman now that Carlos has revealed that he also loves a man. But Julia's rage extends far beyond changing her appearance. She tells Carlos that his betrayal has turned her into a vicious homophobe who cannot see gay men on the street without seething about Pedro: "You've turned me into this monster I've become, prejudiced, angry, resentful." In *Leaving Metropolis*, Violet is also viciously homophobic toward Matt when he comes out to her as bisexual, pulling a kitchen knife on him, calling him "Cocksucker!" and slapping his face. One danger inherent in male bisexual coming-out is the fear of homophobia, which is a feature of the heterosexual world. To be in a bisexual closet — to have one foot in the heterosexual world and one foot in the gay one — is to sometimes be made to witness one's straight friends displaying homophobia, making gay jokes, insults, etc. Understandably, the bisexual male might internalize such negativity. By announcing that one has same-sex feelings, one becomes a representative or an adherent of a hated group; this is a barrier to expressing the feelings at all.

Julia even goes so far as to tell Carlos that she hopes he will contract AIDS and die from his new lifestyle. In Julia's defense, she still loves him and wants him back (as Pedro senses). "Did you ever stop to think how difficult it is for me, Carlos?" she asks, reaffirming not so much the specific problems of bisexual love triangles as those of love triangles in general. The abandoned partner has not been "enough" for her lover, he did not respect the commitment she expected: this pain, which stems from the deepest core of an individual, is often called "fear of abandonment," and has to do with a deeply ingrained, irrational belief that one does not deserve to have even one's most basic needs met. Being with someone who leaves you for someone else can trigger such abandonment issues. But is dependency — or co-dependency — any healthier, in the long run, that the possible pain caused by bisexual infidelity?

Macho Latin cultures seem to encourage a kind of gender-essentialist thinking. Like Julia, Elena in *Second Skin* goes through a process of cutting her hair very short and wearing distinctly unfeminine attire when she feels Alberto straying. She is "sickened" when she learns of Alberto's gay affair. Her suspicions have already been aroused when he leaves his cell phone off for long periods of time, and part of her pain is that he assumes he can get away with it: "You think I'm stupid?" she snaps at him in the scene where she confronts him. During this scene she also gardens nonstop, throwing herself into angrily planting flowers as if to deny the reality of what is happening. The flowers represent her hopes that her marriage to Alberto would grow, hopes that now seem dashed. "It's just that I feel this huge void," she admits tearfully. She blames herself for her husband's bisexuality: "What did I do that drove you into the arms of a man?"

Anger is, of course, only a cover for a deeper heartache, which can be much longer lasting. Like Julia in *Possible Loves*, Manuela in *All About My Mother* has never completely gotten over her marriage to the bisexual transsexual Lola, her first love. When she learns that Lola has slept with and impregnated Rosa, Manuela becomes angry, partly because Lola is up to her old tricks, and partly, it seems, out of lingering jealousy. Her still-sore pain of having to share Lola with the hundreds of nameless men and women whom Lola slept with during their marriage has now narrowed down to a new triangle: Manuela, Lola, and Rosa. It is one thing to accept the idea that one's partner is pursuing an unconventional sexuality, another thing to feel that the partner might actually love someone else, someone with an identifiable name and face. This also seems to fuel Mandy Slade's ultimate sense of betrayal in

Velvet Goldmine, when she attacks Brian for being childish and selfish. But in some ways, Mandy's accusation feels somewhat hollow: she has gone along for the "rock star ride," even helped Brian achieve his stardom. She accepts that he can play at being gay and turn on lots of people, but his love for Curt brings home to her the reality of her husband's bisexual feelings.

Indeed, Mandy, much like Mac in *Kinsey*, occupies the delicate, painful position of being hurt by her husband's bisexual affairs but not wanting to seem like a hypocrite. Both entered their marriages with their eyes more or less open. Mandy was drawn to Brian's androgynous image and sexual adventurousness; Mac understood that her husband's life was invested in progressive sex research. Both women are unconventional enough, in themselves, to be attracted to unconventional men, and brilliant enough to not only keep up with brilliant men but to inspire them in their quests. It is touching to see them react painfully, nonetheless, when the true reality of their situations dawns on them: bisexuality is not just a gimmick for Brian to win over his fans, or a theoretical proposition for Kinsey. But Mandy's and Mac's superior intellects cannot rationalize away what they feel on an instinctive, emotional level, not being able to have their husbands all to themselves, and in fact having to share them with men.

Likewise, the brilliant, troubled Nagiko, in *The Pillow Book*, pushes her bisexual lover Jerome into an affair with her publisher, partly to further her own writing career. At the same time, she is deeply hurt by the fact that Jerome seems to go along with this plan so willingly and seems to be "having too much fun." Where is the line crossed? Jerome can do nothing right: she wants him to sleep with the publisher to prove that he loves her, and she also wants him to reject the publisher as proof of the same thing. Her fantasy of exiling homosexuality from her relationship with Jerome is frustrated, from the beginning, by the fact of his bisexuality, of which she was always aware. But in love, illusions die hard.

An actual bisexual male has offered similar testimony about his female partner's wavering acceptance of his gay side: "At the beginning, she had no problem with [my bisexuality]. We had a lot of fun sitting in a park watching men and talking about the ones that attracted us. Later, she started to have trouble with my 'second' sexuality. In her mind she could never compare to a man and will never fulfill all my sexual wishes."[2] The pain of knowing that one cannot completely satisfy someone whom one loves is, to a large extent, natural and understandable. Many bisexual males in films attempt to lessen what they need from others, as a way of not causing this pain. Sadly, they become used to the idea of standing alone in life, even being somewhat alone within their own relationships. So, Alberto attempts to be as accommodating

8. Fazes and Mazes

This shot from *Kinsey* (2004) literalizes the bisexual love triangle as an actual geometrical shape. Kinsey (Liam Neeson, middle) is involved with both his wife Mac (Laura Linney) and his research assistant Clyde (Peter Sarsgaard). But the triangle's energy is about to shift, when Mac and Clyde also begin a sexual affair of their own.

as possible to Elena when she discovers his secret, asking her what he can do to help save their marriage. "Alberto," she says, looking at him penetratingly, "I can't be a man."

Most of the female partners in bisexual cinema express their anger very demonstratively and directly. By contrast, Elaine's anger in *The Dying Gaul* is far more restrained and passive-aggressive, and because of this, more chilling. She hides behind pseudonymous screen-names to infiltrate her husband Jeffrey's gay affair with Robert. For a long time, she goes on living with Jeffrey, concealing the fact that she knows. In one scene they cuddle in bed, and she tries to harp upon his guilt, murmuring: "I think I see parts of you that no one else does. And you don't know how much goodness there is in there, waiting to stir up a storm." This declaration is completely ironic on her part. Her resentment, of course, is that there are parts of Jeffrey she has *never* seen, or never even guessed, e.g., his bisexuality. The loaded "storm" metaphor is a veiled warning that only something bad will come of his deception. Later, she employs the same quiet, cold-blooded sarcasm against Robert when he advises her to "look for the positive." "Well, good," she says, "I'll look for the positive in you fucking Jeffrey behind my back, over and over again."

Although they appear far less frequently, there are sometimes moments in bisexual cinema where the bisexual man's male partner — "the other man," as it were — expresses a sense of betrayal or anger or jealousy. (Perhaps it is presumed that men dissociate sex from emotions more, or that a gay man would tend to dwell more on the feeling of victory at having "converted" a seemingly heterosexual man.) Again, in *The Dying Gaul*, Robert complains about his relationship with Jeffrey: "I think he's just using me for sensation because his marriage has gotten stale." There are several important negative assumptions in this line. First, Robert feels, on some level, "used" by Jeffrey. He also assumes that Jeffrey is only with him for the "sensation" — as a sexual, physical stimulus and nothing more. His epitaph for Jeffrey's marriage to Elaine further assumes that he needs to see Jeffrey's heterosexual side as a dead letter, over and done with, a non-issue. Neither of Robert's assumptions turns out to be accurate; they arise from an inability to understand the bisexual male for who he is. Jeffrey does feel something for Robert, something more than sexual (though he cannot show it), and he simultaneously loves and has fulfilling sex with Elaine.

This difficulty which the male partner has in understanding the bisexual man stems mainly from the fact that the male partner is generally either fully straight or fully gay. In Téchiné's *Changing Times*, Bilal is a teenaged Moroccan who is seemingly straight but carries on a sexual affair with Sami. At one point, Bilal takes Sami to task at for being indecisive: "You don't know what you want." Bilal couches the accusation as a kind of life-advice, an ironic reprise of the sexual roles they play, in which Bilal, though younger, is "the man" and Sami "the woman." Indeed, because he works hard and has given up drinking, Bilal seems to feel himself to be more of a man than Sami. But is this also part of Bilal's complex act of "rough trade" seduction toward Sami — playing the judgmental, "shaming" conservative to Sami's profligate? Bilal also brings up the subject of Nadia, the woman whom Sami loves and lives with in Paris; so there may be more than a hint of jealousy as well in Bilal's lecture. Ultimately, Bilal might not be able to see a future for himself and Sami, but he seems to resent being relegated to only one corner of the Frenchman's life.

Similarly, in *Possible Loves*, when Pedro senses that Carlos is thinking about going back to Julia, he becomes sulky, peevish, depressed. Pedro comes home from soccer to find Carlos cooking dinner for Lucas and Lucas in Pedro's chair: "When I went out, this seat was still mine," he says in a tone of gentle sadness. "I went out and you put someone in my place." In the same tone, he excuses himself from the table to go and "take a bunch of sleeping pills." No one likes the feeling that he can be replaced at a moment's notice, and this insecurity is one which bisexual males are often accused of conjuring. However, because he truly loves Carlos and recognizes that Carlos still has feelings for Julia that he needs to figure out, Pedro suggests that he does return to her and try to work things out: "Just be careful you don't fall flat on your face. You can't forget that you spent three years living with another man." Again, as we see in bisexual love triangles, the partners of the bisexual male often simply want to be acknowledged, on some level: that they meant something to him, that the love was real, that he was invested in them, and that his identity has been (at least partially) shaped by them. Bisexuality threatens to render attachments meaningless in some ways, and the partners who love the bisexual male do not wish to fall into a kind of interchangeability with each other. But the problem is not that there is too little love, or no love at all, in the bisexual love triangle, but on the contrary, that the bisexual male elicits powerful feelings of love, and that he loves both. Likewise, in *Second Skin*, Diego wants a deeper relationship than the married Alberto can provide. He is upset by all the things which are obstacles to greater intimacy between them: when Alberto's cell phone rings during sex, or when Alberto cannot stay after sex to eat dinner with Diego. At one point, he accuses Alberto of making the other people in his life do "the dirty work," suffering over Alberto's unavailability and inability to wholly commit. Diego tends to be more depressive than angry, taking walks along the beach by himself and staring out to sea.

Like Elaine in *The Dying Gaul*, David in *Leaving Metropolis* is more passive-aggressive in his negative feelings toward his married lover. He also channels them into his artwork. He paints an erotic portrait of Matt, nude and seen from behind, looking over his shoulder as if surprised in the middle of something: he squeezes the blood out of two hearts, one in each fist. The painting's symbolism is obvious: the hearts represent Violet and David, with David's heart clutched, like a guilty secret, behind Matt's back. Throughout the film it seems as if the terminally ironic David gets angry only when Matt always wants to be on top during sex. But after his closest friend dies of AIDS, David has a complete change of heart about everything: he recognizes the instability of his own position as a gay man in love with a man who will sacrifice him at any time in order to maintain his own straight image. In a gay bath house, David has a vision of the ghosts of dead gay men rising from the steam. Suffering confers on David the ability to be self-righteous, a kind of empowerment, as with Robert in *The Dying Gaul*; and also like Robert, David begins to feel that sleeping with a straight man is a betrayal of homosexuality itself. AIDS has re-politicized categories of sexual orientation, drawing divisive lines between gay and straight, and reinforcing allegiances. But the two elements bear a spurious relation to each other: it is not as though AIDS patients "died in vain" if a gay man sleeps with a bisexual man, and certainly not if the gay man chooses to practice safe sex so as not to become infected and thereby add one more to the roster of the dead. After all, liberation means the ability to love and be loved by whomever one chooses. From a human standpoint, David's pain (again, like Robert's in *The Dying Gaul*) is more survivor's guilt than anything truly political — but whether or not these films can "solve" these delicate issues is far less important than the fact that they raise them.

* * *

There is a final structural element of the bisexual love triangle, but it is so rare that it appears in very few films: eventual reconciliation between the female partner and the other male partner, between the straight and gay worlds, so to speak. The two "bottom points" of the triangle meet and come together. They have the understanding that they have both shared the love of the same man, and grow close to each other as a result. Téchiné's *The Witnesses* offers such a moment, when Sara attends the birthday party of her husband's young male lover, Manu, and gives him a tape recorder so that he can record his life story before he dies of AIDS. By the fireplace, Manu asks her if she is afraid to be close to him; she says no, and he challenges her, in that case, to give him a kiss. She kisses him on the lips, a moment which simultaneously transcends any jealousy she might have felt toward her husband's boyfriend and any fear she might have felt at the thought of becoming infected through casual contact with the young man.

The bisexual male's death, or nearness to death, is often the cause of reconciliation between his partners when such reconciliation occurs. After Alberto dies in *Second Skin*, Diego seeks out Elena and, in spite of some initial mistrust, they begin to talk and comfort each other. Sadly, Elena and Diego can come together only when it is too late to save Alberto, but in a sense, what unites them is the fact that, unlike Alberto, they are each comfortable in who they are, their societal roles: straight woman and gay man, ironically, have more in common with each other than with the bisexual male they have both loved.

* * *

Based on the best-selling novel by Michael Chabon, *The Mysteries of Pittsburgh* employs the bisexual love triangle (and bisexual exploration) as a kind of rite of passage for a young man learning to break free from his painful childhood memories and family life; learning to find his own way to adult manhood and learning to love. Art Bechstein (Jon Foster) has just graduated from college and is about to spend his final summer of youth before becoming a stockbroker. He does not really want to be a stockbroker; he is not very ambitious, and is content to work in a bookstore. His father, Joseph (Nick Nolte), prods him to take on more responsibility and direction in life. Joseph Bechstein is a Mafia chieftain, and although Joseph tries to keep his criminal activities out of his son's life, these activities have already permanently damaged their relationship: Art's mother was killed, when Art was nine, by a car bomb meant for Art's father.

At a party, Art meets Jane (Sienna Miller), and his feeling of being stuck in a rut immediately begins to change. Over coffee and pie, she tells him she wants to break through to a new level of honesty and intimacy: "If you tell me something you've never said out loud before, then this moment becomes unique, becomes indelible," she says. He confides to her his fear of death, dating from his mother's death. There are times when he feels as if he vanishes, like a disembodied spirit in a kind of limbo, and no one can see him. The next day, a mysterious man on a motorcycle shows up at the bookstore where Art works. Wearing black leather from head to toe and with his head encased in a helmet, he announces himself as "Death." Art assumes he is a hit man sent to kill him in reprisal for something his father has done, but he gets on the back of the stranger's bike anyway. They ride out to an abandoned factory, nicknamed the Cloud Factory because it still produces puffs of smoke from its smokestack.

The stranger turns out to be Jane's boyfriend Cleveland (Peter Sarsgaard). He tries to seem intimidating, but in a prankish way: Art says in voiceover, "He looked more like a court jester than a criminal." Cleveland pretends to be jealous that Art had coffee with Jane. Then, to help Art overcome his fear of death, he throws him off a walkway high above the factory; the stunned Art lands in a safety net. It is the first of a number of catharses which Cleveland, hell-bent on having fun and being wild, will provide. Cleveland knows Art's secret: an associate of Art's criminal cousins, he knows who Joseph Bechstein is. This creates an instant bond between him and Art. But Cleveland's wild side seems to know no limits: he gambles and runs up serious debts. Art, Jane and Cleveland go to a punk rock club; Art goes looking for Cleveland and finds him in the men's room, performing oral sex on a man. Later that night, Cleveland squabbles with Jane and tells Art to take her home. Is Cleveland pushing Art to sleep with Jane because he secretly wants Art? And whom does Art want? This latter question becomes a source of tension within the trio, a tension which builds during a weekend in the country when Cleveland gets drunk and asks Art: "Do you want to fuck my girlfriend.... Or do you want to fuck me?"

In fact, it turns out that Art wants both of them. When Jane breaks up with Cleveland, Art goes out with her and they end up in bed. Later, Cleveland shows up at Art's apartment and they, too, end up in bed. Jane comes in and finds them sleeping naked together. She sobs and runs out; chasing after her, Art tells her that he loves her, and he loves Cleveland, too. She cautions Art that he will never be able to change Cleveland. Indeed, Cleveland's gambling debts catch up to him, and the mob wants him dead. Art attempts to intercede with his father on Cleveland's behalf. Joseph offers Cleveland a deal: his life in exchange for committing a burglary and promising to never see Art again. Art insists on going along on the burglary, but the job is a set-up; Joseph has notified the police, and they pursue Cleveland and Art. Cornered on top of the Cloud Factory, Cleveland leaps from its smokestack to his death. In the end, Art finds the courage to confront his father and break ties with him forever: "I never saw my father again after that day."

Art begins the film as a heterosexual, albeit seemingly limited in his experiences. He has energetic sex with his manager at the bookstore, a young woman named Phlox (Mena Suvari), but because this sex takes place at work, it is not particularly intimate. They do not take off their clothes; Art says he began the affair out of boredom and likens it to an "obligation." Moreover, there is a hint of Art's homoerotic interest to come: while having sex with Phlox in the sports section, he is distracted by a photo of football quarterback Joe Namath leering at him from the cover of a book. It is not until Art becomes involved with Jane that he experiences heterosexual sex that is truly intimate and deeply connected to emotions; but he simultaneously discovers that he can have the same intimacy and emotions with Cleveland. It is bisexuality which helps Art realize his full potential, both heterosexually and homosexually.

To an extent, bisexuality offers a contorted escape from Art's equally contorted relationship with his father. Afraid of his father's judgments, Art segregates his meetings with him from his friends and romantic attachments, the independent life he is trying to build for himself as a young man. He cannot bring his father together, in his own psyche, with the rest of his life. Jane helps him break through this block: he takes her to dinner with his father on her birthday, but is chagrinned by his father's insistence that Jane is Art's girlfriend. He seems to hesitate to assert his own manhood around his father and thereby challenge his father's dominance: he is stuck at the devalued status of a dependent son who cannot quite graduate to his own masculine identity. It is, therefore, Cleveland who helps Art the most: with Cleveland, Art finds the masculine love his father has withheld from him. Joseph tries to force Art to choose between him and his love for his "friend," Cleveland, but in the end it is Cleveland's death which precipitates Art's decision to make a complete break with his father. Cleveland's and Art's love was not in vain.

Art's individual father-crisis extends to the entire landscape of Pittsburgh. A number of shots and scenes feature the factories (many now closed) that were once the center of the city's industry: giant phallic objects built, owned, powered and finally abandoned by the "fathers'" generation. The young characters are overshadowed by a past they did not create, and which offers them no future. Moreover, many other buildings and interiors are oppressively antiquated and "old world" — in one scene, a gothic stone police station, for instance, resembles an ancient cathedral. Every place where the characters go (except the punk rock club and the scenes set in the country) suggests worshipful, religious veneration of the past. Specifically Catholic values intersect with even the subculture of gangsterdom: when the Mafia wants Cleveland dead, the only thing that can save him is "absolution." Life in this moralistic, conservative environment drives the young characters to rebel by drinking heavily and experimenting sexually, but to what extent are these rebellions empty gestures — gestures which do not overthrow the old order but rather only serve to reinforce its final judgments? A rebellious phase is the fleeting privilege of youth: not to outgrow it is to have to die, like Cleveland.

Finally, who is Art at the end of *The Mysteries of Pittsburgh*? While it is refreshing that he does not agonize about what it has meant for him to have sex with a man, the film's conclusion feels a bit anticlimactic, as he marches off to his stockbroker job, saying only, "I remember my friends, and I love them to this day." The use of the pointedly asexual "friends" seems to denote that what mattered most to Art was the feeling he shared with Jane and Cleveland, rather than the sex. But what does that feeling amount to? He seems to have classified and filed away his turbulent memories a bit too easily. His summer with Jane and Cleveland helped him separate psychologically from his father, his tortuous family life and childhood, but in the end, Art accepts his place in the corporate world anyway — the place his father had earmarked for Art's future all along. Again, the characters expect little more than a brief period of rebelling against the system before growing up and buying it. Was bisexuality nothing more than a "last hurrah" of experimental, footloose youth for Art — a walk on the wild side, as it were, so that he can be content to put away any further thoughts of rebellion and settle for a contented place in the mainstream?

PART 3
Matters of Love and Death

We sing dangerously. We sing the body chaos. Venus to penis: the axis of eros, the meaning in its veins; to remake the world in the image of our desires. The subversive body; under the skin of all oppression, the space of resistance, transfused. — Bradley/Eros

9

The Schoolboy Crush and Its Ambiguous Object

Coming of age as a gay youth can be difficult, to say the least. Although there is more tolerance today than in the past, this tolerance is hardly universal. Peer pressure to be straight, as well as the fear of social stigma and family disapproval, can still cause early adolescence to be a traumatic time for young gays and bisexuals. Moreover, early crushes and first loves can be (as they also can be for heterosexual youths) awkward and misguided — one of the biggest difficulties being that the gay teen often falls in love for the first time with a boy who isn't gay, or who isn't ready to perform same-sex activities or accept a gay identity. Labels with negative connotations can be especially hurtful to a developing adolescent; indeed, the gay teen's own uneasiness about coming out can lead him to identify precisely with a guy who is ambiguous or indeterminate in his own sexuality. In fact, this love object may be, to one extent or another, bisexual, in that he identifies as straight but in some sense "leads on" his gay admirer: whether this ambiguity arises from a shared sense of being misfits, or the natural curiosity of young people about each other, or something more tentatively sexual in nature, the crush is not always as simplistically one-sided as it might seem.

In films, the gay coming-of-age drama has exploded as a thriving subgenre, mainly aimed at making gay teens feel better about themselves. Although there is nothing wrong with this goal (in fact, it is admirable), the aesthetic result sometimes falls somewhere between an "After School Special" and a gay rehash of John Hughes' high school movies. One problem is that these films demonize the ambiguous love object as a kind of strawman villain: specifically, he is seen as standing in the way of gay progress and empowerment. Films which valorize the struggle of teens to be *anything* (much less gay) in the difficult, "awkward years" of puberty are somewhat rare — and in particular, films which honestly depict the strange dance performed between the gay schoolboy and the ambiguous object of his crush.

An intricate and powerful examination of this phenomenon occurs in *The Mudge Boy* (2003), written and directed by Michael Burke. Fourteen-year-old Duncan Mudge (Emile Hirsch) is emotionally traumatized by the recent death of his mother. He has tried to replace her by almost literally becoming her. He rides her bicycle, wears her clothes, and carries on conversations in her voice. He lives on a rural chicken farm with his emotionally distant, withholding father (Richard Jenkins), and tends the chickens which his mother used to adore. The chickens are more like beloved pets to him than livestock, and his attachment to them has earned him the derisive nickname "Chicken Boy" among the local redneck boys.

These same tough boys snicker when Duncan sings in church in a high, cracking, fragile voice. They are sharply distinguished from Duncan's gentleness. They drive around in a red pick-up truck (decorated with the Confederate flag), drink, and try to have sex with girls. If anything, however, Duncan is drawn to them, submissively giving them money to buy beer and genially allowing them to make him the butt of their jokes. One of these boys, Perry (Thomas Guiry), seems drawn to Duncan in return. Perry's family are also farmers, raising cattle. When Perry first sees Duncan petting one of his cows, he approaches the Mudge boy with blatant sexual innuendo: "She'll suck your dick if you let her." The implication is that Perry has tried oral sex with the animal, suggesting that he is opportunistic in his need for sex and does not particularly care how he gets it. Duncan, already smitten, tries to show Perry love the only way he can: he offers to let the boy hold his prized chicken and to give him some eggs. Later, hanging out in Duncan's barn, Perry urinates in front of him and refers to the size of his own penis: "It's big, huh?" "Yeah," Duncan admits, acknowledging that he has looked at it. "You ever fuck a girl, Duncan?" Perry asks, beginning to taunt and tease Duncan with his "superior" masculinity. He goes on to describe, in graphic detail, how the large size of his penis make it difficult for him to find girls who will let him penetrate them. He goes on to tell Duncan about a time when he seduced a girl, sucking on her breasts, playing with her nipples and fingering her until she was begging him to have sex with her. The inexperienced Duncan is uncomfortable throughout Perry's monologue (although that night he plays with his own nipples in bed, the way Perry said he had played with the girl's). Again, Perry's sex talk is blatant but, on another level, difficult to read. On the one hand, it depicts Perry as strongly heterosexual, but on the other hand, it seems significant that he seeks out another boy, the less manly Duncan, as a captive audience to show off his private parts and his "war stories." He shows little respect for the girls he has been with; in this, too, he seems sexually opportunistic.

Perry's mixed messages continue. The two boys go for a hike, Perry lifting Duncan's bike over a fence and then carrying it aloft across a stream; since the bike belonged to Duncan's mother, Perry's stewardship of it suggests that he will accept and care for Duncan's feminine side. (Strictly on a physical level, Perry is bigger and stronger than Duncan.) They go to a trestle bridge above a lake, where he tells Duncan, "Take your clothes off." Perry strips down to his underwear, while the shy, wary Duncan remains fully dressed. Perry throws him into the water anyway, then cannonballs after him, howling Duncan's name. They splash and play in the lake. Then, wearing nothing but their underwear, they hang out in the rafters under the trestle. Perry has a rose tattoo on his arm, a symbol, perhaps, of *his* feminine side (and also a possible reference, on the filmmaker's part, to Tennessee Williams). Duncan asks, "You ever bring a girl up here?" Is he asking out of jealousy, or is he interested in hearing about another one of Perry's sexual conquests? "Fuck

Thomas Guiry plays Perry in *The Mudge Boy* (2003). Perry is a rural boy who begins to question his sexuality when he is drawn to the effeminate Duncan Mudge. On Perry's bedroom wall, the upside-down flag above the nude female pin-ups suggests Perry's rebellion against traditional heterosexuality.

no," Perry says, as if suggesting that this is a special place for Duncan and him. The other boys come along and, noticing Duncan's bike, throw it in the lake. They taunt Duncan to come out, but a train comes along and the boys are forced to flee the bridge. In the moment of relief, Duncan spontaneously squeezes Perry's bicep. Perry jumps back with a look of contempt on his face, then shifts abruptly: flexing his muscles, he says, "Hard as a rock, isn't it?" as if inviting Duncan's worshipful attention.

When it comes to Duncan, Perry is full of such mood-swings and about-faces. He does not hesitate to call Duncan "weird" and keep his distance at times. He seems equally drawn to, and repulsed by, the feminine boy. At a drinking party in the woods, in a kind of chivalrous gesture, Perry beats up a guy who calls Duncan "Chicken Boy." Perry wanders off with April (Beckie King) and she begins to have oral sex with him. Duncan follows and watches from a distance. When Perry notices Duncan watching, he grins and begins to "perform" the sex act more aggressively for his friend's benefit, grabbing April's hair and thrusting his hips. She is called away, and Perry takes his frustration out on Duncan, quite literally in the ensuing scene, where the two guys are back in Duncan's barn. In a touching moment, Duncan thanks Perry for being nice to him, referring to Perry defending him from the "Chicken Boy" insult. But Perry is not in a gentle mood. He makes Duncan put on his mother's wedding dress, telling him to take off his shirt first: "It won't look right." He stares at Duncan, visualizing him as a girl. As the audience, we are aware of Perry's intentions long before the childlike Duncan is. Shoving Duncan and calling him "a bitch," Perry soon enacts a very rough deflowering on the passive, sobbing boy.

When the sex is over, Perry immediately lights a cigarette and changes the subject to the new car his father is buying, as if completely disconnected from what has just happened. The sex would feel exactly like a brutal rape, except that neither of the boys seems to understand it that way. But how do they understand it? We see that Perry has been leading this dance with Duncan from the very beginning; Duncan is too unworldly to make anything happen. For his part, Duncan is falling in love with Perry and eager to please him. But Perry can only understand his sex with Duncan as a purely physical release, an act of desperate lustful need. (During the sex, Perry said, "God, you're so fuckin' tight. It's just like a pussy," as if needing some vestige of heterosexuality to enter into this homosexual act.) This is where the ambiguous, bisexual object of the crush becomes a tarnished figure, a person of bad faith, in gay coming-of-age cinema. He is not liberated, not out. He will not follow through, romantically, on his sexual promises. He is incapable of attaching any sentiment or even conscious awareness to his sex with Duncan. At the same time, as a young man who is still as dependent on his family as Duncan is on his, and still subject to peer pressure of various kinds, Perry does not have full agency to be what Duncan needs: a sort of rescuer, a knight in shining armor.

In a moment of incredibly bad timing, Duncan's father comes into the barn. With his usual reserve, he registers the scene of his son in the wedding dress and says little, but the next day, he forces Duncan to help him burn all of his mother's clothing. Distraught, Duncan runs to Perry that night and desperately appeals to him. Perry has had a change of heart regarding their intimacy: "We can't do nothin' no more. It weren't right. It's queer. I ain't no queer." "I know," Duncan says. The idea of being gay has not occurred to Duncan, who presumably sees himself as a girl around Perry. Here, the nature of the young gay teen — to shun the idea that he is really "gay" the way other gay people are — coincides with the ambiguous object of his crush. They both seek a romantic and sexual understanding without the damning, prejudicial label. Perry sees this is impossible before the needy Duncan ever could.

Bravely, Duncan asks Perry if he ever thinks about kissing him. Perry becomes angry: "You're crazy. No, no way." Then he grabs Duncan's face and kisses him on the lips, shouting, "That what you want?" Perry's denial is bursting at the seams. They kiss some more, but Perry pulls away and says definitively, "You're a fuckin' faggot, Duncan. Get the fuck away from me." The insistent, negative label returns, the label which neither boy wants or can accept. This time, it is Perry's father who catches him outside after "Lights Out." Savagely beaten by his father, Perry later leads the other boys in an attack on Duncan. They grab his chicken and play "keep-away" with it as Duncan tries to grab it back. They restrain Duncan and threaten to kill the chicken in front of him. But at the last moment, Perry ends the torture, telling the other boys to let Duncan go and giving him back his chicken. This is his way of honoring the intimacy he has shared with Duncan, though the other boys make fun of Perry and say he has become "no fun."

The tormented, stormy relationship between Duncan and Perry is somewhat fueled by the problems they both have with their fathers. Just as the boys are opposite in personality (Duncan being passive and Perry being active), so their fathers are different as well. Duncan's father is implosive, a man of grudgingly few words. He holds everything inside, rebuking Duncan in a terrifyingly calm, quiet voice, and letting things simmer until they boil over at random moments: once, he kills two of Duncan's favorite chickens in front of him; another time, he hits him. Perry's father, on the other hand, is explosive, loudly berating his son and pummeling him on a regular basis. Because of this, however schematically, Duncan internalizes everything whereas Perry lashes out. Also, it could be said that Duncan's father sends him the same kind of mixed signals that Perry does, seemingly tolerant and accepting one moment, harsh and punitive the next. Needless to say, when Duncan encounters his father's characteristics in Perry, it brings out the side of him that is like his own mother, and encourages him to love the boy. Perry is seemingly pleased to find, in Duncan, a male who will not constantly challenge and belittle him — in marked contrast to the other males in his world, his father and his buddies.

In many ways, Perry is a victim not only of having been born into a certain kind of family, but of having been born into the often stiflingly narrow circumstances of rural life. His willingness to experiment sexually with Duncan is partly a function of his boredom and his sense that, even at his young age, he has reached a dead end in life. At one point, he says to Duncan: "You have this idea that your life will automatically be different when you grow up, then you start getting older and you realize it's all gonna be the same shit." The end of *The Mudge Boy* suggests that Perry's identity is still up for grabs; he may find a way to navigate a course between the thuggish antics of his friends and the glimpse of male love he has seen in Duncan — in other words, a bisexual course.

A far darker and more one-dimensional look at the schoolboy crush is offered in the Dutch film *Spelen of Sterven* (*To Play or to Die*, 1991), directed by Frank Krom. Young Kees (Geert Hunaerts) is gay, but, in a formula of so many gay coming-of-age films, his parents are too distant and uninvolved in his life to even notice. He, in turn, is taciturn and secretive with them. He has a crush on a popular boy at his school, the handsome Charel (Tjebbo Gerritsma). In class, Charel shouts an obscene rhyme about Kees, making the entire classroom laugh. Kees masochistically laughs and plays along with his own humiliation. Moments later, he willingly offers his homework for Charel to copy. While Charel makes Kees look bad, Kees offers Charel the right answers and makes him look good. (In relationship terms, Kees would like to be "the right answer" for Charel.) It is a disparity of abuse and affection which haunts the relationship between the schoolboy crush and its ambiguous object.

In *To Play or to Die*, the boys' school is an institution based on sadism. The boys are only mimicking the cruelty of their teachers. When the gym teacher catches Charel tormenting Kees in the locker room, he makes Charel wear his pants on his head and sing a nonsense song. Charel tries to turn this embarrassing moment into a game, singing with rousing gusto and trying to get everyone sing along; but he is finally left alone in the locker room with Kees, who stays seemingly to share in Charel's shame. The fact remains: love

9. The Schoolboy Crush and Its Ambiguous Object 167

between these boys is obviously impossible in a world where they are routinely humiliated (by the teachers and by each other) in order to be hardened into men, a process which Charel accepts more than Kees does.

Charel is sexually ambiguous precisely to the extreme extent of the delight he takes in torturing Kees; psychology tells us that so much hatred and aggression often mask repressed, "shameful" desire. But in terms of his ability to respond to Kees, Charel is nothing like Perry is in relation to Duncan in *The Mudge Boy*. Again, in another formulaic element of gay coming-of-age drama, we know that nothing good will come of Kees' bold invitation to Charel to come to his house that night while his parents are away. However, the masochistic acceptance of abuse is part of what makes the schoolboy crush what it is: a painful stage in gay development. We see this same syndrome on the collegiate level, for example, in the desultory yet sometimes truthful *Rules of Attraction* (2002), in which the gay student Paul Denton (Ian Somerhalder) has not yet learned to fully accept himself as gay. He loathes spending time with the openly gay students, who are more stereotypically effeminate and dithering, and prefers instead to "pass" among the straights. But he develops crushes on, and sometimes makes sexual advances toward, straight young men who, no matter what mixed signals they might send along the way, invariably reject him and, in one case, rough him up. The rejection is disappointing to him, but serves a deeper, more unconscious psychological need: to reinforce to him, over and over again, that he *isn't* really straight, but different from the straight young men who seek to protect their roles in the heterosexual pecking order at all costs. (Accepting the label, in all its negative connotations, is the first step toward accepting the identity, and thereby accepting oneself.) The end of *Rules of Attraction* suggests that Paul has already grown and learned from his painful experiences: the part of him that does not wish to be abused seems to gain an edge over the part of him that cannot move on from the trauma of feeling "lesser" than the straight guys. However, in *To Play or to Die*, there is a stronger sense of fatalism and finality: the self-loathing side of the gay youth seeks out the ambiguous object precisely for his power to humiliate and punish him.

And so Charel does exactly this. Although Charel encourages Kees to think that he needs him by asking once again to copy Kees' homework, this is just a ruse: playing nice temporarily to get something that he wants. Charel is not above using Kees, but when push comes to shove (as it literally does, soon enough) his intention is clearly to punish the boy for daring to love him. Why is Charel so threatened by Kees' love? Is he afraid of the temptation to yield to it? The baggage which each boy brings — as a teenager desperate to be popular and to succeed — makes it difficult to say where the weakness of one begins and the strength of the other starts. It is brave of Kees to love

Charel; it is finally weak of Charel to hurt Kees. This is the logic of gay coming-of-age cinema, which (justly) sets out to valorize the struggles of gay youth, but does so (unjustly) at the expense of the strawman villain, the boy who isn't ready or who wants to have it both ways. Of course, Charel is, finally, not deserving of our sympathy, although a more nuanced film might have presented him in such a way that played down his will to power and his black and white view of the relationship between him and Kees.

"So, things are going to happen this evening?" he says, raising his fist to Kees' face. Like Perry in *The Mudge Boy*, Charel begins his ultimate domination of Kees by asserting his sexual prowess and his more extensive experience with the opposite sex. Charel challenges Kees: "Have you ever done it? I have.... She was a nice girl." In a somewhat more overdetermined (because more pointedly hostile) way than Perry's sex talk in *The Mudge Boy*, this exchange calls into question the reasons why some men sleep with women in the first place: because they truly want to, or because they wish to impress, outpace or dominate other males in their peer groups? Charel wants Kees to ask him about it, and when Kees is silent, Charel keeps taunting him, "You don't dare to, eh?" until he knocks Kees down. It is the first of many times Kees will end up sprawled on the floor at Charel's feet. In the same way that Perry does with Duncan, the strapping Charel physically dominates Kees.

Eventually, the games between the two boys turn more and more violent, as Charel proposes a boxing match. He punches Kees several times, knocking him down and bloodying his lip. Flying into rage, Kees attacks Charel, and the two boys struggle before Charel knocks Kees down again. Jumping on top of him, he says, "You fight like a girl!" Again, as in *The Mudge Boy*, being in any way "like a girl" is the worst shame for a young man, at an age when he is learning to assert himself as a man and fears being seen as a failure.

Charel makes Kees beg for mercy, then leaves him alone in the house. The battered, bloodied Kees is sore but aroused, and in a final act of masochism, he masturbates, weeping bitterly as he brings himself to climax. He hears mocking laughter outside the window, and a medicine ball comes crashing through it. When Kees picks up the ball, it is Charel's head, taunting him and spitting on him. This striking surreal image is worth commenting on. If a ball (in all its many shapes and sizes) is the most fundamental emblem of masculinity, certainly of masculine play, then for Kees it will forever bear Charel's face, both in its handsomeness and in its ugly contempt; Charel has imprinted himself on masculinity for Kees, the same way Kees has been imprinted with self-hatred, and it is masculinity itself which condemns Kees. Sent reeling, he tumbles down the stairs and dies. The horrific lesson of *To Play or to Die* is that gay self-hatred and masochism is at its height in adolescence, when the urge to fit in is at its highest and the fear of disappointing one's family is omnipresent; it is at this time of life that a young gay man can fall prey to the seductive charms of a bully who means to harm him. Reaching out to Charel as a peer, he finds that Charel is already hardened, indoctrinated into the adult straight world in which men compete against each other, and do not love.

There are moments of bewildered eye contact between Kees and Charel when it seems as though Charel may be harboring some interest in Kees. For the gay youth, profoundly lonely and isolated, even negative attention seems to get misread as something at least potentially positive: ignored at home, Kees is at least noticed by the boys who pick on him. Their manner of picking on him verges on being sexual: they strip him naked in the locker room and toss his briefs to Charel, who begins to wave them at Kees the way a matador taunts a bull with his red cape. Kees scrambling around nude among the other boys is an image of gay vulnerability within a heterosexual pecking order.

* * *

Kees, as gay youths often do in coming-of-age cinema, may believe that Charel can be reached, if only as a fellow boy of similar age. (After all, they share the same abuse at the hands of adults.) The harsh lesson is taught early in life: do not love "the enemy." But teen sexual experimentation does not have to be tragic, as Alexis Dos Santos' wonderful *Glue* (2006) demonstrates. This Argentinean film concerns the sixteen-year-old Lucas (Nahuel Pérez Biscayart), who worships the Violent Femmes and wears his hair spiky. He sings with a punk rock band, in which his best friend Nacho (Nahuel Viale) is the drummer. Puberty has made Lucas preoccupied with sex; he and Nacho hang around with the awkward, sweet Andrea (Inés Efron), but Lucas is also attracted to Nacho. In voiceover he wonders about his bisexuality: "What is the difference between kissing a boy or a girl? Boys have beards. Otherwise it'd be the same thing."

Lucas' home life is tense. His mother (Verónica Llinás) continually throws his father (Héctor Díaz) out of the house for cheating on her, then takes him back. Angry with his father, Lucas avoids him. While his parents are trying to reconcile, he breaks into the father's apartment with Nacho, and the two boys sniff glue. Sexually aroused, and hovering in a dream-like high, they feel drawn to each other, and end up masturbating each other while watching straight porn. Nacho wakes up later and seems disconcerted by what was happened; he quickly dresses and leaves, worrying that his mother will be "freaked out" if he stays out all night. He leaves Lucas alone, to be awakened later by his father rubbing the dried, sticky glue off Lucas' hands. Resembling semen, the glue is a visual reminder of Lucas' sexual contact with Nacho; but Lucas does not seem ashamed in front of his father, nor does his father get angry at him for breaking in. If sex with another young man is partly a way for Lucas to resolve his negative, distant relationship with his father, the film, in a very refreshing way, suggests that this strategy works: Lucas is calmer and less angry with his father. There is nothing blind or naïve about this: we see that Lucas still has work to do on his relationship with his father, as well as his relationship with Nacho, for that matter. But neither relationship has to be sacrificed to the other; instead, these relationships can grow alongside each other, as Lucas grows through them.

In *Glue*, unlike *The Mudge Boy* and *To Play or to Die*, Lucas' attraction to Nacho is not associated with doomed romanticism; as best friends, the boys are naturally kind, playful and loving toward each other. In some ways, sex comes about more easily between them than with the painfully shy Andrea, because physicality has always been a strong element of their friendship: an extended scene of Lucas and Nacho wrestling together establishes this. In another scene, Nacho, Lucas and Andrea are all together in a nightclub, sharing a drink, and the music is slow, swirling, and romantic; suddenly, Andrea has to go home, and Dos Santos jumpcuts to the two boys, still at the club, dancing to music which is faster, more percussive and jungle-like. For her part, Andrea seems drawn to the two boys in the hope that their impulsivity will help set her free: she thinks to herself that she would rather be a boy, so she could be braver and "more fun." (Andrea's remarks do not strike the viewer as sexist or self-hating. As with so much of what happens in *Glue*, tone is everything; Dos Santos and his gifted young cast capture the tenderness and openness of adolescence, where love is an act of radical empathy, and one almost strives to become what one loves.)

It becomes clear that Lucas has two love objects, Nacho and Andrea. He muses in voiceover: "And Nacho? I wonder what he's doing. Is he sleeping? Am I in his dreams? I wanna touch Andrea's tits." Toward the end of the film, Lucas plays a gig with his band where he sings a song whose erotic lyrics are filled with both masculine and feminine imagery. As the audience cheers for more, we realize that Lucas has figured out a way to turn his bisexuality into creative expression and a kind of rebirth. After the show, he leads his two lovers in a tender, drunken orgy where romantic and sexual contact flows among all three.

There is no violent, painful aftermath to the bisexual sex in *Glue*.[1] In fact, Lucas goes on a camping trip with his family and generally seems to get along better with them after fulfilling his threesome fantasy; moreover, he, Nacho, and Andrea all remain very close friends. Again, Lucas is seen as being

9. The Schoolboy Crush and Its Ambiguous Object

able to have it all: the love of a girl, the love of another boy, and the love of his family. But *Glue* is an exception that only proves the rule, in gay cinema anyway, where sexual uncertainty is often connected to tragic patterns of self-loathing and self-defeat. If he does not adopt an exclusively homosexual identity, a gay youth, it is reasoned, can carry these patterns into adulthood, as we see in the creepy parable *L'Imbalsamatore* (*The Embalmer*, 2002). Although barely involved with male bisexuality per se, this Italian film is worth mentioning in relation to gay crushes and their ambiguous objects. Its main character, Peppino Profeta (Ernesto Mahieux), is arrested developmentally, both in his dwarfism and in his inability to accept his own homosexuality. This lack of self-acceptance leads him to adopt a defensive, macho, even womanizing front, and also to seek out rugged, straight youths, whose company he pays for. When he meets the tall and handsome Valerio (Valerio Foglia Manzillo), he falls in love at first sight, and offers Valerio an apprenticeship at his taxidermy shop. Peppino works by day stuffing animals, but by night he works for the Mafia; this dual identity as solid citizen and amoral criminal mirrors his complicated sexual division. Valerio is slow to understand Peppino's faults, and becomes dependent on the little man financially; they even begin living together, with Peppino plying Valerio with wine and hookers to keep him content and to keep him from noticing Peppino's sexual interest in him.

Apparently, this is Peppino's modus operandi with men: he uses women as a medium by which to experience sex vicariously, as it were. One night, Valerio awakens from an orgy to find Peppino sleeping with his head resting on Valerio's stomach; Valerio leaves the bed in disgust and bewilderment. But Peppino is determined to take advantage of the young man whenever possible. In one scene, Peppino tries to force himself on Valerio orally one night when Valerio is half-asleep; the young man awakens and throws Peppino halfway across the bedroom. In another scene, Peppino undresses and fondles Valerio when the young man is passed out drunk. In spite of all this, the younger man continues to stay friends with Peppino. Partly, this is because he feels obligated to Peppino; it is also because of a kind of macho code which prevents Valerio from admitting that the situation is too much for him and simply walking away. He cannot seem to admit that he was wrong to become involved with Peppino in the first place. Meanwhile, the diminutive Peppino constantly plays on Valerio's male ego, his vanity at being such a physically superior specimen of manhood. Out of immaturity, Valerio is also drawn to the lure of freedom and the "buddy lifestyle" which Peppino represents, so much so that he even considers leaving the woman he has fallen in love with, Deborah (Elisabetta Rocchetti), who is also carrying his child, to go to Cuba with Peppino. But when Peppino threatens Valerio's life with a gun, Valerio shoots him (or Peppino shoots himself; the film is deliberately open-ended on this point), and he and Deborah dispose of the body in a river.

Again, the two men perform a strange dance of attraction and repulsion, admission and denial. In Peppino's homophobic eyes, Valerio's perfection is enhanced by the fact that he is unattainable: he will always reject Peppino sexually. Women function as the go-betweens of repressed male desire, but when Deborah becomes more than a mere plaything to be used and cast aside, she threatens the careful illusion which Peppino has built up, that the friendship between him and Valerio is the narrative's real love story. Peppino's denial is so strong that even when the Mafia Don (Bernardino Terracciano) tells him to "relax," because he understands Peppino is gay and likes young men, Peppino keeps up his defensive routine that Valerio is his nephew. Most of Peppino's manipulative lies are to himself.

Peppino is like an older version of Duncan and Kees, perhaps, hardened out of the youthful vulnerability which helps explain *their* need to suffer for unrequited loves. He has developed, instead, a will to power and a genius for manipulation; however, like the gay youths in *The Mudge Boy* and *To Play or to Die*, he is no less a victim of the world he has created around himself. It is depicted as a world with shaky, crumbling foundations, because Peppino has internalized the world's homophobia to such an extent that he throws himself into his love for Valerio as if into a passive death wish. Hence, the fatalistic ending, in which murder and suicide are conflated: by the logic of his own love, Peppino must either go on feeding parasitically on straight sexuality or make himself a martyr to it so that it can flourish without him.

* * *

Although there is certainly real homophobia in adolescence, there is also the potential for deeply intense first loves, which can be life-altering even if they never come to fruition. Focusing on the trauma of growing up different, being picked on, and often going unloved, gay coming-of-age films repeatedly reanimate the structure of unrequited love and homophobic abuse as a foregone conclusion. Indeed, many of these coming-of-age films have a kind of vested interest in valorizing the gay youth and portraying the ambiguous or bisexual one as a trap to be avoided at all costs, however attractive. What is at stake is precisely the "gay" label, which the gay youth will at some point, presumably, grow to accept, enabling him to perhaps lead a fulfilled life. The recognition that there could be solidarity between a gay youth and a potentially bisexual one would be seen, superficially, as an obstacle to the gay youth's progression from crippling self-hatred to self-acceptance — and finally, as robbing the gay youth of his chance at empowerment. To the extent that this is true, it only serves to pit gay against straight, gay against bisexual, in a way that must be, in the largest sense, unproductive and defeatist for society as a whole. In *To Play or to Die*, for example, it is never suggested that Charel could grow and be enriched from his encounters with Kees. Charel is already meant for the straight world, with its predictable assumptions and demands, while the gay youth passes through this world like a shadow, hardly meriting the attention and effort it takes to crush him. However, the gay youth, in another, equally predictable sense, must either "grow up," or fail to survive, by adopting the heartless logic of the same mainstream society: to remain only with his own kind rather than being free to give his love to whomever he chooses. If gay youths will inevitably continue to fall in love with specific guys rather than labels, and if these guys will sometimes continue to be drawn to them, then the ultimate conclusion of the films discussed in this chapter — particularly *Glue*—can only be that it is not a gayer, or straighter, world which is needed, but a more bisexual, open, and accepting one.

10

Turning It On and Off: "Bi for Pay"

> Of course, if a guy can pay me, hell yeah, here I am for him. I'll sell my ass. I do it on the street occasionally for cash.... But it's when you start doing things for free that you start to grow wings. —
> *My Own Private Idaho*

These words are spoken by the character Scott Favor (Keanu Reeves) in Gus Van Sant's landmark film about gay hustling, *My Own Private Idaho* (1991). Favor is the scion of a business tycoon; he doesn't actually need money, but "selling his ass" to men on the street is an act of rebellion against the staid, conservative values of his father. Favor maintains that he is heterosexual, and that the money is a kind of medium by which gay sex becomes something other than gay activity. If he had sex with men for the pleasure or love of it (in other words, "for free"), he would "grow wings and become a fairy."

In the film, Mike (River Phoenix) is also a hustler and far more lost than Scott, who is his best friend. Abandoned by his family, Mike is a street kid and prone to unexpected bouts of narcolepsy: his body, his only commodity, betrays him under stress and becomes comatose. Mike is gay, and in love with Scott. One night, camping under the stars far from the congested cities of Seattle and Portland where they live, Mike declares his love for Scott. Mike tells Scott that he could have sex with a man out of love, rather than strictly as a job. Resistant at first, Scott relents when he sees Mike's sincerity, and the two make love.

This oasis of feeling within the gritty, criminal, business-like world of these characters has a disturbing impact on both of them. Mike sees it as a sign that Scott truly loves him; Scott, harshly turning away from this moment when he allowed himself to feel something for another man, eventually leaves Mike for an Italian girl, Carmella (Chiara Caselli). In an even more dramatic backlash against his own bisexuality, Scott turns his back on hustling and street life altogether, becoming the respectable heir to his father's fortune.

Although we may choose to read Scott as secretly gay and in denial, the preponderant evidence of the film is that Scott is a situational bisexual: he responds to bisexual urges only under certain circumstances, e.g., to earn money, to aggravate his father, or to respond to the needs of a friend. Situational bisexuality is possibly the most common type of bisexuality: it has almost nothing to do with romantic and sexual attachments, and most typically occurs in male prostitution. An otherwise straight man will consent to have gay sex with other men because of a specific situational inducement: money. In this pointedly unromantic scenario, straight male bodies, usually unattainable to gay men, are made attainable because the bodies in question can be hired. The hustler occupies a special place in gay male imagination, since he fulfills the sometimes common fantasy of wanting to have sex with a younger male, a male who is dependent, or a male who is "totally straight." (The sources of these fantasies may be regrettable, stemming from issues of control or gay self-hatred.) However, although he caters to gay male fantasy, the hustler, for his part, is not technically a true bisexual, since he will often deny that he enjoys the gay sex he engages in for money. Moreover, he often staunchly claims to remain heterosexual (perhaps partly to play into gay male fantasies of "converting" straight male flesh — thereby reifying his initial selling of himself into an endless, shopworn repetition of "the first time"). But then again, in another sense, the hustler *is* bisexual because his experience is that of being involved (sexually at least) with men as well as women. For all of these reasons, the situational bisexual cuts to the very heart of the question central to all issues of sexual identification: is it what he do, our behaviors, that determine who we are, or is it what we profess about ourselves, how we choose to label ourselves?

The hustler deals in fantasy rather than reality. The client who pays him for sex determines how the hustler's psychical identity is to be deciphered. In some scenarios, again, the client enjoys the idea that the hustler is completely straight and only submitting to gay desire because he is forced to, out of economic necessity. Heterosexuality, here, becomes subsumed within gay fantasy, in its enforced conversion to its opposite. In other scenarios, the client may not think at all about the innate wishes and needs of the male body he is paying to use: he may prefer to assume that the hustler is gay, or reciprocally enjoying the sex on some level. In any event, when a male body passes through the looking glass of prostitution, his own desire gets swallowed up in a homosexual order of things. (And indeed, hustlers are hardly monolithic in their "true" sexual orientations, or lack thereof: some are gay, and do not have a heterosexual side; others turn tricks with female clients as well as males, while still others could even be considered asexual in terms of their psychical personality.) The extent to which a given hustler resists homosexuality even while participating in it is also the extent to which he needs to be considered as situationally bisexual.

Intriguingly, the situational aspect of gay hustling gets somewhat reversed in Werner Schroeter's *Diese Nacht* (*Tonight*, 2008), a parable about a fictional city in the grip of war between Gestapo-like police forces and revolutionaries. One of the characters, Juan (Joao Baptista), is a waiter at the Alpha and Omega Club, where he not only maintains the demeanor of a slightly effeminate homosexual, but offers his sexual services to at least one male customer of the club for money. Juan is actually a member of the underground resistance, one of the first to be rounded up and questioned by the sadistic police. Because of his reputation as a gay hustler, the police are prepared to let him go after he acquiesces in showing them his ass. "All sodomites!" one of the police proclaims about Juan and, by extension, the entire city which they are bent on destroying. At this, Juan becomes enraged and attacks the police guard, causing him to be shot numerous times on the desk of the chief of police. The prostituted body sprawled upon a desk suggests would-be sexual usage, but it is, finally, only as a dead body that Juan consents to be "used," and it is only as an emblem of terror and disgust that the police wish to use his naked body: they crucify his bullet-riddled corpse in a loincloth on a kind of altarpiece, and use the sight of him to intimidate other partisans under interrogation. (The imagination of the police runs violently toward the judgment and punishment of surplus desire, not its enjoyment.) Later, we find that Juan was in love with a woman who understood that Juan worked, or posed, as a homosexual, but was nonetheless, with her, "an angel ... an animal!" In Schroeter's film, bisexuality serves as a metaphor for a certain kind of double agency in a political cause. But, in some ways, it is also part of the cause itself. The crucified Juan vividly represents bisexual energies under the most extreme pressure to conform.

Usually, male hustling is not given such a grandiose treatment. A number of films have been made about the lives of hustlers, almost always in poor, drab, urban settings. Many of these films are extremely depressing, focusing on the inevitable tragic circumstances of "the life": degradation, abuse, risk, violence, and homicide. It is not my intention, in this chapter, to examine how hustling in general has been portrayed in films, but rather, how certain hustler characters conceive of their sexual orientation, specifically in relation to whether they are straight, gay, or bi, and what this means for male bisexuality in general.

There is an interview with a hustler running, in voiceover, through Rick Castro and Bruce LaBruce's satirical film, *Hustler White* (1996), which explores the seedy, extensive world of male prostitution on Santa Monica Boulevard in Los Angeles. At one point, the interviewer asks the hustler, "Are you gay or straight?" The hustler laughs and says, "I'm a hustler." This tautological shrug is meant to indicate a few different things. First, one of the damages wrought by prostitution is that, over time, it deadens the prostitute's natural sexual response. Sex becomes a job, and as such, not pleasurable; it no longer attaches to specific love objects (of either gender), but instead to the highest bidder. It does not matter what he "wants": sexual feeling goes numb. Secondly, the hustler must transcend categories of sexual preference if he is to be at all successful in his work. If he thinks about what he would prefer to be doing sexually, he is not likely to accept the conditions of his work, which dictate that he must have no choice in the matter of whom he sleeps with, nor the nature of the sexual fantasies he is paid to fulfill. In LaBruce's often outrageous film, even the worst dangers of hustling — several hustlers fall victim to a creepy mortician serial killer — are presented more as campy black comedy (in LaBruce's inimitable tongue-in-cheek style) rather than as serious, tragic situations. The hustlers tend to become interchangeable: many of the same ones reappear throughout the film in various situations and sexual configurations; many of them strongly resemble each other. They pass like shadows, always taking someone else's place in the line of available "fantasy bodies."

In fact, LaBruce, if anything, mocks the idea that a hustler could be anything but a kind of gay fantasy machine. In one scene, a hustler in a cowboy outfit has been picked up by a john, also in cowboy regalia. The hustler is sitting on a mattress, presumably after a sexual encounter, while the john strums a guitar and yodels. The hustler begins to speak, desultorily, of his heterosexual life before he began to work the streets: "I was married for not even two and a half years. I was in the military for almost a decade. I loved my wife, had a little girl, two years old. It's very painful to lose her. But I guess that's the way things are sometimes. Certainly helped make me grow. Sometimes that's all we need sometimes, is to pull through adversity." This litany is spoken by the actor very flatly, in a stoned monotone that makes it sound patently ridiculous; in other words, at this moment where the gay hustler is professing his straight history and ongoing straight feelings, LaBruce resorts to the rather Brechtian technique of deliberately bad acting, thereby belying the strong, painful feelings which the words, at face value, imply. At the deepest level, LaBruce is saying that the hustler himself is a transparently bad actor, inviting us to ridicule or at least disbelieve the hustler's listless protestations of how straight he truly is. (Though we are simultaneously alarmed by the prominent AIDS-like lesions on the john's bare chest — such is the provocative, confrontational nature of LaBruce's gay cinema.) Indeed, the john shrugs off the hustler's monologue, demanding that the hustler perform for him again, and we see what the "sex" between them consists of: saddling the hustler on all fours, the john rides him like a cowboy on his horse, whooping and celebrating the submission of the straight body to his gay desire.

Time and again in films about hustling, this unromantic nature of situational bisexuality asserts itself. *Twist* (2003), a film from Canada, is a modernized adaptation of Dickens' *Oliver Twist*, with the boys as runaway street kids who have turned to male prostitution. They are managed by Fagin (Gary Farmer), but the entire operation is run by the powerful, mysterious, unseen "Bill." None of the hustlers wants this life, but have been forced into it in one way or another. Dodge (Nick Stahl) is a survivor of childhood sexual abuse at the hands of his father; sex with men fills him with a sense of rage, alienation, and despair, yet somehow puts him in touch with the stolen innocence which haunts him. He is also a junkie. When asked if he turns tricks in order to shoot up, he replies that it is just the opposite: he shoots up so as to able to turn tricks. Dodge has brought in a new boy, Oliver (Joshua Close), who falls in love with Dodge, trying on several occasions to kiss him. Dodge always becomes enraged and pushes him away violently: despising the gay sex he is forced to have, and the gay men he is forced to have it with, he cannot accept love from another man. He refuses to become the thing he hates on a level of acknowledged feelings, though he gives his body to it while in a passive, opiated state.

This split between body and mind (or spirit, or psyche, or awareness, or heart) is, of course, unhealthy and even deranging. Plus, it is a distinction which the straight world — with its often puritanical hatred of the body, its need for the mind to somehow redeem the temptations of the flesh — exploits for the purposes of making sexually unconventional people feel guilty, at odds with themselves. One night, Dodge is robbed by two gay bashers, who beat and stomp him. Taking Dodge's money, one of the bashers sneers, "Whose dick did you have to suck to get this?" For straight homophobes, Dodge's same-sex activity is the only aspect of him that matters; the facts that Dodge himself is homophobic and that he considers himself straight are invisible as far as the bashers are concerned. In this sense, the hustler, or any kind of situational bisexual, assumes the risks of being involved in the gay or bi world without being able to enjoy any of the benefits of community or legal protection from hate crimes and other forms of abuse.

In the end, Dodge explodes: he takes his rage out on Oliver, throwing him to the floor and stomping him repeatedly while shouting, "Fuckin' whore!" Then he returns to the house of his childhood abuse and shoots his family. The tightrope which Dodge has tried to walk (between hating homosexuality and yet participating in it for money) can only resolve itself in acts of destruction, self-annihilation. Another of the hustlers, Charley (Moti Yona), is equally torn about being a hustler, but is kept balanced because he has retained a strong connection to his straight side. He is secretly sleeping with Betsy (Brigid Tierney), one of the girls in the organization and Bill's personal favorite. Betsy sleeps with Bill for money, the way Charley sleeps with men for money, and she gives this money to Charley. She is anxious to keep the others from finding out that she and Charley are in love, because Bill would become jealous. For his part, Charley is jealous of Betsy's activity with Bill. At one point, Bill does find out about Betsy and Charley, and takes swift retribution by beating Charlie severely. If the male hustlers are creatures of gay fantasy on the streets, they are nonetheless pawns of a heterosexual pecking order which verges on the echt-corporate and involves the domination of young men by older, more powerful ones.

Nonetheless, Charley needs to remain blind to this harsh reality, clinging to the idea, not only that he is still straight, but that he can have a "normal" and sincere love relationship with a girl even within the bleak underworld of prostitution and organized crime. (This is strongly reminiscent of Pierrot's tragic love for Ingrid in Téchiné's *I Don't Kiss*.) Charley denies that he is controlled by the mob boss, even though all evidence points to the contrary. Rebellion and resistance are here part of Charley's bisexuality, but unlike true bisexuals in the non-criminal world, who are free to love whom they choose, Charley has nowhere to locate his difficult feelings. How is he able to love in such a loveless environment, and how is he able to turn his feelings on and off?

This last question — about "turning it on and off"— is the fascinating element of Gary Wicks' *Endgame* (2001). In this British film, Tom (Mark McGann) is a young London rent boy, kept by a gangster named George (Daniel Newman). In the film's opening shot, Tom reclines in his underwear in the middle of the sumptuous apartment which George provides for him: one more beautiful commodity surrounded by other beautiful, luxurious commodities, and so perfectly still that he almost seems corpse-like. George has a wife and son, though his marriage is somewhat icy. He visits Tom not only for sexual release but to release the rage that builds up inside him. The sex he has with Tom is sadistic, beating the young man and scratching him until he draws blood. He also uses Tom in his underworld activities, loaning him out sexually to important men in order to secretly videotape them having gay sex and then use the tapes for blackmail. As often happens in films about hustlers, the hustler appears as an emblem of gay sex at its most shameful, sleazy, and taboo.

Tom does not love George, nor does he enjoy George's sadomasochistic abuse. He seems to have traded, in situational fashion, economic security for a miserable existence in which he is more or less raped on a daily basis. Indeed, in one scene, he literally covers up his bruised, scratched body with the expensive, designer clothes which George's money has paid for. Pain and pleasure have become so entwined for Tom as to be nearly indivisible: one always inevitably leads to the other.

Tom strikes up a friendship with Max (Corey Johnson) and Nicky (Toni Barry), a young American married couple who live in his apartment building. Instead of telling them the truth about his living arrangement, he convinces them that he is a highly paid fashion model. One night, after enjoying dinner with his new friends, Tom becomes fed up with George's sexual demands and accidentally kills him. He appeals to Max and Nicky, confessing that he is actually a rent boy. Impulsively, they decide to help him by taking him to their rural cottage to hide. There, the three fall into an impromptu domestic arrangement, and a surprising sexual tension develops between Tom and Nicky. She is curious about what it is like to get paid for sex. Tom says, "I don't know what to tell you — I just get on." Sex for money is survival for Tom. She believes sex is better when love is involved, but he does not agree that the two things go together: "I just do one," he says. "That's what you think," she says, somewhat flirtatiously. He asks her, "Would you do it for money?" but apologizes when he sees her shocked, embarrassed reaction.

Seeing what conventional marriage is like, Tom begins to wonder about the way he has been living. Though he tells Nicky that nothing will change him, he also admits: "I'm different since I met you. You've done something inside of me." She, for her part, is touched by Tom's sincerity, the bruises and scratches on his body, and the fact that he was given up for adoption at birth. She decides to stay at the cottage with Tom when Max goes back to his job in London, and in an interesting twist, she and Tom sexually consummate their feelings for each other. For both of them, this sex is ecstatic, fulfilling, and nurturing. Afterwards, Nicky feels close to him and wants to have sex again, but he is distant. "Do you care?" she asks, angry and hurt. Tom expresses that he is frightened of the emotions she has stirred in him, and that he has difficulty having sex when feelings are involved: "Do you know what it's like to be fucked on demand?... You need to shut down, to detach yourself from yourself." He likens it to a light-switch that he has learned to turn on and off: "You come into my life for, what, three, four days, and you expect me to start finding that switch again." Nonetheless, he grudgingly admits that she has given him the most love and the best sex he has ever said: "I want to, I want to love, I want to know what it feels like...."

Meanwhile, Frank (John Benfield), a corrupt cop who is one of George's blackmail victims, is on a murderous rampage to recover the incriminating tape of him and Tom. He tracks Tom to the cottage and, in the struggle that ensues, Nicky is killed trying to protect Tom. Tom finally kills Frank, and is clearly moved by Nicky's selfless act of love and sacrifice. He kneels over her body, weeping and kissing her. But in the final shot of the film, Tom is in Paris, in the arms of a new sugar daddy.

Part of why Tom may be attracted to Nicky is that he longs for a mother. Unwanted and abandoned at birth, he never knew his real mother. Tom has frequent flashbacks to a brief period of childhood happiness with his adoptive parents; Max and Nicky's cottage reminds him of the farm where he grew up. But the idyll ended violently when his adoptive mother killed his adoptive father to keep him from molesting the child Tom. He remembers seeing her led away by the police in handcuffs. The theme of lost childhood innocence is often endemic to films about hustling, but in Tom's case, it seems important that the memory of his lost, doomed love for a mother seems to fuel his potentially heterosexual side.

"Turning it on and off": Tom tells Nicky that this is precisely what he cannot do, given his history as a gay hustler; he cannot swap sex-as-business with sex-as-love on a dime, so to speak. But the phrase is resonant with larger accusations often made against men who are bisexual. How do they go from heterosexual to homosexual relations, and back again, without feeling a dislocation of self, a dishonesty? The question is a canard on several levels. First, it is likely that bisexual males do feel some sense of dislocation, even guilt, and that this is a particularly difficult component of bisexual identity. Secondly, the idea of turning one thing off and the other thing on implies that the bisexual male is always only one identity at a time; we know this to be incorrect. Although fully invested in both his relations with men and women, he is always still, by definition, attracted to the other gender when he is with the one, and vice versa. In other words, bisexuality is not a practice, as it is in situational bisexuality, where it is contracted to begin and end under certain circumstances and for certain specific inducements, but a way of being, a constant psychical identity in and of itself.

Heterosexuality turns out to be an isolated oasis for Tom. For him, the choice is not between whether he is truly gay or truly straight, or indeed bisexual. The choice is between love, which he does not understand and which frightens him, or cold, unfeeling sex with men for money, which he does understand and which gives him at least a partial sense of control. It is not so much that the woman "must" die at the end of *Endgame*, but that the possibility of love must die, so that prostitution can extend itself, mechanically, into a world which continues to need the temporary release it offers. This happens regardless of the "true" sexuality of the hustler himself, or rather in spite of the fact that he does not actually possess a true sexuality. The hustler, like a corporeal phantom of capitalist energies and the will to power, exists only in the fantasy imagination of the men who pay him.

* * *

College life provides the backdrop for a Catalan film about hustling, *Amic/Amat* (*Beloved Friend*, 1999). David (David Selvas) is a gifted but difficult student; his professors consider him highly intelligent but antisocial and arrogant to a fault. His girlfriend Alba (Irene Montalà) tells him she is carrying his baby; this angers him, and he offers to get her an abortion. "Do you know what love means?" she asks him. "I've never loved anyone," he says matter-of-factly. If David seems to display, here, the hustler's code of separating sex from love, and denying the latter, that is no coincidence: in fact, he is secretly putting himself through school by working as a male prostitute. However, his public and private lives collide unexpectedly one day when one of his professors, Jaume (Josep M. Pou), happens to answer the ad for David's services in the personals section of a newspaper. Though both are startled at first, David chuckles and takes it in stride: "I'm discreet."

The professor is shocked mainly that David, whom he knows has impregnated Alba, sleeps with men for money. "You're not homosexual?" he asks. "No," David says, then goes on to explain somewhat pedantically to the astonished professor that he likes both men and women. "Just pretend I like you.... Just use me," he whispers seductively to the professor, but Jaume takes advantage of this physically intimate moment to confess to David that he has been in love with him ever since he taught him in a seminar. This sentimental, impassioned declaration enrages David, who cruelly tells the professor that he is far past the point where anyone could look at him with love and genuine desire, and will have to pay for sex the rest of his life. After crushing the professor's hopes, he hilariously sits back on the sofa and says, "Shit, I've lost a client."

Undaunted, the professor does make a proposition to David: he asks him to stop prostituting himself, and to stay with Alba and have the baby with her, and in exchange he will pay David's tuition and living expenses. Somewhat bizarrely, this is an instance of homosexuality looking askance at bisexuality and trying to shepherd it back toward exclusive heterosexuality, out of love. The paternalistic implications of the professor's guilt-trip strike a raw nerve in David, who despises his own father, a failed academic who committed suicide. (Like the boys in *Twist*, Tom in *Endgame*, and most male hustlers in films, David is the product of an abusive, unloving, or truncated childhood, a stereotype which works neatly in drama to provide "motive" even if it may not be an adequate generalization about the origins of such situational bisexualities in real life.) David becomes even more belligerent: "I'd vomit on you and you'd thank me.... You can't buy me, queer." Again, we see that the hustler is open about sleeping with both men and women, but rejects the "queer" or "gay" label, which he actually reserves as an insult for men whom he perceives as weaker than himself. Although seemingly proud of being bisexual, David is difficult to like, stubborn, macho, even violent. Indeed, he becomes so angry that he beats up the professor, whom he then defies to call the police.

Jaume does not call the police; however, when another teacher at the college learns about David's bisexuality, his hustling, and his beating of Jaume, he gets David thrown out of school. In the end, David makes peace with Jaume, and accepts responsibility for Alba's baby, but continues hustling. Seemingly, being a hustler goes deeper than any other aspect of David's personality.

At one point, David says that he does not believe "in great ideas. I like to fuck and read." Fucking represents the body; reading, the mind. In characterizing these two activities as his favorites (all he needs in life, as it were), he is implying a split between his body and his mind. Again, this split is often what hustlers in films like to pretend they have negotiated for themselves. David becomes most violent when this artificial split is threatened by Jaume learning his secret; but in fact, it is meant as the start of a healing process in which his two disparate sides can finally be united.

David is almost Nietzschean in his cult of youth, beauty and power. He tells the professor that he plans to kill himself when he grows older and loses his looks; the professor tries to urge a life of compromise on him, but David can see nothing but his own strength — the strength that makes him so attractive to his clientele. Here, hustling is not so much a bedraggled life on the streets as a lucrative enterprise in which David is paid a lot of money for being, or projecting the image of, a superior human specimen. "I'll never be what you and the others expect of me," he boasts to Jaume, showing his delight in confounding people's preconceived notions. David rides a motorcycle, emblem of the self-sufficient, rebellious loner refusing to mingle with the common herd. And his fear of becoming a father seems to stem from a fear of becoming like his own father, a weakling and a failure.

For her part, Alba is strong-willed and independent-minded. In spite of David's reluctance and her own parents' disapproval, she determines that she will be the one to decide what to do about her baby. Her decision to assume full responsibility for it suggests that she does not need David; and it is at this moment, however perversely perhaps, that David commits to helping her — without, however, giving up male prostitution. He will have both in his bisexual life: a heterosexual family and a wide clientele of gay men whose sexual needs he services for money.

College is often seen as a time for young men to experiment bisexually. There are familiar anecdotes about the aftermaths of drunken parties, or paying one's tuition by stripping at gay clubs. But in *The Rules of Attraction*, adapted from the novel by Bret Easton Ellis, being homosexual in college is depicted as rough and risky business. Gay student Paul Denton develops a series of crushes on straight male students. In return for his love, he gets rejection and ridicule; in one case, he is beaten up. He tries to offer them various bribes, drugs or restaurant meals, in the hope that they will be feel beholden to him and therefore sympathetic to his sexual needs; in a real sense, he is trying to turn straight men into situational bisexuals, or "prostitutes." He seems to think that even the most resistant guy has a price, which he merely has to find and name. When Paul meets campus heartthrob Sean Bateman (James Van Der Beek), he lures him back to his dorm room with marijuana. Sean sits shirtless at the foot of Paul's bed while Paul studies him. In voiceover, Paul muses about how "slutty" Sean looks, smoking Paul's pot; Sean becomes a blank slate on which Paul projects his own homoerotic desire. Then the screen splits, and on one half we see Paul's fantasy of pouncing on Sean and falling into his arms for a bout of passionate sex. The reality, however, is that Paul merely masturbates under a pillow while staring at the stoned, oblivious Bateman.

Sean continues to hang around with Paul, taking advantage of Paul's affection by borrowing videos from him which he intends to sell for money. In these woolly gray areas of relations between straight and gay men, the tables turn easily: Paul originally planned to exploit Sean's needs and weaknesses, but ends up having his own exploited by Sean. Ethics, if not sexual orientations, become situational. For Sean, love and sex with young women is a rather complicated dance of having to woo and manipulate them; it can be exhausting. But Paul's love is unconditional, open, there for the taking. If Sean becomes bisexual on any level, it is his willingness to accept Paul's love in one form or another (not sexually, however), whereas the other young straight men in the film will not let Paul anywhere near them, no matter what they might be able to get from him. At the end of the film, having undergone a kind of growth experience, Sean apologizes to Paul for hurting him by leading him on.

Situational bisexuality is hard to defend, precisely because it follows, not the so-called rules of attraction, but only the rules of ruthless self-interest. Unlike true bisexuality, which responds to affection from men and women and can return the same in kind, situational bisexuality does not respect feelings, even its own, from which it cuts itself off by its own rigorous logic of survival. Prostitution allows fantasy to briefly become reality, but only to coldly reveal, in the end, how far apart the two states remain. The most shocking intimacy between people is finally not any act of sex, but the moment when someone opens up to someone else about who he truly is and what he truly loves. A body can make itself available to any fantasy, for a price; but the ultimate truth about that body — what *he* fantasizes — often remains definitively unavailable.

11

Allegories of AIDS

AIDS is a tragic fact of our times, perhaps *the* central fact from a standpoint of social psychology. While denial of the disease itself has eroded, giving way to increasingly widespread educational campaigns about safe sex and increasingly improved medical treatments, denial of the impact of AIDS on our overall humanity is still strong. I do not only mean the impact of the disease on those who are infected and on those who know and love them; I mean the awareness, which belongs to everyone now, that sex and death have become far more linked that we would like them to be. Sex, the refuge, the respite, the relief; death, the reaper, the terror, the end of all. It is a painful, hopeless subject, because, on the one hand, in spite of science's best efforts, the virus remains incurable, and on the other hand, sex remains arguably the main activity by which people express their intimacy for each other and derive their sense of fulfillment in life. Even if the well is poisoned, one still needs to drink.

We have not even tried to begin to really understand the ways in which people have been forced to change as a result of the knowledge that sex can be life-threatening in a categorical sense. Have we become, or are we becoming, collectively more stunted, bitter and mean as a result of our sexual pleasure centers being invaded and short-circuited by thoughts of death? In the Western world, the gay community was hit earliest and hardest by the epidemic, losing nearly two entire generations, and thereby also losing certain links with its own past. Too many voices were silenced, too many relay torches dropped in what should have been a triumphantly evolving progression from one generation to the next. Gay artists of the 1960s and 1970s had only just begun to emerge from the long societal ban on gay thought, imagery and truth. Just as these artists were finally discovering ways, previously forbidden or unimaginable, of expressing their sexual identity, they died en masse, and their lessons to the future were cut short. Furthermore, it is hard, from our vantage point today, to even reach back and reconnect to the artists of those times, since their self-discoveries were directly tied to that moment of sexual openness which occurred in the 1960s and 1970s, in that sex enlarges the creative spirit and helps make people feel real to themselves. They are likely to seem "sex-obsessed" to us, in a naïve or gratuitous way, because we will never exactly know what it was like to feel the very real freedom that they felt, that sense of being on the threshold of a new world. Arguably, gay culture is less stylish, less bold, and less imaginative than it was before AIDS struck: politically, gays are more powerful today, but culturally and artistically, perhaps, less so than they have ever been.

But this is only one segment of the population. Again, in the Western world, AIDS was for a long time an exclusively gay issue, but it has ceased to be so: potential heterosexual transmission of the disease has forced everyone, gay and straight, male and female, to hold the same simultaneous, contradictory thoughts in his or her head — thoughts of pleasure and thoughts of pain, thoughts of well-being and thoughts of illness, thoughts of life-giving sexual energy and thoughts of death.

The promise of history was not supposed to be this way: watch nearly any film from the 1960s, nearly any one at all, and the thought of actual death is the furthest thing from any given "sex scene." Embarrassment of some kind, highly likely; violence of some sort, possibly — but actual death itself? In the 1960s, sex scoffed at death in every multi-orgasmic shudder of its vast universal body. This is certainly not to say that sex was ever wholly uncomplicated by an entire host of negative emotions and worries, only that in the 1960s some of the biggest obstacles had suddenly been cleared out of the way, in heterosexual as well as homosexual experience. (Homosexuality can never be, and will never be, liberated on a societal scale until heterosexuality is: the latter's shame and repression redouble themselves upon the former; in this, again, bisexuality is a key link.) The sexual revolution, as well as technological advances in contraception, freed people from centuries of the biological determinism which prevailed over sexuality. As if overnight, one could experience sexual pleasure without extreme consequences. Because of this, sex was untrammeled from many of the moral and religious strictures which had taken hold in a world where sex truly had a burdensome, hellish aspect, leading to unwanted pregnancies in which the mother was likely to die in childbirth, or to crippling, fatal venereal diseases such as syphilis. If the church succeeded for a thousand years in convincing the human race that sex was a curse, it was because, empirically, it certainly could be. Then, for a brief window of only two decades, sex began to come into a light it had rarely known in modern history. We were beginning to see a possible world in which sex did not have to be demonized.

AIDS brought biological determinism and its cruel logic back into the sexual equation. The consequences of this were as multifarious as they were immediate and bleak. In the 1980s, AIDS was not only a relentless killer, but a remorseless "outer" of men who had tried to hide their homosexuality all their lives. Among celebrities, Rock Hudson remains perhaps the most archetypal case: a movie star who had become famous precisely for playing staunchly heterosexual "he-men" turned out to have been gay. The only upside of this, and it was scant comfort, was that long-held notions of what gay and bisexual men could look like, sound like, be like were beginning to be revised and overturned. In much the same way that the Holocaust eventually led to greater acknowledgment of the humanity of Jewish people, and the lessening of anti-Semitic stereotypes, the brutal early years of the AIDS crisis ended up highlighting a deliberately buried truth: gay and bisexual men were already everywhere among us, and they were people whom one never would have "suspected." Again, this was scant comfort, since the gay and bi men who had been passing in the straight world often wanted to stay that way; nor did they wish to die to prove the point that they were every bit as human as anyone else. Nonetheless, as greater numbers of gay and newly-discovered-to-be-gay celebrities fell, the HIV positive diagnosis wreaked similar, if not worse, havoc on millions of gay and bi men who were not famous, and also on the closets they, too, had carefully maintained.

The bisexual male risks a more complex form of exposure if he contracts the virus: not only is his same-sex activity made public, but he experiences the guilt of possibly infecting the significant female partners in his life. For this reason, bisexual males have been criticized severely, in the AIDS era, for spreading the disease within the heterosexual community. Certainly, it is always a tragic situation when the pursuit of personal desire and happiness must be weighed against one's own life and the lives of one's loved ones. But the public "crucifying" of bisexual males is disturbing in several ways. For one, it reinforces a kind of complacent heterosexual mentality, which has been and often still is very damaging in terms of containing and treating AIDS, that AIDS is a gay problem only, and that the gay community must be closed off from the straight. In other parts of the world, such as Africa, AIDS has always been primarily a heterosexually-spread epidemic — with consequences just as devastating. In the human realm, the false distinction between the well-being of one community and that of another can only be regressive and injurious to both sides. It is, at the deepest level, blindness, ignorance and denial which spread AIDS, rather than sexual activity itself.

Also, because of anti–AIDS hysteria, the image of the bisexual male becomes distorted. Rather than being seen as a sincere individual trying to make the best of a difficult sexual orientation which he did not choose, he is viewed as an opportunistic raider, stealing across the well-defined (and well-policed) borders of identity to sow mayhem and death. The bisexual is actually a conduit between gay and straight communities, and therefore a "canary in the coal mine," so to speak, when it comes to any sexual concern in either community. Yet, he also tends to be depicted, stereotypically, as being in a form of deep denial, rendering him oblivious to health concerns. But the denial, here, is often not on the part of bisexual males, who may, in fact, be *more* cautious than their gay male counterparts. For one thing, bisexual males may already be getting some of their sexual needs met by their activity with women, and therefore are less "desperate" in their search for sex. Also, they may feel more comfortable seeking out males who are predominantly straight or who are bisexual themselves, therefore avoiding contact with the higher-risk gay community. In general, because they fear the risk of being exposed as bisexual, bisexual males may be "choosier" about the men they sleep with. The myth of the bisexual male as a walking set of genitalia always on the prowl is often precisely that, a myth.

Therefore, the denial is on the part of a straight community which prefers not to think that gays and bisexuals exist or matter in the first place. Sexual minorities only become visible when they become perceived as a problem for the heterosexual world, and then they are blamed simply for existing. If their existence had been seen all along, if they had been welcomed into the larger community of mankind from the beginning, AIDS would have been rightly seen from the beginning as a human problem.

Today the straight community is more informed about AIDS than it once was, and more active in trying to prevent the spread of the disease, as the gay community has been since the 1990s if not before. Straight women have been made as much aware of sexual risks as gay men, straight men as much as bisexual men. Therefore, it is, again, disingenuous to paint the bisexual male as a predator taking advantage of his female partners' trusting innocence (or ignorance). In this sense, too, male bisexuality challenges patriarchy's traditional structure of forcing men to play a paternalistic role toward infantilized women. Women *and* men are both becoming more responsible for their sexuality, as they must be. If sex was once where we were all (theoretically) able to become carefree and escape responsibility, it is no longer so; and getting back to my first point, we do not yet know the toll which this painful and rigorous self-responsibility has taken on our general sense of trust and personal freedom. For example, in contemporary U.S. society, the sharp rises in depression, obesity, and compulsive use of pornography may all be directly or indirectly related to the sense, among AIDS-era generations, that sexual desire can equal death. All of these syndromes could be seen as arising from a conscious or an unconscious hopelessness about being able to enjoy complete sexual freedom, and a need to redirect libidinal energies or compensate for their repression.

And yet, people still have and will continue to have sex, just as they fall in love, with all the best intentions and hopes of finding happiness. AIDS has become the cautionary sexual tale of our times, and the films that have been made about it reflect this. There is almost no way of depicting the disease (even in the most enlightened, compassionate of circumstances) without simultaneously raising the specter of "shouldn't have": *shouldn't have* too much sex, *shouldn't have* sex with members of the same sex, etc. It is the inevitable regret, self-blame, anger — all of the shadow emotions of sex which are whipped to frenzy by AIDS, a death sentence incommensurable with the innocent desire for sexual intimacy. AIDS lends itself to a certain shopworn if eternally instinctual and compelling form of allegory: purity, temptation, corruption; forbidden fruit; the skeletal, the marked. Again, we see the link between biological determinism and moralization: where our bodies seem to break down and fail us, the spirit (perceived as the body's ideal authoritarian master) is scourged for failing to resist evil influence. In this, there are certainly historical and literary parallels. In 19th century fiction, a woman became "fallen" if she had a baby out of wedlock; the female body betrayed its owner by getting pregnant. So, Tess of the D'Urbervilles becomes pregnant as a result of rape, but is herself the morally tarnished one; for Emma Bovary and Anna Karenina, being impregnated by their adulterous lovers reveals the sexual deceptions they have practiced. Pregnancy, with its visible biological processes and its inexorable end in childbirth, made the covert overt, and even substituted as a metonymy for death: the death of the "sinner." Today, for gay men, and perhaps especially for bisexual men, AIDS is the biologically determined fate which causes *them* to become "fallen."

The comparison is far from exact, but it is also far from flippant. To be a fallen woman in the 19th century was to court complete social ostracism; it meant, in a very real way, that one could not have a good life, could not have the life one wanted. (In fiction, if not always in reality, though surely there as well, it was also a kind of death sentence: the shamed body fell prey to illness, wore out, gave out — or simply committed suicide.) Today, AIDS is perceived in much the same terms, and indeed, operates in much the same way. This is certainly not to say that AIDS sufferers are fallen, or that they want other people, straight people and people without AIDS, to judge them or try to make them feel regretful about how they came to be infected. In all situations in a given society where there are deep divisions and even deeper inequalities between a majority group and a minority one, the minority tends to guard its most painful and self-blaming feelings from the stigmatizing eyes of the majority, so as not to become all the more vulnerable or give that majority ammunition to use against them. Also, the minority group will (sometimes with very good reason) view the majority as being at least partly responsible for the exacerbated suffering it is experiencing. (Create a social order in which a certain sexual practice is exiled to the public toilet, the back alley, the red light district, and one will soon have all manner of venereal diseases — history has shown this. Create a social order in which a certain segment of the population is inculcated to despise itself and regard itself as second-class citizenry, and one will have a segment of the population unwilling and unable to care for itself, even bent on its own destruction.) But hiding natural emotions, however difficult and painful, only deepens the initial wound of inequality. The resulting inability to be completely open and honest with others or oneself can produce further and more severe self-dislocations on top of those which the minority group is already forced to bear (as we have seen in Craig Lucas' *The Dying Gaul*, for instance).

Consciously or unconsciously, then, even AIDS sufferers internalize straight society's shame and blame about what they have done to place themselves at risk, or how they have been placed at risk. The thicker the closet walls surrounding the gay or bisexual male in question, the more intense these negative feelings are likely to be (although any human being is, understandably, prone to question his own choices under such a severe crisis as the threat of death). Some will twist themselves into hypocritical pretzels in order to avoid awareness of any kind, self- or otherwise. Perhaps the ultimate standard bearer of AIDS hypocrisy is Roy Cohn. A McCarthyite and rightwing New York politician who zealously campaigned against gay rights, Cohn was simultaneously engaging in the furtive gay sex that led to him dying from AIDS. The extremities of Cohn's schizoid identity have caused him to be taken up as a kind of metaphor for denial writ large — a metaphor employed in the struggle of gay activist art to heighten public consciousness about the disease. He appears as a villain in Mike Nichols' *Angels in America* (2003), insisting that the doctor officially change his AIDS diagnosis to the less sexually revealing "cancer." He has also been, along with Jack Smith (of all people), the subject of a provocative one-man show by Ron Vawter. Cohn and Smith would seem to make unlikely "bedfellows." With his films, artworks, writings and impromptu performances, Smith revolutionized the New York art world from the late 1950s through the 1980s. Unlike Cohn, Smith was always very open and confrontational about his gayness. Also unlike Cohn, he did not try to hide the fact that he contracted AIDS in the late 1980s.

Vawter's riveting show, *Roy Cohn/Jack Smith*, was filmed by Jill Godmilow in 1994. This unique film in fact captures one of Vawter's last performances; he himself died from AIDS-related causes. I want to begin, before moving on to two films that deal much more directly with the impact of AIDS on bisexual males — *The Velocity of Gary* (1998) and *The 24th Day* (2004) — by discussing *Roy Cohn/Jack Smith*, because of what it eloquently has to say about the nature of male sexual identity as public pose and lifelong construct, and the way AIDS both disrupts and confirms that identity. We can think of Cohn and Smith as figures out of allegory, Bad Knight and Good Knight, perhaps, Would-Be King and Holy Fool. They will come up again and again as signposts and archetypes.

Cohn, of course, considered himself straight, and desperately wanted to be considered straight by others, although he never, like many secretly gay politicians, went to the trouble of creating a plausible cover of wife and children. In Vawter's impersonation of Cohn, delivering a speech in 1978 to a Family Values consortium, Cohn walks a razor-thin tightrope between preaching about the evils of homosexuality and almost defying his audience to guess that he knows more about his subject than he lets on. He lingers over vivid descriptions of "fisting," and gay men hanging from chains in the backrooms of bars, inadvertently revealing not only his firsthand knowledge of this world but his utter obsession with it. He also reveals what psychiatrists once considered the classic kind of upbringing that produces gay men: weak father and domineering mother.

Cohn's self-conscious bluster demands that we think about a completely different kind of bisexuality: that of a gay man who insists so publicly that he is straight, and campaigns so much against other gay men, that his passionate anti-gay stance takes on a life of its own and assumes the character of a sexual identity in and of itself. At one point, Cohn asks the women in the audience if one of them would like to marry him (boasting that he is still "*young* middle-aged"); only in his public persona, with a podium between his body and the women in the room, does he assume a heterosexual desire. It is, of course, meant as a cover, though, again, not very convincing. Cohn's entire persona is a constant and elaborate, if ultimately thin, camouflage — but does Smith have a kind of cover as well? While I would never make the case that Smith was anything other than gay, the film emphasizes how his entire art and life were shadowed and enriched by an insistent idea of women. The kind of woman Smith revered — actress, "goddess," diva, glamour queen — was every bit as false as Cohn's prospective "wife." And yet, who would Smith have been without her? She is everywhere, from the snippets of Joan Crawford movie dialogue that speak for him in Vawter's show before he himself begins to speak, to the Egyptian harem costume he wears, to the gaudy costume jewelry which fills the toilet bowl beside him. The toilet bowl is significant, for Smith's Woman-in-Extremis is, indeed, both goddess and shit: a reminder of traumatic bodily functions, hateful and contaminating in her all-consuming mode, and yet all-powerful nonetheless. In spite of being gay, Smith would have been the last person on earth to want a world without women in it; indeed, if women had not existed, he would have had to invent them.

So even Smith's aggressive gayness is inflected by a need for women, a need to pay tribute to their beauty, their "superiority," certainly their superior attractiveness to (most) men. Offstage, an actual woman, Chica (Coco McPherson), also dressed like a harem girl, runs the slide projections for Smith. Now and then, he berates her, especially when she shows a slide of an erect penis (is this Smith-as-gay-man or Smith-as-pretend-lady finding the penis disgusting?); once, he holds up a tape recorder and dances "with her" to the music, both of them bobbing their heads in a moment of uncharacteristically sweet simpatico. Often, Godmilow shows us Smith from the wings of the stage, so to speak, with Smith small in the background and Chica large in the foreground, as if the assistant were actually controlling the maestro.

Vawter turns his impersonations into a duel of distinctive, deceptive voices. It is often thought that one can tell whether a man has gay tendencies by the sound of his voice: if he drawls, if he lisps, if he speaks in a high, shrill tone, if he speaks softly. For many, growing into a gay identity, the voice has been a kind of locus of trauma within the self, within the body, something to be feared, disguised, or silenced. In Cohn's case, he seems to love the sound of his own voice: he talks almost nonstop, his nasal tone harsh and brutal, as if to prevent any trace of effeminacy from slipping out. Vawter cleverly has him slur certain phrases into Freudian slips: "ask the common man" becomes "ask the condom man." By contrast, Smith's entire demeanor is proudly effeminate, yet his voice, like his beard, feels somehow out of place. Deep, drawn out, halting, Smith's voice suggests a parody of a Midwesterner looking around the Big City and growing woozy from all the tall buildings. Smith's actual stage voice could be more powerful, and more varied, than Vawter suggests; Vawter has him shout, or go into a higher register, only once or twice, briefly. Like Cohn's, Smith's voice is here presented as a weapon, and also a concealment, a kind of camouflage. Vawter suggests that all of Smith's hemming and hawing before beginning a performance — adjusting a light, fiddling with his headdress, staring at the audience with a glare both bored and reproachful — was really a way of working up to the sound of his own voice, finding and coming to accept it; Smith coming to accept, night after night, every time he spoke onstage, the very thing that one would think he would have no trouble accepting at all: the fact that he did not exactly sound "like a man."

Stigma is inevitable in a society which promotes and thrives upon it. No matter how unique and self-invented a person he is, a person remains, inevitably, a product of his society. Cohn speaks of how homosexuality goes against "three thousand years of sexual morality," citing Biblical passages that advocate putting men who have sex with other men "to death." But isn't Smith, in his Nefertiti drag and his mélange of "everything from ancient Egypt to 1940s," invoking the same judgmental period? The implication of Vawter's piece is that both men succumbed to the internalized command that they be "put to death"—with AIDS as the instrument of execution. Certainly, Cohn and Smith were very different, though Vawter sees them both having in common the fact that they lived in "a society which sought to repress their sexuality." They reacted to this repression in different ways, though in both cases it is a severely wounded male ego lashing out (or lashing inward). Cohn fought aggressively for power, while Smith made an equally aggressive display of his own lack of power, his chronic poverty and hunger. Cohn demanded to be seen as a "real man," while Smith—bearded, bald and in women's attire—threw into crisis the question of what a real man was. Both could be frightening, a defense mechanism to keep people from coming too close. And both were complete constructions, Cohn's homophobia and Smith's androgyny meeting at a point where simply "being" could never be adequate to mend their damaged psyches. When AIDS struck them both, it had the effect of a litmus test, with opposite results. With Cohn, it decimated his pose and revealed it as the bitter joke against himself which it always was. With Smith, it revealed the true seriousness that was always there behind his absurdist comedy, and conferred a less than ironic, less than theoretical reality upon his anxious, "long-suffering" persona.

* * *

Male bisexuality only complicates the difficulties of discussing AIDS: where does responsibility to one's own freedom and happiness leave off, and responsibility for one's partners' well-being begin? *The 24th Day* exploits AIDS paranoia for a dose of heavy-handed psychodrama. The film opens with close-ups of blood flowing through a bloodstream, set to ponderously dark, pseudo-industrial music, then cuts to a crowded straight bar where women are drinking with men. Like a microbe entering a mucus membrane, the camera prowls through the oblivious crowd until it zeroes in on Dan (James Marsden). Dan picks up drunken, gregarious Tom (Scott Speedman) and rushes back to Tom's apartment: he literally chases Tom up the stairs, while a passing neighbor taking his dog for a walk suggests that the film is comparing the two guys, in visual metaphor, to canines. But although Dan seems to be there for obviously sexual reasons, Tom's agenda grows vague once he gets Dan alone in his apartment. He becomes twitchier and twitchier, especially after Dan makes a pass at him. He wants to talk about their respective sexual histories, pressing Dan for the exact number of men Dan has slept with, and whether or not Dan is "safe." "Very," Dan reassures his skittish prey, turning up the charm and using patently evasive answers to tell Tom whatever he thinks Tom wants to hear. Dan displays what seems to be meant as a predatory streak when he admits that it would be more of "a turn-on" if Tom had never been with a man before. Throughout Dan's resourceful, futile attempts at seduction, Tom toys with him, laughing and shaking his head at all of Dan's lines. Eventually Tom reveals that he had a one-night stand with Dan five years ago, which Dan had not remembered.

Dan is now caught off guard, and Tom's strange, taunting, cat-and-mouse behavior turns suddenly violent: he knocks Dan to the floor and handcuffs him to a chair, taking him hostage. He tells Dan that he is responsible for him testing positive for HIV, since Dan is the only man he has ever slept with. He draws a syringe of Dan's blood and, in one of the film's many preposterous moments, runs out to some mysterious, all-night AIDS lab to have it tested, intending to keep Dan his prisoner until the results come back two days later. If Dan's test comes back positive, Tom says he intends to cut his throat and watch him bleed to death.

Dan tries to use psychology on Tom, alternately befriending him with recollections of favorite childhood TV shows and challenging him with remarks about how Tom must feel like a victim of society's homophobia. Tom does not consider himself gay, or even bi; he says, referring to his encounter with Dan, "One night doesn't make me anything." It turns out that Tom found out he was HIV positive when his wife (Thea Chaloner) tested positive after experiencing symptoms of full-blown AIDS. When she received her diagnosis, she crashed her car and died. All of this happened less than a month ago; Tom is on his "24th day" of knowing that he has the virus.

Tom cannot forgive himself for indirectly causing the death of his wife, and also causing her the painful realization of "how the man she's devoted her life to isn't the man she thought he was." The fear of having gay desires discovered by a female partner and being thought "less than a man" is sometimes endemic to closeted bisexual males. As usual, the ideal male role is viewed as a paternalistic one: "I was supposed to protect her," Tom says. Dan makes the point, handcuffed to Tom's living room couch, that it is easier for women to engage in same-sex activity than for men: their boyfriends wouldn't leave them over that, but instead would want to watch or join in, whereas a woman whose boyfriend wants to have sex with another man would "flip her lid." It is true that, according to confining societal roles, men are not supposed to surrender to love for each other, but the logic of the film belies and undermines the compassion of Dan's point, since Tom became infected precisely at the moment when he ventured outside of his traditional male role and allowed himself to be vulnerable with another man.

Indeed, *The 24th Day* directly likens unsafe sex to murder: Tom "killed" his wife; Dan deserves to be killed, in Tom's view, because he spread the virus. "Tell me you killed people.... Tell me you killed me, tell me you killed my wife," Tom says to Dan. At another point, Tom shouts, "We killed her!" As Tom proclaims his sense of personal guilt and responsibility more and more loudly, Dan's deep denial shows in stark contrast: Dan insists again and again that he always wears condoms, always knows his partners, *knows* that he is healthy. Meanwhile, Tom reveals that he has been stalking Dan for the past several nights, watching him pick up anonymous men and take them home: a multiplying network of disease. Tom's seduction is reified again and again as a meaningless, endlessly repeated gesture. The film chronically flashes back to the gay club where Dan meets his tricks; these scenes are staged like a horror movie, luridly lit and featuring scary, hellish music.

Sex certainly isn't love in *The 24th Day*, it's barely even sex, but instead a vehicle for demonstrating how little gay men regard themselves and each other. Sex is also a gateway to violence; it is significant that the film shows absolutely no real tenderness between men whatsoever, rather a series of fight scenes between Tom and Dan in which they are literally trying to kill each other. At one point, Dan takes advantage of Tom's drunken sobbing to try to hug and console him, but he is really reaching for the keys to the handcuffs behind Tom's back; when Tom notices this, he snaps back into angry, violent mode, pummeling Dan. It is never suggested that there could be reasons why men seek out each other for sex except as some kind of orgy of self-obliteration, a metonymy for the annihilation which the sex "inevitably" produces. The nameless young gay men hurl themselves, with vacant eyes and vacant smiles, into their deadly anonymous sex like so much blond, oblivious fodder.

Like Dan's repetition of anonymous sex, Tom dwells in a different kind of purgatory, reliving his moment of apparent "weakness" again and again with endless regret. Dan tries to get Tom to accept some responsibility for having slept with him in the first place: "You made a choice. I owe you nothing." But in one of the script's typically bombastic moments, Dan's infecting of Tom is likened to a playground fight which Tom endured as a kid, when he was clobbered from behind and ganged-up on. Tom's vengeance is, in his mind, like retribution, evening out the playing field.

But in whose elysian fields are these men at play? As if channeling Roy Cohn at his most apocalyptic, Tom revealingly invokes the Ten Commandments, shouting at Dan: "You fuck once and you can never be a virgin again; you steal once and you're always a thief; you lie once and you're always a liar." *The 24th Day* is moralistic to the point of seeming to be anti-sex in general. Tom's marriage is idealized, golden; but all sex outside of wedlock is depicted as rabidly compulsive. Dan becomes trapped by Tom because he can not bring himself to walk away from a potential one-night stand. When Tom offers to release him, early on, Dan lingers by the open doorway for a hug, in the hope that Tom will give in to his advances; after Dan throws Tom to the floor and handcuffs him, he says, "You should have left." "Should have" hangs heavily over everything Tom says and does: he is unable to release himself from the guilt of surrendering once to a forbidden desire, since that *once* turned out to be *once too often*. Desire in every form has become deathly and evil to him. Anyone on the prowl for sex is seen as demonic, deceitful, even vaguely psychopathic. There is a scene where Tom leaves his hostage to blow off steam in a bar, and gets hit on by an older woman (Jona Harvey). She wants to go home with him. From Tom's bemused, heartbroken perspective, she seems predatory, almost salivating as she licks her lips over him. Unwilling to take his quiet "no" for an answer, she first turns vicious, telling Tom he's "nothing special," then tries to use psychology on him, much as Dan does throughout the film, asking him if he knows what it's like to be lonely. The film cuts to one of its insidious, doom-laden flashbacks of Tom leaving the gay club with Dan, five years before, the music like a stalling heartbeat or a ticking bomb. In *The 24th Day*, the wages of loneliness, like the wages of sin, are death.

* * *

The great era of the New York underground more or less came to an end in the late 1980s with the passing of Jack Smith and the AIDS-related deaths of a number of his contemporaries. The bedraggled characters in *The Velocity of Gary* are living in the rubble of that scene, priding themselves on bringing back the heady freedoms and hedonisms of the Warhol Factory crowd, perhaps. But they are essentially pale imitations of their original counterparts, just as the film itself tries mightily to recall *Midnight Cowboy*'s devastating emotional insights into the misfit denizens of surreal urban street life, without achieving the same authenticity, profundity and intensity.

In fact, *The Velocity of Gary* tries too hard in just about every department, from its fussy, pretentious title, to the pro forma freakiness of its local-color details, to its trendy use of non-linear storytelling, in this case more distracting than revelatory or insightful. Also, its characters all wallow in an unearned sense of self-importance. In a way, their central tragedy is their constant denial of how ordinary, and how marginalized, they actually are. They are mythologizing and self-mythologizing to a fault. Valentino (Vincent D'Onofrio) is a porn star, obsessed with fame and self-invention. His porn films are all heterosexual, but he himself is bi. He is in love with Mary Carmen (Selma Hayek), a moody, streetwise bombshell who yearns to be Diana Ross and who cannot hold down even the least demanding waitress job because of her uncontrollable temper and bad attitude. Together, they share a passion for sex and artifice, and a kind of hostile paranoia toward outsiders, the clueless people they call "tourists."

Into their world comes a young, corn-fed newcomer to the city, whom Valentino picks up on the street one day and christens "Gary" (Thomas Jane). Gary has been selling his plasma in order to eat; Valentino drags him off to a job at a gay phone-sex line, and simultaneously seduces him. It is the beginning of an intense love affair between the two men, and also the beginning of a downward-spiraling career in sex work for Gary, who eventually drifts into street hustling.

Valentino does not hide his gay side from Mary Carmen, and immediately introduces his two lovers to each other. The hostility between them is instantaneous, and Valentino says with quiet sarcasm, "Well, I'm glad you guys like each other." Nonetheless, the three of them go to a gay club and proceed to take over the dance floor, putting on a show in which Valentino alternately grinds with Mary Carmen and Gary. We see that Valentino relishes in performing his bisexuality in public, partly because, like any good porn star, he is exhibitionistic, and also partly because the film depicts him as being obsessed with sex in general. When he first meets Gary, he tells him: "Fantasy — now there's a sport for you. People say, if you could fuck yourself you'd never leave the house. The truth is, if you could fuck yourself you'd do it everywhere...." The idea that the world revolves around sex is the closest thing Valentino has to a philosophy, but the double meaning of "fucking yourself" — "destroying yourself" — is brought home by the fact that Valentino is eventually diagnosed with AIDS.

After Valentino becomes ill, the tensions in this *ménage à trois* fissure into faultlines. Mary Carmen and Gary try to pull together at least enough to help Valentino, but their temperaments and lifestyles are not suited to caretaking. Mary Carmen is particularly stressed out, mourning the loss of her and Valentino's formerly carefree life: "Everything's wrong with everything that used to be perfect," she says in one scene, and in another, "Everything used to be so much fun." The grim, dismal atmosphere of the hospital particularly irritates her: "I can't go to the hospital every fucking day," she tells Gary. Anger is a way in which she deals with her sadness over Valentino; Gary's way is to hold his emotions inside and take charge, sorting out Valentino's multiple pill bottles and ordering Mary Carmen not to give him any more cigarettes. Mary Carmen's response is to say to Gary, "I wish it was you who was sick instead of him." Nonetheless, Gary and Mary Carmen each possess qualities that help Valentino. Mary Carmen lifts his spirits with her sheer energy, while the sober Gary tries to keep Valentino's treatment on track, prodding him to keep his doctors' appointments. This is an intriguing reversal on the typical roles of bisexual love triangles in films: usually, it is the female partner who represents responsibility and maturity, and it is the male partner who represents reckless abandon to the illicit and to "pure pleasure."

Mary Carmen sneaks Valentino out of the hospital so the three of them can march in the Halloween parade; they impersonate the Supremes, with Gary and Valentino in matching wigs and gowns and Mary Carmen as Diana Ross, spreading her arms and lip-syncing to "Ain't No Mountain High Enough." It is another moment of glory, of bisexual performativity, for the trio, but Valentino becomes disoriented in the crowd and begins to cough up blood. He lands right back in the hospital, where a nurse cautions him, "You're lucky nothing happened." "It used to be lucky if something did happen," he says.

Valentino is released, and the trio moves into an apartment together. In one scene, Valentino is up late watching *Suddenly, Last Summer* on TV, with Mary Carmen asleep on one of his shoulders and Gary asleep on the other. But Valentino's attempt to construct a bisexual idyll is doomed, of course, not only by the fact that he is dying but also by the fact that Mary Carmen and Gary continue to squabble over everything from Gary liking to watch talk shows to her spending all their food stamps on "Toastettes" and potato chips. She induces Valentino to cha-cha around the apartment, and Gary, seemingly out of jealousy, breaks them up, reminding them about the doctor's orders. "Something has gotta change around here," Valentino says.

Nonetheless, although he has a rough-and-tumble relationship with her, Gary defends Mary Carmen if anyone else insults her; he nearly beats someone up in a pinball arcade for calling her "a crazy bitch." Things spiral even lower for the trio when Mary Carmen discovers that she is pregnant with Valentino's baby and that she, too, has tested positive. Demoralized, she plays jump-rope with some young girls, hopping faster and faster as if to reverse the years and become a happy child again.

This theme of wanting to recapture a lost innocence recurs throughout

The Velocity of Gary. Gary has a vision of his younger self waving to him from a Greyhound bus pulling into Grand Central. In a scene that attempts a certain surrealism but feels somewhat flat (and inexplicable), Valentino acts in a children's theater production of "Grimm's Fairy Tales": as Prince Charming, he awakens a prepubescent Sleeping Beauty with a chaste kiss on her hand. In another scene, Mary Carmen accosts a school crossing guard, Mrs. Sanchez (Gloria Irizarry), and is surprised when the older lady does not remember helping her cross the street when she was a little girl. "There've been so many," Mrs. Sanchez says matter-of-factly. "But it's me, *me*, little Mary Carmen...." "*There've been so many*," the guard reiterates forebodingly, as if the line had a double meaning regarding Valentino's sexual promiscuity. The threatening reality of AIDS has made all three characters question the decisions they have made in life.

Gary follows a man on the street who looks like Valentino; he turns out to be a stranger, but he leads Gary into a church. Gary sits in a pew and listens to the Mass; when he leaves, he seems profoundly shaken. He goes to a porn theater and watches one of Valentino's old movies; he weeps and nuzzles his cheek against Valentino's leather jacket, but leaves in the middle, as if the religious experience in the church had somehow rendered the sexual spectacle hollow for him. He seems to be venturing away from the entire mythology which Valentino's charisma built up around the three of them, like an architecture that was meant to keep them all safe but did not. For his part, however, Gary remains uninfected, in spite of having had sex with Valentino for years and also working as a street hustler; apparently, Gary is a "total top" who only receives oral sex from men.

After Valentino dies, Gary and Mary Carmen continue to share the apartment. She gives birth to a daughter, and, in yet another act of self-mythology, names the baby "Hope." "They told me there's a good chance she's gonna be fine," she proudly tells Gary, offering to let him hold the infant. As in *All About My Mother*, a baby born from an AIDS-infected relationship turns out to represent "hope" for an AIDS-free future. Motherhood seems to soften Mary Carmen; she tells Gary that the baby is partly his, "by association," and that she would like him to help raise the little girl if Mary Carmen should get sick. Smiling, he joins Mary Carmen in her hospital bed and kisses her on the forehead, which makes her giggle; it is a breakthrough of sorts, a reconciliation between Valentino's two surviving lovers, and it suggests that, now that he is gone, they may even form a heterosexual family together. The film ends with a close-up of baby Hope's serene, almost pensive face.

AIDS is the great destroyer, in *The Velocity of Gary*, of Valentino's reckless, lofty bisexuality, his utopian dream of being able to indulge every fantasy, every form of pleasure. This may be why the film seems less transcendent — and the New York underground scene which it depicts, less fertile — than the Warhol films and *Midnight Cowboy*. People are meaner, pettier, and their world more arid, because they can no longer trust that off-kilter romanticism which appears again and again as innocent fun amid the high decadence of the 1960s. I think of the scene of Taylor Mead and Joe Dallesandro dancing to the Beatles in Warhol and Paul Morrissey's *Lonesome Cowboys* (1968)— how far removed from those goofy high-jinks is the thought of what AIDS would later bring. In the 1960s, sex was still a land of plenty to be discovered and explored, sweet refuge from the harshness of urban survival. In the 1990s, bleak, day-by-day survival is all that is left for Valentino, Mary Carmen and Gary.

* * *

Cautionary tales such as *The 24th Day* and *The Velocity of Gary* leave one feeling torn, to say the least. They seem overloaded with mixed messages and symptoms of bad faith, in that they dwell on those aspects of gay and bisexual experience which are morbid and deceitful. The entrance of infection infects everything, retroactively, even the good, the true, the loving. These films' treatment of AIDS, therefore, only serves to further pathologize a pathology (the virus) and even re-pathologize same-sex activity itself, by presenting AIDS not as a tragic turn in the lives of gay and bi men, but somehow as the inevitable outcome of those lives, a kind of readymade judgment. It would probably be too much to ask that every film about AIDS could be as great as Téchiné's *The Witnesses*, in which we understand the all-too human tendency to get caught up in the excitement and freedom of casual sex, in which Manu's illness and death bring out the best, rather than the worst, in his friends, relatives and caretakers, and in which the straight and gay worlds come together to mourn the devastations of the AIDS crisis and to work toward a more hopeful tomorrow. For every heartfelt, balanced masterpiece like *The Witnesses*, there are too many films about AIDS which peep into the gay and bi world seemingly only to get an eyeful of it at its worst.

What is the lesson — I almost want to say, the point — of these films? Gary's "conversion" from church of porn to church of Christ is only one of many moments of ham-fisted moral symbolism in *The Velocity of Gary*, suggesting that the film may, in fact, be covertly religious and antigay. It is the same, in *The 24th Day*, when Tom delivers his monologue about his wife being "up in heaven," knowing the truth about him now and looking down on him. AIDS unfortunately has given people license to demonize male bisexuality and homosexuality. Engaging in same-sex activity becomes, de facto,

The AIDS crisis brings out the best in the characters in André Téchiné's *The Witnesses* (2007). Mehdi (Sami Bouajila, left) is forgiven by his wife Sarah (Emmanuelle Béart, middle, holding infant) for having an affair with a gay man. Both come together with Steve (Lorenzo Balducci) and Steve's lover, Dr. Adrien (Michel Blanc, far right) to combat the disease and bear witness to its devastation.

a form of "going too far" in and of itself. The end always comes down to the worst that can happen when one ventures outside the bounds — but outside the bounds of what? AIDS is humanity's problem, there is no conceivable sexuality that *cannot* spread it. The AIDS sufferer is the human, the all-too human perhaps, but is too often reduced to an emblem of the wages of sin. His corpse has labeled him "gay" for all to see and repeat, even if he himself, in life, never felt comfortable with that label, or truly found it inapplicable. The label is, ultimately, for the comfort of those who survive, who do not have to claim it, who can evacuate their own fears, in cowardly fashion, upon the dying and the dead. As Jack Smith said: "They love dead queers here."

It remains difficult even to talk about AIDS (in many ways, this chapter has been the hardest to write) for precisely the same reasons that it is difficult to dramatize the illness: it truly is the darkest side of gay and bi experience. In a puritanical society such as ours, which demonizes sex, sexually related diseases fall into a category of moral blame, even if very few people are sadistic enough to relish the misguided notion of AIDS as a "punishment." No one makes it a moral issue when someone's consumption of fast food, for instance, leads to diabetes, heart attacks, and cancer. Eating is innocent, even celebrated, and the lie, "I didn't realize what I was eating was so bad for me," is considered a necessary blindness, understandable by all. We don't make them replay, in their minds, all those times they stood in line at the Food Court, salivating, begging, willing to pay hard cash for the calories, grease, sugar and cholesterol that poisoned their systems. There are permissible forms of bingeing, escape, refuge in our society, and there are impermissible ones: in any event, the individual who chooses to eat those fries, light up that cigarette, or swallow that Ambien is alone with his choice. Whereas sex involves others — and this makes a difference.

Just as the risk of infection forces a kind of stalemate of trust between prospective sex partners (romance can falter at the insistence of a condom; also at the refusal of one), so the same stalemate obtains in AIDS films. Who can be trusted to view the problem in ways which do not make the problem worse? This stalemate is likely to remain as long as gay and bisexual lives are politicized by default, as long as those lives are forced to defend themselves from the straight world's disapproval (and from their own). To live in utter denial of the risk is foolhardy to the point of insanity. But, admitting the extent of the power it holds over us all is sometimes like wagging yet another finger in the faces of gay and bi men still struggling to emerge from societal homophobia. The truth can kill, and so can the denial. The effect is as dizzyingly surreal and terrifying as the thought of Roy Cohn coming back from the dead to deliver his own eulogy. Imagine what he might, finally, say? Would he accept that personal responsibility he shirked all his life? Would he rail against the antigay political policies he helped enforce and propagandize? Or would he deny his death the same way he denied his life, stubborn and sad and blithe and corrosive as ever? Would he even, by his own hateful logic, express happiness that he himself had been punished for the gayness within him, labeled for the eyes of the world and put to death?

12

In His Wake: The Strange Power of the Dead Bisexual

In *Velvet Goldmine*, the flamboyant bisexual rock star Brian Slade fakes his own death in the mid–1970s at the height of his success by having himself appear to be shot onstage during a concert. This assassination stunt symbolically marks the end of the glam-rock or glitter-rock era. But it also has personal meaning for Slade, whose androgynous persona has courted public controversy and whose complicated private life (including marriage to a woman as well as a sexual affair with a man) has become overwhelming to him. He seeks a way to escape from the pressure of the larger-than-life bisexual "character" he has created. In the 1980s, he resurfaces under an alias, Tommy Stone, still a rock star but far more mainstream and decidedly heterosexual in his orientation. The bisexual must die for the heterosexual to be reborn. And yet, the faked shooting also serves to build a massive legend around Slade, who continues to haunt Tommy Stone as a discarded piece of himself—perhaps the best and most brilliant piece—which he cannot quite outlive or outrun.

There is a dual syndrome at work here. First, the restless, untamed energies of the bisexual male — and the societal controversies which they awaken — become something which only his death (figurative or literal) can contain. Second, those bisexual energies and controversies prove to be so strong, so compelling and puzzling, that not even death can contain them. This same template has appeared in various forms in several other recent films: the death of a bisexual male is merely the beginning of a strange kind of afterlife in which his survivors — fans, lovers, family, friends, enemies — are left trying to solve the ongoing riddle of who this man was, whom it was he truly loved, and why he had to die.

One of the better-known of these films is Patrice Chéreau's *Ceux Qui M'Aiment Prendront le Train* (*Those Who Love Me Can Take the Train*, 1998). Somewhat like Robert Altman's ensemble dramas, *Those Who Love Me* decentralizes its narrative over an array of characters gathering for the funeral of the famous, brilliant, irascible painter, Jean-Baptiste (Jean-Louis Trintignant). Jean-Baptiste has insisted on being buried in the country, thereby forcing his loved ones to journey from Paris in order to pay their last respects. In the long opening montage, impressively conceived and edited, we hear the painter's voice speaking over shots of the disparate mourners arriving at the train station and then settling in together, uncomfortably, on the train. This voiceover is the painter's last taped interview, conducted with his biographer and ex-lover François (Pascal Greggory), and it is as if Jean-Baptiste's spirit, reaching out from beyond the grave, were connecting the various mourners, who include other ex-lovers of both genders. During this montage, the camera's viewpoint is radically displaced over a variety of people whose identities and connections to each other are not made immediately apparent — the viewpoint of a disembodied spirit, perhaps, but significantly, the spirit of a bisexual artist, drawn to watching both men and women.

One of the mourners is an androgynous young man, Bruno (Sylvain Jacques), who, we learn, is infected with AIDS and who seems to be on the verge of coming between François and his current lover, Louis (Bruno Todeschini). Bruno and Louis make significant eye contact in the station and, later, physical contact in the bathroom of the train. Louis' attraction to Bruno becomes problematic when he learns that Bruno has AIDS, but throughout the film he is attracted to the young man more and more, in spite, or perhaps even because, of the threat of infection. It is an example of how Jean-Baptiste's extremely nihilistic, death-obsessed philosophy seems to float freely among the mourners, casting a certain spell over them, as it were, and leading them to commit their own acts of destruction and self-destruction.

Chéreau's film is very much a manifesto and cry of despair about the AIDS crisis, and a somber tribute to the hundreds of thousands of gay men who have died of AIDS. Not once but twice, his camera prowls over a sprawling cemetery as if summoning up the vision of a vast necropolis populated by deceased AIDS sufferers, as well as commenting on the omnipresence of death in the sexual lives of all gay men. In the second of these solemn tracking shots, at the end of the film, the camera seems to be adopting Jean-Baptiste's point of view, his spirit seemingly set free to fly over his burial place and witness his friends as they go their separate ways. Louis reaches the difficult conclusion that as a gay man he owes it to Bruno to return his love, to "take care of him," as he says. Louis proposes to François that the three of them live together as a *ménage à trois*, but François rejects this idea. If anything, the film condemns François as a person of bad faith for not loving Bruno. By judging Bruno for potentially spreading the virus, François displays a lack of gay solidarity. After witnessing the sexual coupling of Louis and Bruno through a hotel window, the sulky François rides off alone in a cab, his health protected, perhaps, but his life condemned to isolation. (Ultimately, watching others make love, and being excluded from their bliss, may be the closest we can come to experience what death feels like, in life; therefore, for François to avoid literal death in one sense is only to acutely suffer it in another.) AIDS activism made ubiquitous the idea that when one sleeps with anyone, one is sleeping with everyone whom that person has ever slept with — what is called, in sexual parlance, "taking a train" (multiple partners at once) — and I believe this is the secondary meaning of Chéreau's title: if a gay man truly loves another gay man, he will take him with his sexual baggage and all, will "take the train" of his ex-partners and thereby share in his HIV status precisely as an expression of human and political solidarity.

The disturbing implications of this as a philosophy — Chéreau is no stranger to nihilist death cults, having devoted much energy to an epochal staging of Wagner's Ring Cycle — are difficult to accept. (I myself tended to sympathize with François, who wanted to stay healthy.) The romantic idea that one should risk exposure to AIDS so as not to be like the judgmental, shaming homophobes is certainly dubious; the only way that Louis's actions toward Bruno make sense is that he is enacting, much like other mourners do throughout the film, the implicit command of Jean-Baptiste, from beyond the grave, to submit to the death instinct, to follow him into the void. The power of the dead bisexual, in *Those Who Love Me Can Take the Train*, is to call out to his survivors to join him in death. He who has already "done it all" (slept with both genders, become a great artist, been a drug addict) and initiated so many of his acolytes into behaviors they might never have otherwise tried, still holds this lure of the edge, a siren song teasing lesser, weaker beings to see if they are strong enough to live in the nihilistic way he did, and indeed, to die the way he did.

Because the painter's male lovers far outnumber her, they tend to belittle Lucie (Marie Daëms), the one woman among them who claims to have slept with Jean-Baptiste, even, at times, accusing her of exaggerating her place in his life. At one point she rather smugly claims that Jean-Baptiste was fascinated with her because she was "the unattainable woman"; but François contradicts her, saying that she was the one who threw herself at him because he was the unattainable man. Strangely enough, one of Lucie's most vehement adversaries is not a gay man but a woman, Claire (Valeria Bruni Tedeschi). Claire is the ex-wife of Jean-Marie (Charles Berling), the painter's nephew and also one of his male lovers. Claire dismisses Lucie's claim to having loved or been loved by Jean-Baptiste with the hostile summary: "You raped him once in Madrid, ages ago." Claire may be speaking from jealousy; some intense feelings are implied to have existed between Claire and Jean-Baptiste. (Perhaps they slept together as well; the film becomes so dizzyingly incestuous that one begins to imagine everyone connected in a zigzagging lineage of blood or semen or both.) It may also be that Lucie — as a sort of fussy, old-fashioned, would-be *grande dame*— strikes the others as having been unworthy of the uncompromising artist. But it seems telling that the film builds hardly any bridge between the gay and straight characters; on the contrary, it reinforces preexisting barriers. The gay men seem intent on taking possession of Jean-Baptiste's legacy by resolving his complex attachments in favor of strict homosexuality, while the female lover seems to want to plump up her role in the story wherever possible. In Chéreau's film, the spirit of the dead bisexual confuses and divides.

Again, it is partly the extent to which Jean-Baptiste was bisexual that becomes problematic in this extremely pro-gay film. Two of his male lovers who are themselves bisexual are the two mourners who are singled out for the most hatred, both being seen as selfish, destructive and weak. Thierry (Roschdy Zem) is the male nurse who took care of the dying painter; he was also his drug buddy and part-time lover. In the early scenes, he is shown driving the painter's coffin in a station wagon alongside the train as the obsessed mourners stare from the train windows for any glimpse, however vestigial, of Jean-Baptiste's body. "Now he's got a kid, he's become a family man," one of the characters says of Thierry, an observation at odds with his dangerous, antisocial lifestyle as a junkie. Thierry speaks with deep pain about how Jean-Baptiste had wanted to die in his arms. But unlike Jean-Baptiste, whose bisexuality has been, again, contained by death, Thierry is seen, not as a romantic free spirit, but a maddening imp of the perverse, cut off from others, prone to rages. Similarly, Jean-Marie has led his life in the shadow of his formative experience with Jean-Baptiste, whom he strives to imitate by carrying on his uncle's rebellion against the bourgeois spirit of the family itself. At Jean-Baptiste's graveside, Jean-Marie delivers a eulogy against procreation, declaring that he intends the family line to end with him — a speech which is calculated to hurt Claire, who is pregnant with his child. Rather than valorizing Jean-Marie or at least acknowledging his helpless pain at having been psychologically imprinted by his charismatic uncle, Chéreau makes Jean-Marie seem feckless and fatuous, throwing petulant tantrums, making messes for other people to clean up. Chéreau also focuses on the disapproval of Jean-Marie's father (also played by Trintignant) toward his son's life choices, as well as Claire's pain at having been abandoned. In fact, as pro-gay as this film is, Chéreau shows great identification for the pain of depressed, neglected women, suggesting that he finds room in his vision of homosexuality for expressing the regret that it so often excludes women — all the more surprising that his film extends so little sympathy to the bisexual males, depicting them as betrayers, more or less without nuance, and depicting bisexuality as a state of confusion, bringing pain to others.

* * *

Those Who Love Me is impossible to understand outside the cult of the great artist — the artist as sacred monster, certainly, but also as media superstar and cottage industry whose work supports a variety of other people. Jean-Baptiste's power over others is finally the power of art itself, to speak to people, to bring out their contemplativeness, their sensuality, their thirst for life, and their remorse. Art is always bisexual (even if artists are not), moving its audience regardless of gender or orientation. It comes from, and aims at, a place where what is human transcends all prefabricated categorization, while remaining supremely alive to what "turns it on."

A different, equally charismatic kind of bisexual artist — a young rock star on the verge of fame — is depicted in *Chacun sa Nuit* (*To Each His Night*; U.S. title: *One to Another*, 2006), directed by Pascal Arnold and Jean-Marc Barr. *To Each His Night* is, I believe, a remarkable film, which should be better known outside the category of gay cinema to which it has been relegated. Rich, profound, elegiac, while retaining a chillingly hard edge, the film is the work of naturally gifted directors. (Barr, also a veteran actor, is a compatriot of Lars von Trier.) The film is based on a true-crime story which occurred in France, and centers around four best friends who play together in a rock band: Pierre (Arthur Dupont), Nicholas (Guillaume Baché), Sébastien (Pierre Perrier), and Baptiste (Nicholas Nollet). Pierre is the band's leader and singer; he is also bisexual. He is extremely close to his sister Lucie (Lizzie Brocheré). Pierre disappears one day, and Lucie devotes herself to finding out what happened to him. When his body is discovered, beaten to death, she keeps searching for answers until she goes insane and has to be committed to a mental hospital. For her, everything has been betrayed, turned inside out. Pierre's utopian drive for constant, endless pleasures of the flesh has ended in a brutal homicide. His body, which had formerly given itself to acts of love, has become a mangled, broken sacrifice — indeed, the ultimate sacrifice for its own unbridled passion, its need for physical contact, and even, perhaps, its need to be punished for "going too far."

12. In His Wake

Lucie (Lizzie Brocheré, left) sunbathes with her brother Pierre (Arthur Dupont, middle), who is also her lover, and her lover Nicholas (Guillaume Baché), who is also Pierre's lover. *To Each His Night* (2006) employs incest as an extreme metaphor for the broken bonds of intimacy among alienated, contemporary French youth.

Does the seemingly guiltless Pierre actually feel guilt? Throughout the film, there are suggestions of sexual tensions among the close circle of friends. Lucie and Pierre have an intense and incestuous relationship; she is only too happy to indulge his narcissistic needs when he cuddles naked with her in bed and asks her to tell him how beautiful he is. They discuss their other partners, and she assures Pierre that sex is "never better" than it is with him. Lucie also sleeps with Nicholas and Sébastien, who both conclude that she is hopelessly in love with Pierre and unable to love anyone else. Sébastien harbors resentment toward Lucie for her bond with Pierre, and after Pierre dies, he tells her: "You're selfish like your brother, always using people. What you did together was sick. You've been punished." Pierre is also having a sexual relationship with the secretly bisexual Nicholas, a secret which must be kept or Nicholas "would do himself in." At one point, Pierre tries to lure Nicholas into prostitution, to which Nicholas angrily replies: "It's disgusting. You're sick.... It's fucked up!" Baptiste, insecure about his sexual prowess after being dumped by his girlfriend for not being good in bed, asks Sébastien if he can watch him have sex sometime, in order to learn to do it better. But it is Pierre who coaxes and coerces Baptiste into joining him in a sexual threesome with Julie (Marion Donon), though Baptiste is made very embarrassed and uncomfortable by this, and ends up sitting naked on the edge of the bed, with his back to the couple as they make love. Like the lyrics of Pierre's songs, which boast of casual one-night stands that leave him feeling disgusted and bored, Pierre's omnivorous carnality defines the group of friends, each of whom must negotiate his own awkward relationship to Pierre.

Some moments in the film imply that both Pierre and Lucie indulge in a kind of cult of youth and beauty. Pierre interrogates Lucie about whether she ever gets "fed up" with all the repetitions of daily life: eating, pissing, shitting, itching, shaving, etc. Although this scene is played as light banter, it suggests that Pierre would, perhaps, rather die young than grow old in a stale, unfulfilling life. Lucie stares at herself in the mirror, pulling down the bags under her eyes, and asks her mother (Valérie Mairesse) when she first began to feel old. "The first time you asked me that," the mother replies. Although it is too easy to say that Pierre truly *wants* to die, *To Each His Night* resonates with the classic doomed romanticism of the lyric poet who peaks, and dies, young: a mini-tradition within western culture that includes Keats, Kleist, Rimbaud (not to mention Joy Division's Ian Curtis, whom Pierre somewhat resembles). "Deprived of his youth," Lucie says at one point, waxing philosophical, "man becomes the accomplice to his death." Or, put otherwise: live fast, die young, leave a beautiful corpse. To a large extent, the illusions which Pierre fostered about his life—that he was in some sense invincible, that pleasure could always solve every problem—drive his survivors insane as they try to make them congruent with the blunt reality of his death.

Grieving and overcoming grief require bonds of kinship deeper and more authentic than merely sexual ones. This touches on a larger societal problem: how do people who have rejected tradition (or who have been cast out of tradition) manage to forge bonds of kinship around wholly new rituals and traditions? Lucie says at one point: "Life lacks rituals, don't you think?" Like the bickering mourners in *Those Who Love Me Can Take the Train*, the young people in *To Each His Night* face the difficulty of acknowledging the true emotional weight of certain group moments, since their lives are so devoted to apathetic pleasures and the steadfast avoidance of cliché.

Still, they speak of missing Pierre; in death, he stirs their need for kinship, but without his immediate presence they seem to feel somewhat lost. (As if to emphasize the importance of Pierre's sheer presence, the narrative is nonlinear, with scenes of Pierre alive mixed in with scenes of the other characters trying to cope after he has died.) Worship of Pierre is signaled in the scenes where he is singing with his band; he is filmed from a low angle, the point of view of someone staring up in adoration. But this adoration becomes more and more insubstantial and diffuse when Pierre himself is gone, much like the difficulties of maintaining any faith in an incorporeal deity. The opening shot of the film shows Lucie and the four men dancing, but as shadows against a stony wall: the image suggests primitive cave paintings, and sets the tone for the film, as a study of people trying to live essentially pagan lives in a post-pagan world. In retrospect, the use of shadows rather than actual figures and faces comes to seem not only ageless and universal (again, like cave paintings) but rather sinister as well, suggestive of something not entirely human or differentiated. Even in the taboo-breaking world of Pierre and Lucie, a certain amount of conformism (to emblems which symbolize their rebellion) is the inevitable coin of the realm. For example, to augment their close bond, Pierre and Lucie have matching strawberry tattoos on their right buttocks. Like similar pagan rites, bodily ornamentation becomes an expression of tribal solidarity. And the symbol becomes, in some ways, more important than the feeling of love itself: although Lucie does not seem to mind sharing Pierre with Nicholas, she slaps Nicholas angrily when he invades her sense of ritual by showing that he has gotten the same strawberry tattoo on his buttock.

When Lucie discovers that she is pregnant, she convenes the surviving members of the band at the spot where Pierre was killed — "like an exorcism," she says. It is another kind of non-traditional group ritual she is seeking, something to fill her the way Pierre did: "We're here to ward off bad fate. I wanted to share this with you." Again invoking Pierre's ongoing presence in death, she looks around at the bleak, rocky scene with wildly staring eyes and says: "Pierre saw this before he died." She announces that her unborn child is a boy and that she will name him Pierre. She also says the baby is Sébastien's, but will belong to all four of them. This is reminiscent of *A Home at the End of the World*, where the bisexual triangle attempts to raise a baby as a trio. It is also distantly reminiscent of Goethe's novel *Elective Affinities*, where the offspring of two enmeshed love triangles bears an uncanny resemblance to all four of its "parents," and is doomed to die in infancy. The same doom hangs over *To Each His Night*: even as Lucie and the three men hug each other, there are strange feelings of guilt, resistance and madness in the air; she eventually gets an abortion.

In another scene that speaks to the characters' expressed need for new rituals, they watch as Pierre's body is cremated. Lucie says, "It was unimaginable. None of us had ever been to a cremation before. Pierre keeps teaching me things." The influence of Pierre lives on — and also, by the simple fact that he has become the first to die, he remains the one among them who pushes forward into the future, trying new things and dragging the others along behind him. The fact that even what she is witnessing with her own eyes — a coffin with Pierre inside being slid into a furnace — is "unimaginable," speaks to the nature of the beautiful young bisexual Pierre as an almost mythic creature. Death can kill him, claim him, burn him up; but it cannot seem to end him, so boundless were his physical and sexual energies. He has almost superhuman powers for Lucie, who says that being with him was like being able to grab onto eternity. Even after death, Pierre has the power to stop and start time for Lucie: "Today, I'm ready to know. Pierre is dead.... Tomorrow I can forget again."

Being able to arrest time, however momentarily, is one of the aspects of sex which makes it so intoxicating. It is Pierre's sexuality — his determined use of his body as a vessel of pleasure — which has the greatest impact on Lucie after he dies. He had described himself to her as being "a kamikaze with a cause.... I'd engage my body." It is a fascinating metaphor, since a kamikaze mission, of course, can only be performed once; its end goal is death, obliteration. Pierre's performance of sex is repetitive, endless, always seeking new outlets, new forms of expression, and new combinations of partners. The illusion, here, is that one can commit an act with the gravitas of a kamikaze mission, but without the same literal consequences. The camera, recording Pierre's child-like delight at his own theorizing about himself, cannot help but reveal Pierre's fatuity at this moment, even if the entire film remains as fascinated and adoring of Pierre (whenever he is onscreen) as Lucie is. And indeed, as if taking up precisely this sort of sexual kamikaze mission, Lucie begins to use her body to try to get information about Pierre's death from a series of men: Paul (Karl E. Landler), the autistic clairvoyant who hung around the band; Romain (Guillaime Gouix), a young skinhead who had threatened Pierre; and the lieutenant (Pierre Beziers), a police detective assigned to Pierre's case. Ironically, the lieutenant — one of the few male characters in the film who identifies as wholly straight — is also terrible in bed, apologizing to Lucie for his premature ejaculation problem. He is also controlling and sexist, the opposite of the sensitive, free love promoted by Pierre and his friends.

Does Pierre go too far in his insistence on sexual freedom? Exposing Nicholas to the shame of potentially being outed, involving his sister Lucie in an incestuous relationship, making his other male friends feel sexually inadequate in his presence — all are unintended "crimes" against the fabric of the group. For Pierre, there is only the religion of staying true to himself at every moment; but Baptiste, Sébastien, and Nicholas seem at times as if they would be content to be more or less ordinary young men. In a key scene of hostile confrontation between the band and a homophobic skinhead gang, Pierre admits that he and his friends could have ended up just like the fascist bully boys. The option to break free from conformism remains more difficult than the ingrained, reflexive tendency to give in to it. And by the end of the film, when the friends are in disarray and consumed with nameless remorse, it becomes almost fatalistically unsurprising that Pierre's three best friends, Nicholas, Sébastien, and Baptiste, turn out to have been his killers.

For Lucie, this marks the ultimate betrayal of the fragile utopia the five of them were attempting to build up around the figure of the bisexual Pierre. Even after confessing, none of the guys expresses any motive. "They don't know what came over them," Nicholas' father says. Even when the truth emerges, it is shrouded in a mystery that not even the killers can elucidate. "I'm condemned to searching for the unanswerable," Lucie says, reifying not only the fathomless motives of the killers but the extreme hold which her brother's enigma continues to have over her. He still holds sway over his other lovers as well. In prison, Nicholas becomes homosexual, calling out Pierre's name each night while his cellmate rapes him. Having in some sense sacrificed Pierre to it, Nicholas can now assume the gay identity which formerly shamed him.

Some of the themes of *To Each His Night* parallel another film, Larry Clark's *Bully* (2001), in which a high-school-aged bisexual male is also murdered by his circle of friends. Bobby Kent (Nick Stahl), the "bully" of the title, is a spoiled rich brat and arrogant womanizer who constantly abuses his best friend, Marty Puccio (Brad Renfro), physically and emotionally. He constantly punches Marty and orders him around, often expressing remorse immediately afterward ("I'm really sorry, you're my best friend") in the pattern of an abusive boyfriend. Seemingly out of jealousy or possessiveness, Bobby tries to steal or drive away any girls who seem interested in Marty. He also sadistically forces Marty to strip in gay nightclubs for money. Bobby seems turned on by the idea that Marty secretly enjoys performing for men (which Marty vehemently denies), but equally turned on by watching Marty have sex with girls.

Like *To Each His Night, Bully* is based on a true-crime story (out of Florida) in which the real-life Bobby and Marty did dominate older submissive gay men to con them out of money. Clark takes such telling details and weaves them into a psychosexual nightmare of epic proportions, in which Bobby emerges as a secretly bisexual male with a huge amount of self-loathing and repression toward his gay side, causing him to lash out at everyone. In perhaps the film's most disturbing (also most over-the-top and potentially campy) scene, he beats and rapes a girl, Ali (Bijou Phillips), while forcing her to watch gay porn, which she finds disgusting. Whereas Pierre's influence over his friends is pervasive but mainly benign, Bobby is an explosive terror intent on destroying whatever crosses his path. Both Pierre and Bobby are forces of nature and, again, almost mythic beings even to the people who appeared to know them best. Both men highlight the ultimate "unknowability" of the bisexual male — which is partly just a reaction against his stubborn refusal to be categorized.

Bully builds its grueling tension by having the gang's plots to kill Bobby simmer and boil over again and again, while Bobby remains, as usual, cocky and oblivious. In *To Each His Night*, the murder remains a mystery until the end of the film, while much of *Bully* consists of elaborating the various murder plans conceived by the habitually stoned Marty and his equally strung-out friends. Indeed, what makes Clark's film such a painful masterpiece, which gets under one's skin and lingers, is that it is hard to say what is more frightening: Bobby's turmoil as he helplessly surrenders to his own sadistic impulses, or the drug-induced numbness of the killers, who view the taking of life as little more than snuffing out targets in a video game. Eventually, the conspirators lure Bobby to a swampy, deserted canal in the Everglades and carry out their grisly massacre. As hateful as Bobby has been, the injustice of his brutal murder seems to prey on his killers' sense of guilt as well as their paranoia — again, an instance of the dead bisexual, in all his mystery, seeming to reach out supernaturally from beyond the grave. In the final scene, the killers turn on each other in the middle of a shocked courtroom.

The bisexual male proves hard to ultimately kill in *To Each His Night* and *Bully*, because he continues to loom large in people's erotic imaginations, which turn toward him in spite of the violence of their denials. Like the young hustler Pierrot in Téchiné's *I Don't Kiss*, who indulges every sexual contact except the most basic human intimacy, the bisexual is available to every physical apotheosis except death. Is it so surprising that a man who has lived his whole life in utter transcendence of nature — through his refusal of innate, essentialist gender roles and categories — should also transcend nature's ultimate revenge against the living? In fact, as tragic as it is, death seems to set him free to become an even more ubiquitous, larger-than-life legend, immortalized, frozen at the seeming height of his perfection.

* * *

So far, the films discussed in this chapter have involved unconventional sexuality "going too far," as it were, and getting struck down. The lives of Jean-Baptiste, Pierre, and Bobby Kent are steeped in risk and, to a certain extent, imbued with death already. Can we imagine a bisexual male character who is not completely tragic — whose life is happy and whose death comes unexpectedly, as a kind of cheat? A bisexual male who, in his extreme openness to all the possibilities of life, can inspire, even in death, an awakening to such possibilities in others?

The Italian film *Le Fate Ignoranti* (*His Secret Life*, 2001) centers around this latter kind of life-loving and life-inspiring bisexual male. The literal translation of the title is "The Ignorant Fairy"—"ignorant" in the sense of "willing to look the other way," for the film is largely about the allowances people make for those whom they love. *His Secret Life* begins in a museum gallery where Antonia (Margherita Buy) is looking at ancient sculpture; a man in a tuxedo approaches her and tries to seduce her, but she tells him she is waiting for her husband. They leave the gallery together, and it is only in the next scene that we realize this "stranger" was really her husband, Massimo (Andrea Renzi), romantically staging a game in which he could seduce his wife as if for the first time. Indeed, their life together seems idyllic, until the sudden moment when Massimo is killed in a traffic accident. In an incongruously cartoon-like effect, Massimo's body is struck and sent flying through the air by a car from one side, only to be struck and sent flying back through the air by a car from the other side—obeying a certain swirling weightlessness, Massimo seems to be revealed, by death, as what he was all along, in life: a kind of spirit trapped in the physical world.

In deep mourning and depression, Antonia finds an intimate inscription on the back of a painting which Massimo owned, titled "The Ignorant Fairy" (an abstract portrait of a genderless face). The inscription is signed, "Your ignorant fairy." Convinced that Massimo was having an affair, Antonia searches for the painting's purchaser; the trail of receipts leads her to the apartment of a Mariani, which she assumes to be the last name of a woman. Instead, it turns out to be that of a young man named Michele (Stefano Accorsi).

Michele's apartment is warm and inviting, a sanctuary crowded with colorful figures including a blue-haired Turkish refugee named Serra (Serra Yilmaz) and an AIDS sufferer named Ernesto (Gabriel Garko). In spite of herself, Antonia is drawn into their chattering, joking, squabbling cosmos. In good Italian fashion, she begins to bond with them around cooking and eating a sumptuous meal. However, when Michele confirms that he was her husband's gay lover, she becomes enraged and slaps him. He argues back: "You can just burst into my house whenever you want, but I could never get close to your perfect little house, so spare me the melodrama, because if anyone should be angry it should be me, not you." At this early stage of unfamiliar awareness, each one is intent on what he or she feels the other has "stolen" from him or her. And yet, almost in spite of herself, Antonia continues to seek out Michele, wanting to understand him and, through him, the side of Massimo she never knew.

At first, Michele seems cold-hearted in his need to disabuse Antonia of her illusions. "He's not here anymore," he tells her flatly, "for you or for me."

But this is merely the hardened exterior he has learned to build up, to protect himself as a gay man. As Antonia comes to win him over, Michele begins to soften and admit to his deep feelings: "You can avoid saying his name, thinking about him, you can even forget him, but Massimo is still here with us...." The power of Massimo in death, his victory perhaps, is that his spirit and his love are strong enough to bring together the two people whom he loved the most. There is a beautiful scene where Michele finally visits the house where Massimo lived with Antonia. He looks at the two deck chairs on the patio, the two hammocks in the backyard; everything in the house is a sign of married life, domesticity, monogamy. He realizes that this world was as real for Massimo as the gay world the two men inhabited together, and he breaks down in Antonia's arms, sobbing, "Forgive me!" She comforts him, and surprisingly, the two begin to kiss passionately, as if trying to conjure Massimo in the body of the one other person who was closest to him. It seems as if they are even about to make love, but they stop abruptly, recognizing that it is not sex they want or need from each other but support, succor, memory. Indeed, one of the central themes of *His Secret Life* is how a loved one can live on in one's memory, and how these cherished memories can be strengthened by sharing them with others rather than possessively hoarding them to oneself. When his lovers share with each other, they amplify the power of Massimo's love. Although starting out as a battle of memories, in which Antonia's version of Massimo is pitted against Michele's, with each one denying the other's validity, the film ends in fusion: in death, as he wished to in life, Massimo finally belongs to both of them. (This tragic phenomenon is sometimes referred to as the "bisexual double closet.") Ironically, as a bisexual male, he becomes most whole and visible only in death.

Indeed, as marginalized and persecuted members of society, the gay characters keenly feel the invisibility of ghosts, how the living and the dead can seem to trade places. The ailing Ernesto speaks of the rendezvous where he used to meet his long-lost, deceased lover: "Maybe we're still there, but no one sees us, because no one ever understood our love. Or maybe I'm the only one who's still there." A large part of what Antonia learns from Michele and his friends is how hard it is to be gay; this helps her to understand Massimo. She comes from a heterosexual world where people are, or are supposed to be, equal to their appearances, and where love follows naturally from telling the truth about oneself. But as one of the gay characters informs her, gently trying to show her the reasons behind Massimo's lifelong deception: "If you tell the truth to someone you love, they might not love you anymore." Truth, like love and like life itself, is a luxury in the gay world, but all the more precious, for this reason, whenever and wherever it can be told. Indeed, the most basic test of kinship is whether or not it can accept the truth about oneself, as one bisexual male has stated: "My good friends take me as I am."[1]

Kinship, for this reason, is immensely important in *His Secret Life*, and is shown to grow stronger wherever society attempts to suppress it. When the straitlaced Antonia begins to open up in the company of Michele's effervescent, free-spirited circle of friends, it is impossible not to be reminded of the poignant scene in Douglas Sirk's *All That Heaven Allows* (1955) where Jane Wyman attends the dinner party with Rock Hudson's nonconformist friends and discovers that there is an entire world, free of judgments and filled with spontaneous fun, beyond her drab suburban routines. Director Ferzan Ozpetek adds other Sirkian touches; for example, in one shot where Antonia is questioning how much of her life has been real and how much has been illusion, she catches sight of her pale and murky reflection in a storefront window. Sirk's characters often reveal their inner dislocation or displacement when they are shown reflected in mirrors. The background music is also reminiscent of old Hollywood melodramas, swelling orchestral passages which underscore key emotional points. And yet, *His Secret Life* uses the melodrama form critically. In a distinctly postmodern way, the characters are aware, and wary, of being trapped inside the conventions of melodrama. They call attention to this frequently, as when Michele tells Antonia, "spare me the melodrama," or when Antonia says that her mother's advice on love sounds like "soap opera." It is as if they are looking for a way out of the emotional stagnation, the doom, which melodrama so often requires of its victimized heroes and heroines. Sirk himself would have approved of their struggle to live, not an imitation of life, but an authentic life all their own. In this, they are also guided by the spirit of Massimo, who used artifice as a way of bringing passion to both of his relationships: the game of seduction with Antonia in the museum gallery which begins the film; the elaborate ruse of pretending to haggle over the only copy of a rare book of poems which enabled him to meet Michele in the first place. We see from these examples that certain illusions are only a means for getting to those moments of real life in which we strive to live, moments expressed in the sharing of feelings.

Intent on healing and on building a bridge between the gay and the straight worlds, *His Secret Life* reveals that Massimo's power in death is to impart lessons to his loved ones, lessons which he could never impart to them when he was alive. One of these lessons is embittering, but also empowering, and stems from the fact that he was never wholly a part of either of the worlds he inhabited: in the last analysis, we are all on our own, and we must live the life we make for ourselves. Antonia chooses to travel alone in the end, stepping bravely into the future, seemingly ready to start living without possessing all the answers in advance. Michele is also alone at the end of the film, and facing an ambiguous future. No matter what society can give or take away, it is the self in all its contradictory impulses which must always be confronted and embraced. The other lesson is more hopeful, and has to do, of course, with that society at its most helpful and generous: we have the ability to reach out to others, to enter unfamiliar territories and make ourselves at home there. The recognition of their shared love for Massimo brings Antonia and Michele together, in spite of the fact that they could just as easily see each other as enemies, jealous rivals, opposites who cancel each other out. What they are able to put together is the whole of Massimo, as a bisexual male, and this acceptance makes both of them more whole, as well. Their common humanity, as a straight woman and a gay man, is that they both loved and were loved by the same man.

13

At the Limits of Heterosexuality: The Woman's Viewpoint in *Anatomy of Hell*

Many films about bisexual males follow a pattern. The male begins in a relationship with a woman, then discovers his sexual urges for another man and becomes involved with him as well. Then the male's bisexuality is discovered, in turn, by the woman, who experiences it as a betrayal. Rather than viewing the male as being always already bisexual, the films have him "changing," with the woman as victim of this change. This means that some films which purport to be about bisexuality actually reinforce the idea that sexual orientation is an all-or-nothing proposition, in which the woman represents a dogmatic, tradition-bound vision of hearth and home. Where is the agency of women in these films? It is not only a matter of the female characters being barred from stepping outside the bounds of patriarchal heterosexuality; they flock to patriarchal heterosexuality and defend it with a vengeance. With a female partner who is un-liberated and a male partner who is, perhaps, too liberated, the bisexual male is depicted as a challenge to heterosexuality, marriage, the family—even though, precisely as a bisexual male, he might be in complete sympathy with heterosexuality. He is not abandoning his straight side, only searching for another side as well.

But this is where the perception problem arises for many people, who cannot accept heterosexuality as only one option in a fairly crowded field. Heterosexual bliss is supposed to have been, from time immemorial, the end of the "fairy tale." With bisexuality, it is neither end nor beginning, but one point along a circular continuum of sexual existence. Real love cannot be shared by half-formed beings in hiding, afraid of their own deepest impulses. Both partners must be encouraged to fully realize their potentials. Arguably, feminists recognized this as an important struggle within the sexual politics of heterosexuality: a man could only oppress a woman to the extent that he himself was bound up in patriarchal, traditionalist concepts of masculine and feminine roles. And yet, there have been very few films in which a woman expresses her agency, her liberation, her break with traditional patriarchy, by knowingly becoming involved with a bisexual male—even fewer in which a woman does this without simultaneously courting humiliation, disaster and death. Catherine Breillat's *Anatomie de l'Enfer* (*Anatomy of Hell*, 2003) goes farther than most films in suggesting a potential, covert alliance between feminists and bisexual males, but nonetheless remains trapped, like the heroine of the film, in a confining sense of genders and sex roles as being immutable, eternal, imprisoning facts of destiny.

Breillat begins *Anatomy of Hell* with a close-up of a man on his knees, fellating the penis of a standing figure whose face is not seen. They are out of doors, implying a sense of freedom in this sexual act, and the kneeling man's rapt devotion to the penis he is sucking (his eyes are closed) suggests a lack of shame, as well as the lack of any need to justify the act. In fact, they are behind a gay club, and inside, gay men swarm on the dance floor. None of the men is alone; each is paired off with another man, dancing or kissing. In the middle of this spectacle of homosexual lust and abandonment, a woman (Amira Casar) stands in the corner, seemingly seething with rage. She is isolated in this crowd, not least of all by her gender, but also by her outfit: her soft white blouse and pink skirt are superficial emblems of feminine "purity." She catches the eye of a man (Rocco Sifredi), kissing another man across the club. She begins to move toward this man, elbowing her way angrily through a cluster of dancers, but as she approaches him with slow determination, she ends up walking past him, and in the next shot she is sitting on a toilet in the rest room, slicing her wrist with a razor.

The Man follows her into the bathroom and finds her bleeding. "Why did you do that?" he asks. "Because I'm a woman," she says. "I don't understand," he says. "You understand very well." She is flattering his male ego: as a woman in a gay bar, she wants to die because she is invisible to him, unwanted by him. He takes her to an all-night pharmacy, where her wound is bandaged; staring at her in the pharmacy, he has a vision of her cutting her throat. This vision is somewhat mystifying: does he wish to protect her from harm, or is he projecting onto her his own sadistic desire to see her hurt, to see her dead?

They walk along the street. There is blood smeared across her skirt, suggestive of menstruation. The Woman becomes an emblem of femaleness, her open, abalone-pink coat flapping on either side of her like the inner lips of a vulva. She asks him why he came to find her in the bathroom. He says that

13. At the Limits of Heterosexuality 221

she touched him as she brushed past him: "At first I paid no attention to it. Then I got scared...." She contradicts him, insisting cynically that he went to the bathroom "to get sucked—like all men." He slaps her and calls her, "Dumb bitch!" Indicating how easily she has been able to manipulate his emotions (fear, worry, anger, even arousal of sorts), she says, "You're all alike." The implication is that, even though he is gay, the Man cannot escape reacting to her in the same ways that a straight man would. She seems to want to bring him even closer to heterosexuality when she sinks to her knees and wordlessly performs oral sex on him. He responds physically, becoming erect and ejaculating into her mouth. Performing oral sex is often characterized as a submissive gesture, but in this case, the Woman's performance of it on the Man has seemingly been to further prove her point, that he is exactly like any other (straight) man.

She offers him a deal: she will pay him money if he will help her with an experiment. "You don't like women," she tells him, "you can look at me ... impartially. Watch me when I'm unwatchable. No need to touch me. Just say what you see." "It'll cost you a lot," he replies matter-of-factly. The strange language of her proposal implies an experiment not only in male-female relations, in which a woman usually has little control over how she is seen or "watched" by men, but an existential investigation into her deepest selfhood. "Unwatchable" is a loaded word, usually applied, intriguingly, to films that are shockingly brutal. In the case of a person, it suggests a judgment on her behavior or appearance—and also a sense of what is unseen or invisible about her, since one cannot watch what is not visible to the eye. Of what does her unwatchableness consist? And what is the relation of male desire to her unwatchableness? Straight male attention and desire are characterized as bearing an active relation to her (these things can confer watchableness upon her, perhaps, or conversely, cannot be made to look at all when she is not playing by their rules), whereas gay male attention and desire are seen as neutral, objective, without a vested interest in her actions per se. But will these distinctions remain as obvious as they first seem to be?

On the first night, he arrives at her house, which is perched on a hilltop overlooking some craggy cliffs and, far below, the ocean. She flirtatiously implies that she wants to have sex with him. He is diffident and business-like, telling her that he will only watch, and reminding her about their financial agreement. "I'll pay for everything," she reiterates, with a serious, even somewhat rueful expression: normal gender roles are being reversed here, in which a man is more likely to pay for a woman's attention and company. In fact, the Woman finds herself in a position that is identical to that of gay men who patronize straight male hustlers: the Man has all the power, since he is not sexually oriented toward her, and does not "want" her, and since she is placing a monetary value on his presence. His power expresses itself when he sneers at her, as she begins to strip: "At last. It's about time." We can identify a certain "situational bisexuality" taking hold of the Man, here. If he does involve himself with her sexually, it will presumably be because she is offering money; this inducement allows him a refuge in terms of how he thinks of what he is doing with her, whether or not he will accept it as part of his true identity. Just as straight male hustlers can countenance having sex with other men when money is involved (doing it for money does not make them "gay"), so the Man in *Anatomy of Hell* can presumably shy away from the psychical implications of what he is doing with the Woman.

Indeed, he actively voices disgust of her body, her flesh, her private parts, and her being. He looks at her, lying naked on the bed, and says: "The fragility of female flesh inspires either disgust or brutality. Women depend on one or the other." In some ways, he is "blaming" the Woman — all women — for his own dislike of them. He is also extending a blanket license to heterosexual men who brutalize women, reading their sadism backwards as, again, a response which has been directly elicited by the women themselves. She has anticipated his negative response, and speaks wearily of how "brutality" does not frighten her. She prefers it to "nothingness," and says that usually men are too slow to act on their desires: sex becomes artificial the longer it takes for action to catch up to desire, or during "the ages" that pass between when an offer is made and "when it's taken up." But who is bluffing whom, here? Which of them is overcompensating? Why would a gay man care at all about "female flesh," care enough to have a complex opinion about what he does not like about it, unless he was uncertain, to begin with, about what he claims to like? And how vulnerable is she truly willing to make herself?

Visually, the film shows us that a paradox is taking place: he turns away from her and looks into a mirror across from her bed. In a single shot, Breillat shows us the Man looking into the mirror, and the reflection of the Woman's naked body in the mirror itself. On some level, which has yet to be determined, they are the same: Man fearfully looks into a mirror to remember who he is, and sees, not himself, but Woman. Breillat seems to say that this fear — the fear that, at his deepest core, a man might actually be a woman — is the basis of sexism and misogyny. For her part, the Woman seems to want to bring this out: the extent to which she is already part of the Man's psyche whether he has placed her there or not. Likewise, Breillat reinforces this concept by speaking both of their voiceovers herself, on the soundtrack. Both the Man's and the Woman's innermost thoughts are brought together and transmitted in a female voice.

13. At the Limits of Heterosexuality 223

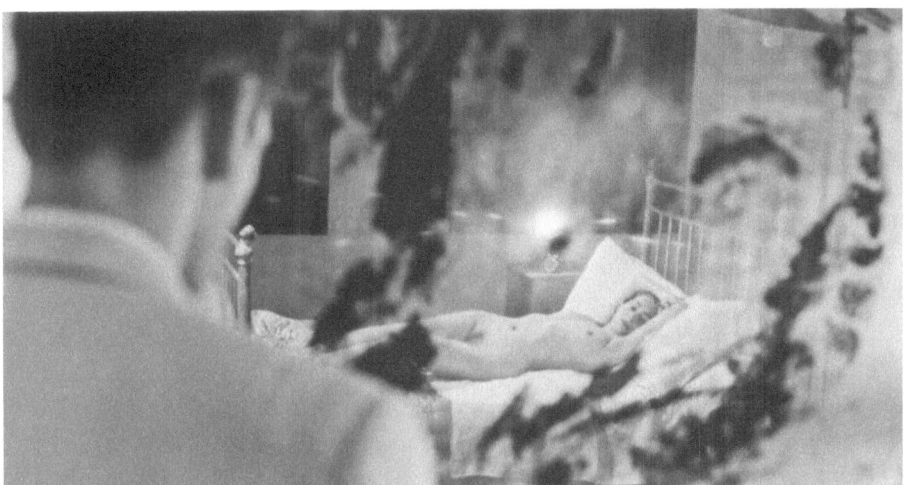

In *Anatomy of Hell* (2004), the Man (Rocco Sifredi) looks into a tarnished mirror and sees the reflection of the Woman (Amira Casar) lying naked on the bed behind him. In this shot, writer-director Catherine Breillat seems to imply that a man's deepest fear is that he might actually be a woman.

He continues to elaborate on the biological basis of woman's "obscene nature": "Men who don't like women envy that obscenity, and men who do like women hate them for it." He reinforces her own supposition that male hostility toward women is an inescapable fact. "So we can't do a thing about it," she sighs. He goes on to say: "Your denial of the obscenity is what frightens us the most...." She lies on the bed, almost corpse-like, staring at the ceiling; but in this verbal chess game, he is unwittingly giving her the opening she will need to mount her counterattack. If she is to be hated and punished for the mere fact of existence, then she has virtually nothing to lose; if passive, demure, respectable "denial of the obscenity" is the worst crime in the male imagination, then she only has to give in to obscenity, take control of it and express it comprehensively. "I was learning what I knew, but was afraid to hear," she admits, while Breillat shows a close-up of her hand both covering her "revolting" vagina and penetrating it with her fingers. To pass through abuse, she must surrender to it.

The Man leaves the bedroom to get a drink. It is the first of many times he will be forced to flee the confines of the room, an admission of his weakness. When he comes back, she is in a more dominant position, sitting up on the bed, and she stares at him defiantly. He feels the need to defend his drinking: "Man or woman, it makes no difference.... When an opening in the flesh is promised, I lack thoughts, words.... I need alcohol.... I need to forget that bestiality, that loneliness." Here, he is revealing (perhaps in the moment of first discovering it) that he is bisexual, at least to the extent that he is secretly disturbed by bodily orifices of either gender and by the need to penetrate them. He must numb or alter his consciousness before he can bring himself to sexually perform.

He joins her in bed. He puts his finger into her vagina and eats the drop of glistening come he brings out. In an exploratory way, he puts his finger back inside her, and his whole hand disappears. She laughs mockingly and deliriously as he reacts with solemn horror: "I bless the day I was born immune to you, and all of your kind." He describes a woman's vagina as different from "a boy's anus," in that the latter does not lie about its "elasticity." A vagina, on the other hand, is "a trap," revealing the bottomless horror of physical, animal lust hidden beneath a cover of respectability and love. Buried within this speech are two reasons that have sometimes been cited by males about why they might prefer sex with other males to sex with females: first, the anus itself is tighter and therefore more pleasurable; second, males are straightforward with each other. Although he is still insisting on his homosexuality, and denigrating the Woman, the Man is beginning to think more and more in bisexual terms, in that he is now comparing the genders directly, placing them within the same realm of sexual pleasure if not on the same par. "I'm sick of your dallying!" she says. "You've hardly looked at me. Look at me when I can't see myself." She says this last sentence twice: her goal is still to become visible to a man, beyond the illusions and dishonesty of sexual desire, but it is beginning to feel as though she needs to become visible to herself most of all, and though she will use the Man to accomplish this, this process of becoming visible will be on her own terms. Finally, her earlier assumption that a gay man will look at her "impartially" comes to seem delusional, or perhaps it was only a calculated strategy on her part to get him to accept her deal: the drift of the film is that no one, not even a gay man, looks at women impartially.

For the second time the Man leaves, this time turning out the lights in her room and walking out of the house. He stands on a cliff overlooking the ocean and smokes a cigarette, feeling "helpless against the whole world." When he returns to the bedroom she is still lying motionless in the same position where he left her. It is as if she were indulging the male fantasy that a woman always waits, that he can control her even when he is not there. He gets a tube of red lipstick from her bathroom medicine chest, and uses this somewhat comical phallic object to draw a red ring around her anus and vagina, and then a big, clownish smear of red across her lips. She is inert as he does this, letting him move her limbs and head as he wishes. In the next

13. At the Limits of Heterosexuality 225

shot, he is naked and erect, and he penetrates her; she barely stirs from her slumber. Afterwards, he slumps at the end of the bed, weeping like a baby. She is moved enough to half-heartedly comfort and encourage him: "It doesn't matter. It's just the first night."

On the second night, he fingers her vagina again and realizes she is menstruating when he pulls them out covered in blood. He licks some of this blood from his fingers, and shudders. He again leaves the house, reaffirming a need, on the part of the Man, to escape, to come and go from female space at will; as usual, he leaves only to return momentarily, this time armed with a rake from the garden shed. In a kind of frat-boy gesture of trying to insult the Woman and claim ownership of her body, he inserts the handle of the rake into her vagina and leaves it sticking out. She reacts slightly to this, but then turns and stares at him impassively through the three metal prongs of the rake. In fact, he has inadvertently revealed that she has exhausted his own phallus. He passes out drunk in a chair, and when he wakes up, she is the one who is watching him: an uncanny, chilling moment. He can never quite get the drop on her, so to speak. This is because, by focusing on her as a "hole," he invests her with the ultimate power of any hole: to lie in wait, to always be there, to trip someone up. A phallus comes and goes, and, like any kind of matter, can be destroyed; but a hole can only be permanently filled, or else grow larger until it swallows everything. This is implied on the third night, when he steals toward the house from far away, like a marauder, but finds the door already wide open. He finds her in bed again and reproaches her: "Anyone could have come in."

This hint of jealousy is enough to place her on surer footing. "That's what men can't stand," she says. She pulls him down onto the bed and rolls on top of him: "In fact they're afraid women don't belong to them." What has oppressed her most are male attempts to contain and imprison her, with physical restraints such as belts and locks, and with psychological ones such as "morality." She tells him to pull out her tampon: wordlessly he obeys and holds it up in fascination. It is soaked in blood; commenting on how men are afraid of the "impurity" of menstrual blood, she steeps the tampon in a glass of water, turning the water a hazy reddish color. Then she offers the glass to him: "Don't we drink the blood of our enemies?" she asks.

He drinks, then she drinks, too — the shared cup like a grotesque and oddly touching parody of a wedding sacrament. Throughout this scene, the Man's entire attitude toward the Woman changes: instead of challenging her or saying anything at all, he listens to her, shaking with rapt attentiveness; he cannot take his eyes from her. The Woman's personal mission finally becomes clear. In order to create a man who can appreciate her as an individual rather than an object, she has had to take a gay man and make him bisexual. He must be in between gay and straight, so that a romantic and sexual interest can be aroused in him toward her, but so that he will still be caught off guard by her, will experience this interest as something new. In this way, she can shed her deep bodily shame in the presence of a non-judgmental male. Her anger in the gay club stemmed from the fact that she recognized it not only as a space from which women had been banished, but a space which men had specially engineered for their desires to be satiated without shame. As a woman, she carries her shame with her all the time, in her body; she is unable to deny it. Gay men, because they are men (Breillat seems to say), constantly proclaim their right to be, and create a free-floating space around themselves to dispel shame, because shame is female, and men cannot live with shame, or doubt, the way women must.

As a gay man, he would reject her; as a straight man, he would have sex with her without seeing her. But, at the moment when he becomes flooded with bisexual awareness (in the form of an alien heterosexual desire) he looks at her with a personal reverence. She has become his teacher, and what she teaches him is that her vagina is not a hole to be filled: the fact that it can be filled, with nearly anything, is immaterial to what it is first and foremost. To embrace themselves, women must be on familiar terms with absence, incorporeality, and with the immaterial — which is to say, not only that which lacks physical presence and shape, but that which is considered "beside the point" as evidence of anything, unrelated to the main subject of discourse (always the male world of space-filling, penetration, measurement, etc.). Like fabled "conversions" of straight men by gay men, this is, finally, for her, a political victory of sorts: she is winning, or fashioning from the ground up, an adherent to female power and pleasure. But it is not heterosexuality, as an abstract category, to which she converts him (this would make him an oblivious straight man, after all), but rather, sex with *her*, a specific person. Categories can be manipulated to deny and repress feelings; they become uniforms, programmatic behaviors. But to truly see and love one individual, beyond categories, is the point of Breillat's film. This time, when he has sex with her again, it is an act of love (he even kisses her toes as he holds up her leg to penetrate her), and she is now a fully conscious participant in the act.

But this moment is a temporary one. After sex, his penis is covered in her blood, and he returns to his former disgust. "You think I've put a curse on you," she says, "ruined your penis forever." He admits his fear of women's life-giving potential. He says that penetrating a man is less awe-inspiring and threatening: "Men can't give life." She says that it is man's role to take life instead of give it.

He takes his money reluctantly and leaves, but remains haunted by her. Getting drunk in a bar, he feels the need to denigrate her to another man (Jacques Monge). Calling her "the queen of sluts," he brags, "I reamed her pussy so hard no one will want her again." He is falling into the male role of destroyer, taker of life. He is amazed that she let him do everything he did to her, and always wanted more: this brings up the latent male anxiety about not being able to satisfy women, not being able to fill the hole, so to speak. "I should have ripped out her guts and made her eat them." She has transformed him too much perhaps, but there is no going back. He leaves her money on the bar, indicating that his bisexuality is no longer "situational." He returns to her, wanting to begin all over again and not wanting to realize that "nothing that has been done can be done again." This is the viewpoint, associated with the Woman, that sex should be about breaking through to a new intimacy, rather than the pointless repetition of the same sensation, with one person or another. A true intimacy cannot be repeated. He finds the house empty except for a blood-stained sheet. Outside, in dream-like slow motion, he encounters her on the cliffs and pushes her off the edge, into the ocean.

The Woman creates a bisexual male from a gay male so that he will see beyond simplistic categories of pleasure and experience. Thus, he can love a specific person, and confer on her a wholeness and a reality which no man has ever given her, and which can strengthen her subjectivity. But in Breillat's pessimistic vision, falling in love with the Woman only brings the Man to his own biologically determined fate: to seek to kill what he loves and cannot fully possess. The need to hide in abstract, dualistic categories (man/woman; straight/gay) is simply too strong. And yet, Breillat herself reinforces this dualistic thinking in her very pessimism. Instead of imagining a male bisexuality that could truly represent the growth of feeling and response in a man, she forces the Man into the role of killer in order to justify the Woman's original futility and oppression. She liberates her characters from artificially constructed sexual identity only to nail them back into their respective categories all the more forcefully, like the crucifix in the film which depicts Christ with an erect penis on the cross — the blunt, brutal facts of biology supersede any attempt at transcendence, and are finally all that survive of such attempts.

* * *

Anatomy of Hell is an important film about male bisexuality, precisely because it was made by a woman and it examines male sexual identity from a feminist point of view. For this reason, it does not provide the entire picture of male bisexuality, but in the extremity of its battle of the sexes, it offers a side of the subject not usually covered in films by men, films which concentrate on the male characters and relegate the woman to a subsidiary role as the abandoned, passive or reactive element. Breillat's feminism is harsh and confrontational, and rooted not so much in politics and social roles (these are only symptoms of a larger human condition) but in the deepest part of womanhood, where gender and sexuality enact themselves at the core of a woman's being, as deep-seated, innate shame and a struggle not to be objectified by men.

Breillat's female characters are never bisexual; the truth is, they are extremely heterosexual and therefore dependent emotionally and sexually on men: this is their curse. It would be easier for them if they could work up some feeling of love for themselves and their gender (not necessarily a sexual love: what her female characters often lack on the most superficial level, but sometimes grow to discover, is *self-esteem*). However, the truth is, they have no way of seeing themselves apart from, and outside of, male desire; they must work out their struggle for selfhood directly with the men who erode their autonomy and well-being. In *Romance* (1999), a woman (Caroline Ducey) is driven to a series of casual encounters with men because her boyfriend (Sagamore Stévenin), whom she truly loves, is too narcissistic and "frigid" to have sex with her; at the end of the film, she triumphantly kills her boyfriend on the eve of delivering his baby. For Breillat, female sexual liberation often becomes a case of life and death. In *À Ma Soeur!* (*Fat Girl*, 2000), a plain, overweight teenager, Anaïs (Anaïs Reboux), tells her pretty, older sister (Roxana Mesquida) that she does not want to lose her virginity to a boy she cares about, because the act will be humiliating. The occasionally bullying sister scoffs at Anaïs' advice, but later falls into the trap Anaïs has described: she is seduced and abandoned by an Italian boy (Libero Di Rienzo) who has claimed to love her, and whom she believes she loves. Finally, Anaïs loses her virginity in an act of rape, by a maniac (Albert Goldberg) who has just killed her sister and her domineering mother (Arsinée Kahanjian) in front of her. The blessings are mixed: her self-centered, tormenting family is decimated; Anaïs is alone but free amid the wreckage.

Breillat has always reminded me of poet and rock musician Patti Smith, in that Smith's early poems and songs were often desperate, heated arguments with her own femaleness. In "Female" and "piss factory," she writes about wanting to be a boy. In "Female," womanhood is depicted as a biological predestination leading inevitably to the "humiliating" conditions of being penetrated and impregnated.[1] But her yearning to be male does not seem to stem from a rejection of female heterosexual desire, which she acknowledges. In fact, the rhapsodic language in which she describes the smells and penises of boys in "piss factory" reveals her deep attraction to men.[2] Like Breillat's

Woman character in *Anatomy of Hell*, Smith is seeking to escape the shame and disempowerment she feels *as a woman* desiring men. Becoming a man feels intuitively like a way to do this; indeed, Smith became famous when she recorded the garage-rock classic, "Gloria," a song about the seduction of a woman at a party, told from the man's viewpoint.

But becoming male is not the only way: another way, as Smith's writings also show, is to explore, and even revel in, the idea of sex as violation. The idea of rape functions both as a means to assume the power of masculinity, while also preserving the female element against willingly surrendering to the "humiliation" of being penetrated. So, in Smith's poem, bluntly entitled "rape," she writes from the viewpoint of a marauding man who does not understand why his demure female prey is sobbing and upset after he has had intercourse with her. Male energy is, somewhat ironically, likened to the power inherent in rock and roll, while female energy is passive, inspiring torrents of fantasy but remaining trapped at a level of internalized feeling. The collision of these energies is a kind of rape, by definition, since it forces feeling to act itself out; but it is also the primal basis of Western romanticism. In a breathtaking use of sleazy slang and innuendo, as well as an underlying current of fear, the poem "rape" reveals how the perception of rape itself is subjective and perhaps gender-dependent.[3] In a later poem, "robert bresson" (named for the film director), Smith constructs a scene from both the rapist's and the victim's viewpoints: a young man has caused a car to crash by pouring oil on a road; he rapes the daughter while her father dies in the wreck. Both feel the meaning of this act of sacrilege, that it is a kind of artwork, and that the victim, by giving in to the violent seductiveness of taboo, becomes a work of art herself.[4] This scenario is remarkably like the ending to Breillat's *Fat Girl*, in which Anaïs is raped by the drifter who has just massacred her family: being forced to engage in sex removes the onus from disempowered female power, since it means, by definition, that the man has wanted it more, but it also, significantly, liberates the female from her subservient position within the patriarchal family structure. One loss of "guilt" triggers another loss of guilt on an entirely different level. Indeed, both "rape" and "robert bresson" mix the horror of sexual violation with a kind of queasy romanticism that implies transcendence — another way of transcending the limitations of the body or of gender itself.

In her personal life, Smith has acknowledged being in love with, or being influenced by, gay and bisexual men. When she was young, she had a romantic and sexual relationship with the photographer Robert Mapplethorpe. Later, Mapplethorpe became exclusively homosexual, but he and Smith continued to remain lifelong friends, supporters and artistic collaborators. She refers to him often in Steven Sebring's gorgeously filmed documentary, *Patti Smith: Dream of Life* (2008). In a particularly moving scene, she shows several mementos that she still has of him, including some of his cremated ashes in an ancient Persian urn. Sifting the ashes in her hand, she beams with happiness and pride: "It's nice to have him. I can travel with him, or take him places." It seems clear that her creative, free-spirited personality was drawn to an unconventional man like Mapplethorpe, equally creative and free-spirited, and that they inspired and pushed each other to new heights within themselves.

* * *

Heterosexual romance is possibly the last institution in our culture which still infantilizes women as a rule. In fact, it has become the last refuge against all the psycho-social heterosexual anxieties which feminism and gay rights have unleashed. In the college, the workplace, the military, we have criminalized the "old-fashioned," the "chivalrous," the "sexist"—not that these ideas never occur anymore, but at least they no longer represent the official faces of the institutions themselves. But these ideas continue to have their special day in the realm of male-female sexual relations, perhaps due to a fear of letting the infantilization of women slip away completely. For oppressors and oppressed, control is a difficult thing to give up overnight. Even (or perhaps especially) a feminist artist such as Catherine Breillat, ever alert to issues of male abuse of women, can imagine only the death of women as the inevitable outcome of shedding romantic illusions and gaining sexual freedom.

This might be because the "chivalrous" itself was never anything but a thin cover for the abuse of women in the first place. To jettison patriarchy's smiling face is to be left with nothing but the bitter sexism behind it. And the stakes have always been high, for all parties concerned: the straight, the gay, the bisexual; women and men. For all human beings, annihilation is the dialectical complement that gives love its dramatic meaning, its savor. Without one extreme, the other ceases to maintain its psychological hold. We are forever meeting on hastily prepared common ground, which is forever turning back into a field of battle in spite of our tenderest efforts to exorcise the ghosts of conflict. No matter who extends it, love yearns for the slightest help, all the help it can get.

But just as love and annihilation are connected, so one love deepens and strengthens another love, weaving a wider and wider grid of understanding. No one else in our culture comes to understand, the way some bisexual people do, the fact that love can be as kind, and feel as good, with both men and women. This knowledge must start somewhere, for everyone.

Ultimately, it is less than human to cling to categories at the expense of feeling. Whenever people become dogmatic in their behaviors, it is always in an effort to feel less, to think less — to shut out the scary unknown, the unexplored wilderness, always somewhere beyond, which reminds us that we have unfulfilled desires in the first place, unrealized parts of ourselves. Our shared feelings constitute our common humanity, wherever and however they are shared, and whomever does the sharing. The stories in this book have been human stories.

Conclusion: "It's All Good"

> [Bisexuality] allows us to love each other regardless of our gender, race, etc.; to know each other; to learn from one another; to understand each other without fear; to dream together; to respect those who don't belong.... To me, being able to identify with people to this degree is essential to the world.[1]

> Categories of gender and sexual orientation are human inventions; they differ from culture to culture and through different periods of history. At best, categories are methods of summarizing our experiences. They profoundly influence our sense of identity.[2]

Back in the mid–1990s, the catchphrase "It's all good" was used as a kind of unofficial argot by bisexual males to advertise their taste for both genders. It was a genial, welcoming expression, suggesting that no kind of pleasure could ever be bad, and that love was love, wherever it happened to exist. A world where everything is "good" is a world of tolerance and forbearance, and this is partly what bisexuality has always promised: the willingness to reach across to "the other side" — actually, to abolish the whole idea of separate, different sides — and always see only the happiest aspect of human (sexual) interactions.

That probably sounds more naïve than I intend, or more than the subject of male bisexuality might seem to warrant. Of course, the world in which we live is not that world, no matter how strong the effort of certain brave, adventuresome souls to make it so. In part, the phrase itself was already a throwback to even earlier times, in which stoner mythology, pop music, and sexual exploration were fused in a constant, ongoing celebration of personal freedom, joy, what makes life worth living. But let us not idealize specific eras of the past too much: in any decade, it has always been difficult, albeit possible, to find kindred spirits in the social margins of sexuality. In fact, the implied division between the margins and the main text, as it were, may be yet another artificial, self-serving division which needs to be abolished before we can begin to think in unrestricted terms. *All* forms of sexuality require that walls of separation be removed, that human beings learn to trust one another.

However, bisexuality requires this human trust more, perhaps, than any other sexual preference. People speak of feeling insecure in relationships with bisexuals, because of the fear of losing their partner to either a man or a woman: twice the options means twice the competition. And yet, this view of relationships presupposes that, even under the most straightforward and simplistic of circumstances, we have the ability or right to "own" or "possess" or "control" one another. We certainly don't; and the more this control is exerted over someone, the more it tends to make him want to rebel.

The films discussed in this book have encompassed a wide range of bisexual males and male bisexualities. Some have been more romantic than others; some have been very unromantic indeed. But even at their most unromantic, bisexual males are often best depicted as looking for, and exploring, that thrilling, painful, slightly surreal moment when fantasy becomes reality, when the gift of love comes from an unexpected source, and when that human trust seems (for a short while, anyway) to reveal the best in people. Often, when that trust is misplaced, bisexuals themselves end up being victims of it, as much or more than the partners they sometimes deceive. It can be very lonely to live with a secret, in two worlds, as it were — at home in both, perhaps, but belonging completely to neither.

It is futile to predict the future of a sexual orientation, or society's acceptance of it. It helps to always keep in mind that acceptance is relative to time and place, and varies greatly with both; sexuality, on the other hand, is not and does not. Among human behaviors, sex truly can be called "ageless": every imaginable sexuality was present at the dawn of human life, and will likely remain until the end of human time. When any people engage each other in actual, real-time sex acts, they could be in the ancient world or the far-distant future, so little have the desires, sensations, positions, and (indeed) body parts changed over thousands and thousands of years. What does change is how we think about the sex acts we perform, and how we feel about ourselves for performing them. If the bisexual male is often accused, today, of being indecisive or opportunistic, it is my belief that, over time, people will evolve more and more toward bisexuality.

"There is still much work to do before homosexual or bisexual people are accepted as they are, and not as interesting freaks."[3] And yet, as the world grows ever smaller and more populous, this evolutionary movement toward bisexuality will hopefully accompany a simultaneous understanding that we all have more in common, as humans, than we have differences, and that we can ill afford to reject any part of that shared humanity. In our current era of partisan "culture wars," bisexuality — which resists cultural identification just as it resists organization and definition — may yet point the way out of the thicket of toxic cultural chauvinisms. In a war-torn, hostile world, marked by men's conflicts with other men, the openness of male bisexuality, with its tendency to tear down divisive walls, may yet save the day. But evolution is, at best, painstakingly slow.

Chapter Notes

Introduction

1. This is from the mission statement of *Anything That Moves*, a bisexual-themed journal of theory and literature quoted in Marjorie Garber, *Vice Versa: Bisexuality and the Eroticism of Everyday Life* (New York: Simon & Schuster, 1995), 56.
2. Commentary track, *Kinsey* DVD.
3. Garber, *Vice Versa*, 20.
4. Interview, *Barocco* DVD (Pathfinder Home Entertainment, 2003).
5. Garber, *Vice Versa*, 137.
6. "The Journey Home" (making-of featurette), *A Home at the End of the World* DVD (Warner Home Video, 2004).
7. Garber, *Vice Versa*, 47.
8. Martin S. Weinberg, Colin J. Williams, and Douglas W. Pryor, *Dual Attraction: Understanding Bisexuality* (New York: Oxford University Press, 1994), 34.
9. Ibid., 39.
10. Garber, *Vice Versa*, 66.
11. Weinberg, Williams, and Pryor, *Dual Attraction*, 49.
12. Ibid., 190.
13. Eve Kosofky Sedgwick, *Epistemology of the Closet* (Berkeley: University of California Press, 2008), 157.
14. Weinberg, Williams, and Pryor, *Dual Attraction*, 158.
15. Robyn Ochs and Sarah E. Rowley, *Getting Bi: Voices of Bisexuals Around the World*, 2d ed. (Boston: Bisexual Resource Center, 2009), 123.
16. Weinberg, Williams, and Pryor, *Dual Attraction*, 8.
17. Ibid., 35.
18. Ibid., 32.
19. Ibid., 35.
20. Ibid., 37.
21. Ibid., 36.
22. Ibid., 225.
23. Garber, *Vice Versa*, 160.

Chapter 1

1. Weinberg, Williams, and Pryor, *Dual Attraction*, 29–30.
2. Commentary track, *Sins of the Fleshapoids* DVD.
3. Weinberg, Williams, and Pryor, *Dual Attraction*, 90.
4. Stephen Frosh, *The Politics of Psychoanalysis* (New Haven: Yale University Press, 1987), 31.

Chapter 2

1. Garber, *Vice Versa*, 430.
2. Antoine is reborn twice in *Changing Times*: on both occasions he is caught in an eruption of waste matter which is either literally shit or its closest substitute (mud). These unlikely eruptions serve to feminize Antoine and make him helpless, but they also open doors, shamanistically, through which he can evolve toward higher (i.e., more and more loving) cycles of selfhood. He becomes a male heterosexual sacrifice on an altar of love, love which is akin to polymorphous perversity in its ability to break down the rigidities of selfhood and render it diffuse. The anus is the closest a male comes to understanding the female's possession of a vagina, as a reminder of the porousness and vulnerability of the body and, by extension, the self. Therefore, this understanding overturns, or finds a way through, Freud's insistence on the

fear of castration as the great motivator in the formation of personality, in the sense that the reminder of an absence, a hole, becomes, not a terrifying trauma, but an opportunity to experience oneself as more completely human.

3. Since Tennessee Williams' *A Streetcar Named Desire*, at least, the depiction of sexual relations between older women and adolescent males has been a way of encoding gayness within heterosexuality, of homoeroticizing heterosexuality, in the sense that the maternal instinct is questioned, and masculine youth and beauty are privileged.

4. Sedgwick, *Epistemology of the Closet*, 133.

5. It is illuminating to compare Téchiné's films, on this point, with *À Tout Vitesse* (*Full Speed*, 1996), directed by Gaël Morel. In *Full Speed*, the young novelist Quentin (Pascal Cervo) violently and homophobically rejects all possibility of a sexual relationship with Samir (Mezziane Bardadi), a young Moroccan who has been a victim of racist and antigay violence; Quentin's refusal of Samir's love is shown to correspond with his subsequent betrayal of his childhood friends and ideals. The somewhat more schematic execution of *Full Speed* makes explicit one of the more delicate points in Téchiné's sexual politics: "bisexual willingness" is often a sign of whether an ostensibly straight male can be trusted as an ally by sexual and racial minorities.

6. In the context of colonialism, sexual relations between white-identified men and men of color have always been problematic "testing grounds," as Téchiné acknowledges. Is the white man who gives himself passively ceding part of his power to the man of color, or exploiting that power all the more fully? A lot depends on how much agency the man of color feels himself to have in the exchange.

Chapter 3

1. Vanessa Van Petten, "Teen Trend: 7 Reasons Why It's Cool to Pretend to be Bisexual," www.radicalparenting.com, July 2008.
2. Weinberg, Williams, and Pryor, *Dual Attraction*, 117.
3. Ibid., 194.
4. Ibid., 193.
5. Ibid., 246.
6. Ibid., 212.
7. Ibid., 247.
8. Ibid.
9. Ibid., 240.

Chapter 4

1. Mandy is herself bisexual, so this joke might also signify that she prefers to sleep with women; at any rate, her sexual incompatibility with her husband is stressed throughout the film, undermining a comfortably bisexual reading.

2. The brooch migrates from one male character to another, becoming an emblem, a mark, of homosexual desire. It once belonged to Oscar Wilde. Curt received it from Brian, and toward the end of the film, Curt in turn offers it to Arthur. Arthur rejects it, but then finds it magically in his beer. The implication is, if it's in you, it belongs to you and you cannot get rid of it. Brian is the only character in the film who steals it without having it offered to him.

3. *Velvet Goldmine* may owe some of its narrative structure to Orson Welles' *Citizen Kane* (1941), but it is stylistically closer to *Sunset Boulevard* (1950), in which Billy Wilder uses eerie, portentous dolly-shots to signify when the "veil" is about to be lifted on the world of Hollywood illusion. And closer still to the sexual-political phantasmagoria of *Performance*.

Chapter 5

1. Rainer Werner Fassbinder, *The Anarchy of the Imagination: Interviews, Essays, Notes*, edited by Michael A. Töteberg and Leo A. Lensing, and translated by Krishna Winston (Baltimore: The Johns Hopkins University Press, 1992), 84.
2. Ochs and Rowley, *Getting Bi*, 135.
3. Ibid., 59.
4. Ibid., 111.
5. Loraine Hutchins and Lani Kaahumanu, *Bi Any Other Name: Bisexual People Speak Out* (Boston: Alyson, 1991), 159.
6. Fassbinder, *The Anarchy of the Imagination*, 198.

Chapter 6

1. Garber, *Vice Versa*, 140.
2. Ibid.
3. Commentary track, *Kinsey* DVD.
4. Male arousal is continuously privileged in *Kinsey*; the women tend to be passive vessels, liberated in their willingness to say yes to male advances, but unable to take charge of the sex itself. This may be historically

accurate to the days of pre–feminism, or it may be part of the film's way of delineating the homoerotic side of Kinsey's bisexuality.
5. Weinberg, Williams, and Pryor, *Dual Attraction*, 96.
6. Ibid., 94.

Chapter 7

1. Ochs and Rowley, *Getting Bi*, 177.
2. Hutchins and Kaahumanu, *Bi Any Other Name*, 165.
3. Ibid., 159.
4. Ibid., 45.
5. Interview, *The Trio* DVD (TLA Releasing, 2000).
6. "An Intimate Conversation with Pedro Almodóvar," interview with Annette Insdorf, *All About My Mother* DVD (Columbia Tristar Home Video, 2000).
7. Ochs and Rowley, *Getting Bi*, 121.
8. Weinberg, Williams, and Pryor, *Dual Attraction*, 221.
9. Ibid., 53.
10. "The Journey Home."
11. Ibid.
12. Weinberg, Williams, and Pryor, *Dual Attraction*, 283.
13. "The Journey Home."

Chapter 8

1. Hutchins and Kaahumana, *Bi Any Other Name*, 123.
2. Ochs and Rowley, *Getting Bi*, 124.

Chapter 9

1. Male bisexuality is also treated positively in Dos Santos' second feature, *Unmade Beds* (2009), two of whose young male protagonists engage in bisexual activity without feeling the need to agonize over it, categorize themselves, or even discuss the matter. Again, Dos Santos winningly depicts a youth culture in love with the authentic emotion of indie-rock music, and pursuing sexual pleasure with friends of both genders.

Chapter 12

1. Ochs and Rowley, *Getting Bi*, 124.

Chapter 13

1. Patti Smith, *Seventh Heaven* (Boston: Telegraph, 1972), 44.
2. Patti Smith, *Early Work 1970–1979* (New York: W. W. Norton, 1994), 38–40.
3. Ibid., 52.
4. Ibid., 142–147.

Conclusion

1. Ochs and Rowley, *Getting Bi*, 157.
2. Hutchins and Kaahumana, *Bi Any Other Name*, 43.
3. Ochs and Rowley, *Getting Bi*, 124.

Works Cited*

Almodóvar, Pedro. *Todo Sobre Mi Madre [All About My Mother]*. Spain: El Deseo S.A., 1999.
Araki, Gregg. *The Doom Generation*. USA: Blurco Studios, 1995.
———. *Nowhere*. USA: Blurco Studios, 1997.
———. *Totally F***ed Up*. USA: Blurco Studios, 1995.
Arévalo, Daniel Sánchez. *Azuloscurocasinegro [Dark Blue Almost Black]*. Spain: Canal+ España, 2006.
Arnold, Pascal, and Jean-Marc Barr. *Chacun Sa Nuit [One to Another]*. France-Denmark: Toloda, 2006.
Arteta, Miguel. *Chuck & Buck*. USA: Artisan Entertainment, 2000.
Avary, Roger. *The Rules of Attraction*. USA-Germany: Kingsgate Films, 2002.
Barthes, Roland. *Mythologies*. Translated by Annette Lavers. New York: Hill & Wang, 1972.
Benet, Josep Maria. *Amic/Amat [Beloved/Friend]*. Spain: Canal+ España, 1999.
Breillat, Catherine. *Anatomie d l'Enfer [Anatomy of Hell]*. France: CB Films, 2004.
———. *À Ma Soeur! [Fat Girl]*. France-Italy: CB Films, 2001.
———. *Romance*. France: Flach Film, 1999.
Bresson, Robert. *Pickpocket*. France: Compagnie Cinématographique de France, 1959.
Buñuel, Luis. *Un Chien Andalou [An Andalusian Dog]*. France, 1929.
Burke, Michael. *The Mudge Boy*. USA: First Cold Press Productions, 2003.
Carey, Benedict. "Straight, Gay, or Lying?: Bisexuality Revisited." *The New York Times*, July 5, 2005.
Castro, Rick, and Bruce LaBruce. *Hustler White*. Germany-Canada: Dangerous to Know Swell Company, 1996.
Chéreau, Patrice. *Ceux Qui M'Aiment Prendront le Train [Those Who Love Me Can Take the Train]*. France: Téléma, 1998.
Condon, Bill. Commentary track, *Kinsey* DVD. 20th Century-Fox, 2005.
———. *Kinsey*. USA-Germany: Fox Searchlight Pictures, 2004.
Dos Santos, Alexis. *Glue*. Argentina-UK: Diablo Films, 2006.
Fassbinder, Rainer Werner. *The Anarchy of the Imagination: Interviews, Essays, Notes*. Edited by Michael A. Töteberg and Leo A. Lensing; translated by Krishna Winston. Baltimore: The Johns Hopkins University Press, 1992.
Faure, Étienne. *In Extremis [To the Extreme]*. France: Alliance Limited International, 2000.
Fontaine, Anne. *Nettoyage à Sec [Dry Cleaning]*. France-Spain: Cinéa, 1997.
Fraser, Brad. *Leaving Metropolis*. Canada: Film Tonic, 2002.
Frosh, Stephen. *The Politics of Psychoanalysis*. New Haven: Yale University Press, 1987.
Garber, Dr. Marjorie. *Vice Versa: Bisexuality and the Eroticism of Everyday Life*. New York: Simon & Schuster, 1995.
Garrone, Matteo. *L'Imbalmasatore [The Embalmer]*. Italy: Fandango, 2002.
Godmilow, Jill. *Roy Cohn/Jack Smith*. USA: Good Machine, 1994.
Greenaway, Peter. *The Pillow Book*. France-UK-Netherlands-Luxembourg: Kasander & Wigman Productions, 1996.

*Films are cited under the director's last name.

Harrison, Greg. *Groove*. USA: 415 Productions, 2000.
Haynes, Todd. *I'm Not There*. USA-Germany: Killer Films, 2007.
———. *Velvet Goldmine*. UK-USA: Channel Four Films, 1998.
Huntgeburth, Hermine. *Das Trio [The Trio]*. Germany: Arte, 1998.
Hutchins, Loraine, and Lani Kaahumanu. *Bi Any Other Name: Bisexual People Speak Out*. Boston: Alyson, 1991.
Ireland, Dan. *The Velocity of Gary*. USA: Cineville, 1998.
Jordan, Mary. *Jack Smith & the Destruction of Atlantis*. USA: Tongue Press, 2006.
"The Journey Home" (making-of featurette). *A Home at the End of the World* DVD. Warner Home Video, 2004.
Krom, Frank. *Spelen of Sterven [To Play or to Die]*. Netherlands, 1990.
Kuchar, Mike. Commentary track, *The Sins of the Fleshapoids* DVD. Other Cinema DVD, 2005.
LaBruce, Bruce. *Skin Gang*. Germany-Canada-UK-Japan: CAZZO Film Berlin, 1999.
Lucas, Craig. *The Dying Gaul*. USA: Rebel Park Pictures, 2005.
Lynch, David. *Blue Velvet*. USA: De Laurentiis Entertainment Group, 1986.
Mayer, Michael. *A Home at the End of the World*. USA: Hart-Sharp Entertainment, 2004.
Morel, Gaël. *À Tout Vitesse [Full Speed]*. France: Magouric Productions, 1996.
Ochs, Robyn, and Sarah E. Rowley. *Getting Bi: Voices of Bisexuals Around the World*. Boston: Bisexual Resource Center, 2009.
O'Hara, Frank. *Lunch Poems*. San Francisco: City Lights Books, 1964.
Oshima, Nagisa. *Ai No Korîda [In the Realm of the Senses]*. Japan-France: Argos Films, 1976.
Ozon, François. *Les Amants Criminels [Criminal Lovers]*. France: Canal+, 1999.
———. *Gouttes d'Eau sur Pierres Brûlantes [Water Drops on Burning Rocks]*. France: Fidélité Productions, 2000.
———. *Une Robe d'Été [A Summer Dress]*. France: Fidélité Productions, 1996.
Ozpetek, Ferzan. *Le Fate Ignoranti [His Secret Life]*. Italy-France: R&C Produzioni, 2001.
Pasolini, Pier Paolo. *Teorema [Theorem]*. Italy: Aetos Produzioni Cinematografiche, 1968.
Penn, Robin Wright. Interview, *A Home at the End of the World* DVD. Warner Bros., 2004.
Piccirillo, Tony. *The 24th Day*. USA: Big Teddy Films, 2004.
Ray, Nicholas. *Rebel Without a Cause*. USA: Warner Bros., Pictures, 1955.
Schlesinger, John. *Sunday Bloody Sunday*. UK: Vectia, 1971.
Schroeter, Werner. *Diese Nacht [Tonight]*. Portugal-Germany-France: Alfama Films, 2008.
Sebring, Steven. *Patti Smith: Dream of Life*. USA: Clean Socks, 2008.
Sedgwick, Eve Kosofsky. *The Epistemology of the Closet*. Berkeley: University of California Press, 2008.
Shepard, Richard. *The Matador*. USA-Germany-Ireland: Stratus Film Company, 2005.
Smith, Patti. *Early Work 1970–1979*. New York: W. W. Norton, 1994.
———. *Seventh Heaven*. Boston: Telegraph Books, 1972.
Téchiné, André. *Alice et Martin [Alice and Martin]*. France-Spain: Les Films Alain Sarde, 1998.
———. *Barocco*. France: Les Films de la Boétie, 1976.
———. *Les Égarés [Strayed]*. France: FIT Productions, 2003.
———. Interview, *Barocco* DVD. Pathfinder Home Entertainment, 2003.
———. *J'embrasse Pas [I Don't Kiss]*. France-Italy: Bac Films, 1991.
———. *Ma Saison Préferée [My Favorite Season]*. France: D. A. Films, 1993.
———. *Rendez-vous [Rendezvous]*. France: Films A2, 1985.
———. *Les Roseaux Sauvages [Wild Reeds]*. France: Ima Films, 1994.
———. *Les Témoins [The Witnesses]*. France: UGC Distribution, 2007.
———. *Les Temps Qui Changent [Changing Times]*. France, Gemini Films, 2004.
———. *Les Voleurs [Thieves]*. France: Canal+, 1996.
Thurber, Rawson Marshall. *The Mysteries of Pittsburgh*. USA: Arclight Films, 2008.
Tierney, Jacob. *Twist*. Canada: Various Films, 2003.
Van Petten, Vanessa. "Teen Trend: 7 Reasons Why It's Cool to Pretend to be Bisexual." www.radicalparenting.com, July 2008.
Van Sant, Gus. *My Own Private Idaho*. USA: New Line Cinema, 1991.
Vera, Gerardo. *Segunda Piel [Second Skin]*. Spain: Antena 3 Televisión, 1999.
Weinberg, Martin S., Colin J. Williams, and

Douglas W. Pryor. *Dual Attraction: Understanding Bisexuality.* New York: Oxford University Press, 1994.

Werneck, Sandra. *Amores Possíveis [Possible Loves].* Brazil: Cineluz–Produções Cinematográficas Lda., 2001.

Wicks, Gary. *Endgame.* UK: Various Films, 2001.

Index

Page numbers in **_bold italics_** indicate pages with photographs.

Accorsi, Stefano 215
Adjani, Isabelle 50
AIDS 4, 13, 19, 41, 43, 44, 48–49, 55, 62–63, 64–65, 74, 80, 131–133, 135, 149, 153–154, 178, 186–203, 205–206, 215
Alice and Martin 41, 45
All About My Mother 131–134, 149, 200
All That Heaven Allows 217
Almodóvar, Pedro 23, 131–134
Altman, Robert 205
Amalric, Mathieu 45
Anatomy of Hell 219–228, ***223***, 229
Angels in America 191
Anger, Kenneth 32
Anything That Moves 235n
Araki, Gregg 23, 51–63
Arévalo, Raúl 129
Arnold, Pascal 23, 208
Auteil, Daniel 41
Ayres, Lew 11
Azabal, Lubna 44

Baché, Guillaume 208, ***209***
Bad Monster–Worse Monster trope 102
Balducci, Lorenzo 48, ***202***
Bale, Christian 65
Baptista, Joao 176
Bardadi, Mezziane 236n
Bardem, Javier 143
Barocco 50
Barr, Jean-Marc 23, 208
Barry, Toni 180
Barthes, Roland 104
Basic Instinct 4
Bätscher, David 61
Béart, Emmanuelle 41, 43, 47, ***202***

Beloved Friend 182–184
Benicio, Murilo 12
Berling, Charles 119, 207
Bernard, Christophe 49
Bexton, Nathan 52
Beziers, Pierre 212
Bi Any Other Name 5
Binoche, Juliette 40, 45
Biscayart, Nahuel Pérez 169
Bisexual Center of San Francisco 4
The Blackout 73
Blanc, Manuel 39
Blanc, Michel 43, ***202***
Blue Velvet 49
Boisson, Christine 110
Bouajila, Sami 43, ***48***, ***202***
Bouchez, Élodie 40
Bowie, David 64
Boyce, Alan 54
Breillat, Catherine 220, 226, 228, 229, 230
Bresson, Robert 105, 115, 229
Brocheré, Lizzie 208, ***209***
Brosnan, Pierce 103
Bully 213–214
Buñuel, Luis 37–38, 122
Burke, Michael 162
Burroughs, William S. 69
Buy, Margherita 215

Cabaret 8
La Cage aux folles 39
Cammell, Donald 8
Cantó, Toni 131
Carey, Benedict 20
Casar, Amira 220, ***223***
Caselli, Chiara 174

243

Index

The Castle 84
Castro, Rick 177
Cervo, Pascal 236*n*
Chabon, Michael 154
Chaloner, Thea 195
Changing Times 41, 44–45, 50, 152, 235*n*
Charles, Sébastien 32
Chéreau, Patrice 205–208
Chicago-Toronto study 20–23
Un Chien andalou 37–38
Chuck & Buck 139–140
Citizen Kane 236*n*
Clark, Larry 213–214
Clarkson, Patricia 72
Close, Joshua 178
Cohn, Roy 191–194, 197, 203
Collette, Toni 66
Colt, Beth 139
Condon, Bill 7, 99, 101, 102
Corazza, Vince 145
Crabbe, Buster 11
Criminal Lovers 37, 93–99, **95**, 140
Cruz, Penélope 131
Cumming, Alastair 66
Cunningham, Michael 140
Curtis, Ian 210

Daëms, Marie 206
Dallesandro, Joe 8, 32–33, 201
D'Angelo, Beverly 52
Dark Blue Almost Black 129–131, 133, 134
Davis, Bette 133
Davis, Hope 107
Dean, James 91, 92, 130
Death Instinct 38, 206
de la Torre, Antonio 129
de Melo, Emilio 13
Demme, Jonathan 102
Deneuve, Catherine 41
Depardieu, Gérard 41, 50
Depardieu, Julie 110
Díaz, Héctor 169
Dickens, Charles 178
Di Rienzo, Libero 228
D'Onofrio, Vincent 198
Donon, Marie 209
The Doom Generation 51, 52, 55–58, **55**
Dos Santos, Alexis 23, 169–171, 237*n*
Dry Cleaning 115, 118–122, **120**
Dual Attraction 4
Ducey, Caroline 228
Dupont, Arthur 208, **209**
Duval, James 52, **55**
The Dying Gaul 72–82, **78**, 83, 87–88, 146, 151, 152, 153–154, 191
Dylan, Bob 66

Edison 11
Efron, Inés 169
Eitner, Felix 115
Elective Affinities 211
Ellis, Bret Easton 184
Elomri, Idir 44
The Embalmer 171–172
Endgame 179–182, 183

Farmer, Gary 178
Farrell, Colin 135, 136, **137**
Fassbinder, Rainer Werner 8, 72, 82, 86–87
Fat Girl 228
Ferraz, Carolina 12
Ferry, Bryan 68
Finney, Albert 9
Firgens, Mackenzie 59
Flynn, Errol 11
Fontaine, Anne 115, 118, 119, 122
Fosse, Bob 8
Foster, Jon 155
Freud, Dr. Sigmund 2, 38, 107, 114, 125, 235*n*
Friedlander, Benedict 43
Full Speed 236*n*

Gable, Clark 12
Garber, Dr. Marjorie 4–5, 16, 23, 235*n*
Garfield, John 12
Garko, Gabriel 215
"gaydar" 92
George, Götz 115
Gerritsma, Tjebbo 166
Getting Bi 5
Gil, Ariadna 143
Gilliat, Penelope 25
Giraudeau, Bernard 82
Glue 169–171, 173
Godmilow, Jill 192
Goldberg, Albert 228
Goldenhersh, Heather 100
Good Bisexual–Bad Bisexual trope 80, 82, 86
Gorny, Frédéric 41
Gouix, Guillaume 212
Goulart, Beth 12
Greenaway, Peter 123–129
Greggory, Pascal 205
Groove 59–61
Guiry, Thomas 162, **163**
Guttiérrez, Quim 129

Hain, Jeanette 115
Hall, Philip Baker 104
Hamlet 46

Index

Harvey, Jona 197
Hayek, Selma 198
Haynes, Todd 64–71
Head, Murray 9
"heterosexual privilege" 49, 54–55, 75, 81, 106
Hirsch, Emile 162
His Secret Life 215–218
A Home at the End of the World 14, 16, 134–141, *137*, 211
Hopper, Dennis 49
Hudson, Rock 188, 217
Hugo, Candice 110
Hunaerts, Geert 166
Huntgeburth, Hermine 115, 118
Hustler White 177–178
hustling 43, 46–48, 68, 174–185, 221–222; *see also* situational bisexuality
Hutchins, Loraine 5

I Don't Kiss 39, 43, 44, 46–48, 49, 50, 179, 214
I'm Not There 66
In the Realm of the Senses 125, 127
internalized homophobia 35, 65, 70
interpersonal fascism 87
Interview with the Vampire 19
Irizarry, Gloria 200

Jackson, Glenda 9, 24
Jacques, Sylvain 205
Jagger, Mick 8
Jane, Thomas 198
Johnson, Corey 180
Joy Division 210

Kaahumanu, Lani 5
Kafka, Franz 84
Kahanjian, Arsinée 228
Keats, John 210
Kechiouch, Salim 94
Kinnear, Greg 104
Kinsey 7, 99–103, 150, *151*, 236–237n
Kinsey, Dr. Alfred 15, 99–103
Kinsey Scale 15
Kirkwood, Denny 59
The Kiss 11
Krom, Frank 166
Kuchar, George 32
Kuchar, Mike 32

LaBruce, Bruce 60, 61, 177–178
Landler, Karl E. 212
Lassez, Sarah 58
Leaving Metropolis 145–147, 148, 153–154
Libéreau, Johan 43, *48*

Linklater, Hamish 59
Linney, Laura 100, *151*
Llinás, Verónica 169
Lonesome Cowboys 201
Loret, Alexis 41
Lucas, Craig 72, 73, 80, 87, 191
Lynch, David 49

MacLachlan, Kyle 49
Mahieux, Ernesto 171
Mairesse, Valérie 210
Mangenot, Frédéric 32
Manojlovic, Miki 96
Manzillo, Valerio Foglia 171
Mapplethorpe, Robert 229–230
Marsden, James 194
Marvel, Elizabeth 74
Marx, Zeppo 12
Masters, Steve 61
Mastroianni, Chiara 52
The Matador 103–107
Mayer, Michael 14, 23, 136, *137*
Mazar, Debi 52
McGann, Mark 179
McGowan, Rose 55, *55*
McGregor, Ewan 65, 124
McPherson, Coco 193
Mead, Taylor 201
Meister, Nanou 120
Merhar, Stanislas 119, *120*
Mesquida, Roxana 228
Midnight Cowboy 7–8, 197, 201
Miller, Eden 61
Miller, Sienna 155
Mineo, Sal 91, 92
Miou-Miou 119
Mollà, Jordi 143
Monge, Jacques 227
Montalà, Irene 182
Morel, Gaël 40, *42*, 236n
Morrissey, Paul 8, 32–33, 201
The Mudge Boy 162–166, *163*, 167, 168, 170, 172
Muni, Paul 11
The Music Lovers 8
My Favorite Season 41
My Own Private Idaho 174–175
Myra Breckenridge 8
The Mysteries of Pittsburgh 154–157

Namath, Joe 156
Neeson, Liam 99, *151*
Newman, Daniel 179
Nichols, Mike 191
Noiret, Philippe 40
Nollet, Nicholas 208

Nolte, Nick 155
Nowhere 51, 52–53, 54, 58–59, 61–63
Nyro, Laura 135

Ochs, Robyn 5
O'Donnell, Chris 100
Oedipus 46
Oedipus complex 114, 124, 125, 139
Ogata, Ken 123
O'Hara, Frank 12
Oida, Yoshi 123
Oliver Twist 178
One to Another see *To Each His Night*
Operation Margarine 104, 107
Orbison, Roy 49
Oshima, Nagisa 125
Ozon, François 23, 31–38, 72, 82, 84, 93–99, 140
Ozpetek, Ferzan 217

Pasolini, Pier Paolo 8, 118–119
Patti Smith: Dream of Life 230
Performance 8, 64, 236n
Perrier, Pierre 208
Pflieger, Noé 119
Philippe, Ryan 58
Phillips, Bijou 213
Phoenix, River 174
Pickpocket 105, 115
The Pillow Book 123–129, 133, 150
Plato 38
The Player 73
Possible Loves 12–14, 145, 148, 149, 152–153
Pou, Josep M. 182
Powell, Dick 11
Prince, Harold 8
Pryor, Douglas W. 4

Rachati, Nadem 44
Ravache, Irene 13
Ray, Nicholas 91–92, 97
Rebel Without a Cause 91–92, 130, 135
Reboux, Anaïs 228
Redl, Christian 115
Reeves, Keanu 174
Regnier, Natacha 94, *95*
Rendez-vous 40
Renfro, Brad 213
Renier, Jérémie 94, *95*
Renzi, Andrea 215
Rhys-Meyers, Jonathan 64, *67*
Rideau, Stéphane 42, *42*
Rimbaud, Arthur 98, 210
Roberts, Dallas 135, *137*
Robertson, Kathleen 54
Roch, Sébastien 110

Rochetti, Elisabetta 171
The Rocky Horror Picture Show 8, 19, 64
Roeg, Nicolas 8
Romance 228
Ross, Diana 198, 199
Roth, Cecilia 131
Rowley, Sarah 5
Roxy Music 7, 68
Roy Cohn/Jack Smith 191–194
The Rules of Attraction 167, 184–185
Ruptash, Troy 145
Russell, Ken 8
Russo, Vito 23

Sadler, William 102
Sagnier, Ludavine 84
Sanchez, Lucia 34
Sanguinetti, Jérémy 110
Sardà, Rosa María 132
Sarne, Michael 8
Sarsgaard, Peter 72, 100, *151*, 155
Schlesinger, John 7
Schroeter, Werner 176
Scorpio Rising 32
Scott, Campbell 72, *78*
Sebring, Steven 230
Second Skin 143–145, 147, 149, 154
Sedgwick, Eve Kosofsky 17
Seigner, Mathilde 119
Selvas, David 182
Shaech, Jonathon 55, *55*
Shakespeare 46
Shear, Jon 26
Sheila 32, 33
Sifredi, Rocco 220, *223*
The Silence of the Lambs 102
Simmons, Jaason 58
Sirk, Douglas 217
situational bisexuality 42, 175, 184–185, 222, 227; see also hustling
Skin Gang 60–61
Smith, Jack 32, 191–194, 197, 202
Smith, Patti 228–230
Somerhalder, Ian 167
Something for Everyone 8
Spacek, Sissy 135
Speedman, Scott 194
Stahl, Nick 178, 213
Stamp, Terence 118
Stévenin, Sagamore 228
Strayed 41–42
A Streetcar Named Desire 133, 236n
Suddenly, Last Summer 199
A Summer Dress 31–38, 93, 94–95, 96
Sunday Bloody Sunday 7, 9–10, 23–26
Sunset Boulevard 73, 236n

Index

The Supremes 199
Suvari, Mena 156
Szafran, Alberto 13

Taylor, Cherilee 145
Téchiné, André 10, 23, 39–50, 140, 154, 179, 201, **202**, 214, 236n
Tedeschi, Valeria Bruni 206
Terracciano, Bernardino 172
Theorem 8, 118–119
Thieves 41
Thomson, Anna 85
Those Who Love Me Can Take the Train 205–208, 210
Tierney, Brigid 179
To Each His Night 208–214, **209**
To Play or to Die 166–169, 170, 172, 173
To the Extreme 110–115
Todeschini, Bruno 205
Tonight 176
Totally F***ed Up 51, 52, 53–54
transgression 96
Trintignant, Jean-Louis 205, 208
The Trio 115–118, 121
True, Rachel 52
The 24th Day 192, 194–197, 201
Twist 178–179, 183
Tyler, Parker 12

Ulliel, Gaspar 41
Unmade Beds 237n
Urbania 26

Van Der Beek, James 184
Van Sant, Gus 174
Vawter, Ron 191
The Velocity of Gary 192, 197–201
Velvet Goldmine 64–71, **67**, 132, 141, 150, 204, 236n
Vera, Gerard 143
Verdi Requiem 84
Vertigo 50

Viale, Nahuel 169
Vice Versa 4, 235n
Vincent, Hélène 43
Violent Femmes 169
Visconti, Luchino 8
von Goethe, Johann Wolfgang 211
von Kleist, Heinrich 210
von Trier, Lars 208

Warhol, Andy 12, 32–33, 197, 201
Water Drops on Burning Rocks 72, 82–88
Waters, John 8
Weinberg, Martin S. 4
Weissmuller, Johnny 11
Weitz, Chris 139
Welles, Orson 236n
Werneck, Sandra 12, 13
Westmoreland, Micko 65
White, Mike 139
Wicks, Gary 179
Wieners, John 12
Wiik, Aurélien 110
Wild Reeds 40, 42, **42**, 50
Wilde, Oscar 65, 236n
Wilder, Billy 236n
Williams, Colin J. 4
Williams, Tennessee 163, 236n
The Witnesses 41, 43, 44, 48–49, **48**, 50, 140, 154, 201, **202**
Women in Love 8
Wood, Natalie 91
Woof, Emily 70
Wright Penn, Robin 135, **137**, 139, 141
Wu, Vivian 123
Wyman, Jane 217

Yilmaz, Serra 215
Yona, Moti 179

Zem, Roschdy 47, **207**
Zidi, Malik 44, 82
Ziggy Stardust 8

www.ingramcontent.com/pod-product-compliance
Lightning Source LLC
Chambersburg PA
CBHW051217300426
44116CB00006B/614